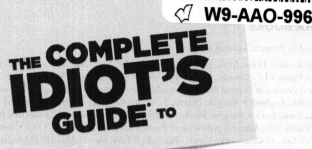

# THE COMPLETE IDIOT'S GUIDE TO

# Writing a Memoir

by Victoria Costello

## ALPHA

A member of Penguin Random House LLC

## ALPHA BOOKS

Published by Penguin Random House LLC

Penguin Random House LLC, 375 Hudson Street, New York, New York 10014, USA • Penguin Random House LLC (Canada), 90 Eglinton Avenue East, Suite 700, Toronto, Ontario M4P 2Y3, Canada (a division of Pearson Penguin Canada Inc.) • Penguin Books Ltd., 80 Strand, London WC2R 0RL, England • Penguin Ireland, 25 St. Stephen's Green, Dublin 2, Ireland (a division of Penguin Books Ltd.) • Penguin Random House LLC (Australia), 250 Camberwell Road, Camberwell, Victoria 3124, Australia (a division of Pearson Australia Group Pty. Ltd.) • Penguin Books India Pvt. Ltd., 11 Community Centre, Panchsheel Park, New Delhi—110 017, India • Penguin Random House LLC (NZ), 67 Apollo Drive, Rosedale, North Shore, Auckland 1311, New Zealand (a division of Pearson New Zealand Ltd.) • Penguin Books (South Africa) (Pty.) Ltd., 24 Sturdee Avenue, Rosebank, Johannesburg 2196, South Africa • Penguin Books Ltd., Registered Offices: 80 Strand, London WC2R 0RL, England

004-189938-December2011

International Standard Book Number: 978-1-61564-123-9
Library of Congress Catalog Card Number: 2011908147

19  18        10  9  8  7  6

Interpretation of the printing code: The rightmost number of the first series of numbers is the year of the book's printing; the rightmost number of the second series of numbers is the number of the book's printing. For example, a printing code of 11-1 shows that the first printing occurred in 2011.

*Printed in the United States of America*

**Note:** This publication contains the opinions and ideas of its author. It is intended to provide helpful and informative material on the subject matter covered. It is sold with the understanding that the author and publisher are not engaged in rendering professional services in the book. If the reader requires personal assistance or advice, a competent professional should be consulted.

The author and publisher specifically disclaim any responsibility for any liability, loss, or risk, personal or otherwise, which is incurred as a consequence, directly or indirectly, of the use and application of any of the contents of this book.

Most Alpha books are available at special quantity discounts for bulk purchases for sales promotions, premiums, fund-raising, or educational use. Special books, or book excerpts, can also be created to fit specific needs.

For details, write: Special Markets, Alpha Books, 375 Hudson Street, New York, NY 10014.

**Publisher:** *Marie Butler-Knight*
**Associate Publisher:** *Mike Sanders*
**Executive Managing Editor:** *Billy Fields*
**Executive Editors:** *Randy Ladenheim-Gil, Lori Cates Hand*
**Development Editor:** *Megan Douglass*
**Senior Production Editor:** *Janette Lynn*

**Copy Editor:** *Megan Wade*
**Cover Designer:** *William Thomas*
**Book Designers:** *William Thomas, Rebecca Batchelor*
**Indexer:** *Heather McNeill*
**Layout:** *Brian Massey*
**Proofreader:** *John Etchison*

*To my fellow memoirists and the great writers who continue to inspire us, many of whom you'll find on the pages of this book.*

# Contents

## Appendixes

# Introduction

As memoirs surge to the top of bestseller lists, the number of people writing one also grows. As a result, we now find ourselves in a vibrant community of memoirists, each of us learning from the others by sharing our work; trading tips on craft; and gathering online for support, ideas, and inspiration.

I invite you to use this book as your entry into this wonderful writing community. Keep it next to you as you work so you can avoid the many potholes that can inhibit a new writer's progress: confusion about what goes in and what stays out of your memoir, procrastination, a fear of offending others by writing "your truth," or a lack of experience with the theory and craft. Use the inspirational quotes and excerpts from the work of published memoirists that appear in every chapter to keep you on track.

In this guide, I apply what I've learned as a five-time published author of memoirs and nonfiction books to lay out the essentials of craft you need to write your own memoir. I include the techniques we borrow from novelists, journalists, and screenwriters to tell a story that is true but just as compelling as our favorite novel, news story, or movie. With exercises and writing prompts, I demystify plot, voice, character, dialogue, setting, and theme and apply these techniques to the peculiar needs of the memoir form.

Memoirs come in many genres, each with their own expectations and rules. You might have a travel story to tell in which you want to add your favorite found recipes. Or perhaps there's a business success you want to tout. You might be a survivor who wants to inspire others in your same predicament. Or maybe you simply want to leave your examined life behind as an heirloom for future generations. All these memoirs share the goal of adding meaning to lived events and experiences. On the following pages, you'll find everything you need to carry out your purpose. Please join me for what I guarantee you'll find to be an amazing journey to self and back.

If you are considering or have begun to write a memoir about your life for meaning, healing, fun, or profit, this book is organized to help you get from your initial idea to the end. As a new writer, or as a writer proficient in other areas, you will soon see that the memoir form is unique. No other form of writing fuses the expectations and techniques currently applied to fiction writing and journalism in one place. When you're writing a memoir, you're expected to have the flair for dialogue and plotting of a novelist and the veracity of a newshound.

So how do you quickly get up to speed on all these different expectations and techniques?

## How This Book Is Organized

You begin in **Part 1, Writing Your Life,** where you find an inventory of what makes a memoir true versus "sort of true" or fictionalized. There is a guide to research sources, including genealogical databases and how to find out about long-lost members of the family with only a shred of information to go on.

In **Part 2, The Ingredients of Memoir,** you dig into the craft, learning how to find your voice, put it into dialogue that rings true, and then put these elements into scene and plot.

**Part 3, The Bigger Picture: Theme and Genre,** is where you encounter the particulars of major categories or genres of memoir. These include life passages, relationships, illness, travel and adventure, and business memoirs.

In **Part 4, Getting Read,** you learn all your options for getting your memoir into the hands of readers. These can be family and friends or readers unknown to you. Legal and ethical issues are reviewed here, and the worlds of trade publishing and self-publishing are demystified, with strategies for dealing with either or both.

## Extras

*The Complete Idiot's Guide to Writing a Memoir* also includes the following sidebars:

**DEFINITION**

Key literary and craft terms are defined.

**QUICK PROMPT**

Suggested writing exercises for putting theory into practice and guiding your use of the techniques.

**TAKE IT TO HEART**

Inspirational quotes from published memoirists on the craft and content of their works.

**POTHOLE AHEAD!**

Things to avoid in your writing and distribution efforts.

## Acknowledgments

I wish to thank my agent Marilyn Allen and former Alpha editor Randy Ladenheim-Gil, who brought this lovely project into being.

## Trademarks

All terms mentioned in this book that are known to be or are suspected of being trademarks or service marks have been appropriately capitalized. Alpha Books and Penguin Random House LLC cannot attest to the accuracy of this information. Use of a term in this book should not be regarded as affecting the validity of any trademark or service mark.

# Writing Your Life

Everyone, it seems, is reading and writing memoirs. You've been harboring the desire to write one for years, and the time has finally become available for you to do it. In this first part, I cover the basics: what is memoir, how true must your true life story be to deserve the title of *memoir*, and how on earth do you recall the details of events and conversations that happened two or three decades ago? I lay out the tricks used by professional writers for such common problems as getting past writer's block and dealing with first drafts that are, well, less than what you had envisioned for your opus. There is guidance ahead on research sources at your disposal for delving into family history and many prompts to get your fingers tapping on the keyboard or pen moving on the page.

# Why Write a Memoir?

## In This Chapter

- Know your purpose to focus your memoir
- How to tell whether an event is "memoir-worthy"
- Finding the universal in the particular
- Picking a purpose to discover your genre and theme

You love reading them. And lately it seems like everyone is writing one, or at least talking about one. This might be true, but the more likely scenario prompting you to pick up this book is that something keeps tugging at you to write a *memoir* of your own. Perhaps an amazing experience or a relationship with someone you loved is calling out to you to memorialize. You may have survived an ordeal and feel compelled to share it with others. Or maybe you simply wish to create a family record as a legacy to great grandchildren you might never meet. You have journals spanning years, but you've never shown them to a soul, let alone thought about publishing them. There are different rules for memoirs that won't go beyond your inner circle of family and friends and those you wish to have read far and wide. I cover both kinds with an emphasis on how to write a memoir that can travel beyond your kitchen table and touch readers on the other side of town—or the world.

**DEFINITION**

A **memoir** is a historical account written from personal knowledge, so it's a story only you can tell. The word *memoir* derives from the French *memoire* and the Latin *memoria*, for "memory." The author of a memoir is a *memoirist*.

If your memoir were a piece of furniture, it would be Grandma's antique rocker. You've been saving that old piece in the attic so that one day you can restore it to its former glory. You've never restored anything before, but how hard can it be? You've even bought the tools. Meanwhile, the chair accumulates dust, waiting for you to say yes, today is the day I'm going to start that project!

Perhaps the free time you've never had before has suddenly materialized or you've made a pact to fit a couple of hours of writing time into the wee dawn hours before you leave for work.

If you have the burning desire to tell your story, this book is designed to give you everything you need to get the job done.

# Memory and Writing

Every memoir writer starts with an unruly stockpile of slippery memories, some familiar, others vague but still calling out for attention. Your first job will be to stand these guys and gals up next to each other in a long line. From this virtual casting call, you'll then choose which ones will make the final cut and land in your memoir and let the others slide back into the recesses of your mind.

**TAKE IT TO HEART**

"The scariest moment is always just before you start. After that, things can only get better."

—Stephen King

"Uh oh," your panicked thinking begins, "I just have a feeling about what I want to write, but nothing concrete. Where do I start?" Not to worry. The first secret I'll share about the art of writing has already been spilled by mega-selling author Stephen King. This sense of dread that bubbles up as you stare at a blank page or screen is familiar to every writer. It doesn't matter if it's his first or fifteenth book. The trick, writers soon learn, is to tell that feeling to go wait outside while you simply start…one word after another, just like you learned to walk by putting one foot in front of the other—and occasionally falling down. You should definitely *not* worry about the quality of what goes on the page, at least not yet. In fact, writers' second secret is that all first drafts are terrible. They're supposed to be that way, so that you can get past the warm-up to the good stuff.

And then consider this: you are doing what you were born to do!

Encoded into the DNA of our human species is a unique talent for storytelling. Neuroscientists tell us that narrative is part of the scouting-for-trouble capability that has evolved as part of human nature, an ancient cognitive skill that does for each of us what scouts used to do when they sat on a high hill keeping watch for enemy tribes.

Other mammals don't have it, evolutionary scientists say, because, beyond watching and remembering, storytelling also requires a singularly human talent: the ability to reflect. The link between memory and reflection is a critical one for memoirists. Your reflections are what will guide you to choose among tens of thousands of memories your brain has stored to find only those that belong in your memoir. The recollections that are worth leaving for posterity are those that contain just enough of the personal and the universal to be of interest to you and others besides you.

## The Universal in the Particular

Our experiences matter to us merely because they happened. They are meaningful to other people because of their larger implications, their echoes. To find those echoes, hold your experiences up to the light and examine them carefully. This is the first and most important lesson for writing a memoir if you want it to be read by others. If that is not so important, then you have much more room to indulge yourself.

Look and listen for those experiences that might resonate with other people. Not because they're ordinary. In fact, it's better if they're unique in some way. But a memoir-worthy memory must have a touch of the universal about it. Here's one example. Every daughter is embarrassed by her mother at some point in her life. For gossip columnist Jeannette Walls, whose mother became homeless and lived on the same streets of New York City where her daughter lived and worked, the experience was heightened and yet highly relatable and very poignant. Perhaps that's why Walls's memoir, *The Glass Castle*, has been a bestseller for over two years.

## The Beauty of the Ordinary

At the risk of contradicting myself, I offer this seemingly opposite advice. Don't rule out something that happened to you for inclusion in your memoir simply because it is commonplace. Your job is to find an extraordinary angle on the ordinary. Your version of birth, first love, marriage, and loss will never be the same as anyone else's if you allow yourself to dig deep down into the experience and tell it in a way that reflects who you really are—with your unique personality, sense of humor, flaws, and history. Just as you have a unique set of 46 chromosomes and a destiny like no one else's, chances are that you have at least one fabulous story that is hiding in plain sight waiting to be told. And while people write memoirs for many reasons, there is one common purpose they all share: a desire to give meaning to something that occurred in their past. The essential question you must answer then is not *if* you have a story to tell, but whether you will tell it. Will this story travel beyond your private musings? If your answer is yes or maybe, please read on.

# Memories Are Like Old Friends

When most people reflect on their lives, they find that the same memories tend to pop up in their minds. Like reliable old friends, these familiar faces, lines of conversations, favorite songs, and images of pivotal events are always there, making them the most likely suspects for inclusion in a memoir. At the very least, these memories will give you some starting places from which to begin brainstorming.

## The Backward Glance

Many religions paint a poignant picture of an end-of-life rite of passage in which, before gaining admittance to paradise, every departing soul must pass through a gate with a gatekeeper. The gatekeeper's job is to help the individual carry out an exhaustive review of the life just completed. All the good and not-so-good deeds of the past are said to fly by as if in a movie, with each action or omission up for review and discussion. Another term for this conjectured experience is *judgment day.*

Writing a memoir is like getting a jump on judgment day and stealing some of the gatekeeper's thunder by carrying out at least part of this life review while you're still alive and well. It's an empowering process of taking random events and putting them together into a single coherent picture—and then giving that picture the nuances of meaning you believe it deserves.

**QUICK PROMPT**

There's no time like the present to begin brainstorming your memoir. Let's try this idea: you've arrived at the pearly gates of Heaven where you are greeted by *the* gatekeeper. His first question: What is the most important thing you've done? Second: What have you left undone? Answer these questions. Save your answers for later.

## Serve Yourself Well

Even a celebrity who is constantly followed by paparazzi, her life an open book, prefers to be in control of what goes in and what's left out of that book. This is evident by the sheer numbers of memoirs penned by celebrities (or their ghostwriters) on bookstore shelves.

Famous or not, someone's autobiography is not the same as her memoir. The autobiography covers more time in a life, is broader in scope, and includes the author's assessment of her place in history. Gore Vidal, in his own memoir *Palimpsest*, gave a personal definition of memoir: "A memoir is how one remembers one's own life, while an autobiography is history, requiring research, dates, facts double-checked."

Often, an autobiographical writer wants to put her own spin on events that were dramatic or controversial; in effect, to have the last word on a public life. Nearly every modern president and prime minister has written one. Bill Clinton, who wrote a 1,056-page autobiography titled *My Life*, hoped that his account of two contentious terms in the White House would set several records straight. "A lot of presidential memoirs, they say, are dull and self-serving," Clinton quipped. "I hope mine is interesting and self-serving."

Humorist Will Rogers put it more irreverently: "Memoirs means when you put down the good things you ought to have done and leave out the bad ones you did do."

Sometimes, famous people take the opportunity to apologize in a memoir. More than one spurned wife has received a mea culpa from a cheating husband on the pages of his memoir. So, too, have grown children whose famous parent missed much of their childhoods while they were busy entertaining others or changing the world.

Wanting to settle a score or make an apology are valid motives for writing a memoir. That doesn't necessarily mean either will result in an engrossing story. Ego and pride can get in the way of a good yarn. What matters most at this beginning stage is to figure out your own motive for putting pen to paper. You don't have to know all that your memoir will cover. But it does help to know *why* you're writing it.

# First, Know Your Purpose

You will soon find that the intention you bring to writing a memoir determines virtually everything else about it. That includes how you focus your story, where and when it takes place, as well as its voice, tone, and theme. Each of these critical elements of memoir will be discussed in detail later. For now, we'll stick to determining your purpose. Here are some common reasons memoirists give for wanting to write about their lives:

> • You want to record the details of your life (and the lives of your ancestors) for the benefit of your grandchildren and great-grandchildren whom you might never meet.

- You've got an amazing story to tell.
- You want the catharsis of making a confession on paper.
- You want to achieve self-understanding.
- You want to memorialize a personally significant relationship.
- You're not sure why, but you can't not write it…the urge to put your life down on paper is so strong.
- You want to cheat death and become immortal on the page.
- You believe the story of how you overcame an obstacle or adversity can inspire and help others.
- You want to settle a score.
- You've built a business and want the world to know about it.
- You would like the camaraderie and shared intimacy of joining a memoir writers' group.
- You've thought about writing all your life but were too busy and/or scared of being judged. Now you're determined to face your fear and do it anyway.

Do any of these reasons resonate for you? Perhaps you have more than one reason for writing a memoir. Once you've come up with your primary motive(s), the next step is to decide on a category of memoir that offers the best vehicle to carry your story forward. That can seem like another daunting choice to make at this stage of the game. But knowing your purpose and category will give you a major jump-start in writing your memoir. Dip your toe in the water by reading the category descriptions that follow. See if any sound like what you are imagining for your memoir. By the way, another word for a category of memoir (or novel or play) is *genre*.

Your genre and purpose should be mirror images of each other— when these two are in sync, you will arrive at a theme. Check out how this three-way reciprocal relationship works in these examples.

| Purpose | Genre/Category | Theme |
|---------|----------------|-------|
| How I survived childhood poverty | Coming-of-age | Self-discovery in adversity |
| How I became the first woman astronaut | Business-career | Gender/A woman in a man's world |
| How I married my childhood sweetheart at age 65 | Relationship | True love is forever |

# Memoir Categories

Every memoir serves its writer in some way, whether to tout a success, inspire others, or as a revelatory exercise for self-healing—to name a few reasons for writing and publishing one's own true story. Part 3 contains an in-depth discussion of the major categories of memoir, their conventions, and classic memoirs that have been written in each genre. For now, here's a quick look at some popular memoir categories.

## Life's Passages

When people speak of passages, they're referring to the universal turning points in every life, when one stage ends and another begins. According to the Freudians, change at these turning points doesn't come without conflict. In a memoir about an important passage in your life, you depict the struggle you went through to give birth to a new you. Here are the most common passages seen in memoirs.

- **Coming of Age**—The passage from adolescence to young adulthood is especially rich for memoirs.

- **Wild Youth**—These are written by reformed gang members, cultists, outlaws, or any other older but wiser writers out there.

- **Second Coming of Age**—A midlife crisis and a post-divorce renaissance are two examples of this category.

- **Marriage/Divorce**—When the occasion is bliss or the disaster is manmade.

- **The Other Woman**—Usually written when you are the other woman and you've opted out for a more promising candidate.

- **First Love/First Love Rekindled Much Later**—Readers never tire of reading about first loves and heartbreaks, and—increasingly, thanks to social media—second chances at love.

- **Birth or Adoption**—These are about mothers (and sometimes fathers) trying to have a baby, having a baby, or loving a child despite the trials he or she brings.

- **Parent's Death**—A rite of passage with deep reverberations for an adult child.

- **Return to Ancestral Home**—When you go home to a place that has only existed in your mind's eye.

- **Old Age**—It's baby boomers' new favorite subject, look out!

## A Survivor Overcoming Obstacles

This is a big category fitting to survivors of poverty, war, crime, abuse, and natural disasters, among many other obstacles. Here are some of the common obstacles writers encounter in their lives which they then deem worthy of sharing in a memoir.

- **Illness**—A narrative account from the patient or caregiver's perspective, leading to an unexpected cure or a lesson learned from pain.

- **Addiction**—It's own sub-sub category of overcoming an illness, open to any addictive substance.

- **Grief**—Bearing up over any of the losses that try our souls.

- **Confession**—When the writer reveals a long-held secret, usually about himself, it's a confessional or tell-all memoir.

- **Self-Healing**—Using memoir to gain a better understanding and resolution of troubling events or relationships in the past; breaking down to break through to a better you.

- **Crisis**—In business or personal life, this category focuses on overcoming an unexpected or difficult predicament.

## Conquering the World

How you became the master of your little part of the world is the focus of this category:

- **Travel**—Exotic places are toured and memorialized, often with a twist involving an unexpected event or mishap.

- **Travel Romance**—When place becomes a backdrop to new passion.

- **Adventure**—These writers have lived unusual lives. He or she has fought in a war, worked as a spy behind enemy lines, done important scientific research, or took on Mother Nature.

- **Business-Career**—Goes behind the scenes with the self-made man or woman. These memoirs usually offer secrets of success. This category is also written by entrepreneurs who use memoir as a self-marketing tool.

- **War**—Battlegrounds experienced as an innocent, a soldier, or a reporter.

- **Man (or Woman) Against Nature**—Boulders, tsunamis, and wild bears are just some of the adversaries in these memoirs.

Are you getting your own purpose and genre pinned down? You may have more than one memoir in you. Where do you think your first idea for a memoir fits best? Try to picture it sitting on a shelf in the bookstore. Where would it fit best?

# Who Are You Writing For?

This might or might not seem like an important question when you've barely just begun writing. But how you answer it can be extremely helpful for establishing your parameters and shaping your writing process. Perhaps no one but you will read it. That gives you a lot more room for self-indulgence of the best kind. If you plan to restrict the reading of your memoir to family and friends, you can make certain assumptions—for example, an inherent interest in your life that will not be true of strangers.

As you go outward in concentric circles from you to others known and unknown, the audience changes and so do the expectations for your memoir. Will you put it out on the Internet anonymously? Well, then it doesn't matter what you say about anyone, or does it? Do you plan to share what you write chapter by chapter with your writers' group? That assumes a certain preexisting intimacy between you and your readers, and also an expectation on your part for constructive criticism. Does that mean you'll take more or fewer creative risks? As you consider these questions about why you're writing and who might read what you write, keep any answers you come up with in mind as you take on the next question: what part of your life will you write about?

# The Pivotal Event

Most of the memoirs that really work are about one aspect of the authors' lives, one particular element of the human experience. For this reason, you'll need to concentrate your story on one incident, a pivotal event, relationship, perhaps a single major life change, or a distinct thread of events in your life. This thread may be personal or professional. And while each can include some of the other, either your personal or professional life is usually favored. If it's a "rags to riches" story, for example, there might be a parent or spouse who inspired and helped you succeed, but the focus is on your exterior accomplishment, not your relationships.

> **TAKE IT TO HEART**
>
> Before you decide something is worthy of inclusion in your memoir, test drive it. Tell the story to a half-dozen friends and see how they react. What questions do they ask you? Do they draw the same lesson from the experience that you did? If you have already written the story, ask them: Does this work for you? Where do you get bored? Where are you interested?

The key to narrowing down your story is to identify the turning point(s) that leaps out at you as most memoir-worthy. Your story might not have begun until you were 20; dropped out of college; and backpacked across Asia, where you discovered your life's work as a an acupuncturist. Or it may not have begun until you were 45 and, against all odds, gave birth to twins, or until age 50 when you gave up a lucrative career as an international businessman to open a charity for girls saved from sex traffickers.

## Your Top Ten List

Here's an exercise to help narrow down what matters for your memoir:

1. On a piece of paper, write the 10 most important events in your life. Jot them down as they come to mind without editing or revising.

2. After you have 10, rank them in order of their importance.

3. Look over your list and ask yourself why these events are there and others aren't. Do they relate to each other and add up to something overarching?

Your answers will tell you the part of your life that you should be writing about. If you don't yet grasp the "why" part of your response to this prompt, don't worry. It will come.

After you've made your list of top 10 life events, you may find that several link together to form a single narrative. For example, the day you married might be there, along with the birth of your first child, a son. Then there could be the day you sat across from a doctor and learned that your son had a serious disease. You may also have a climax to these events: when your child achieved remission or the morning you awoke to the devastating news that you had lost him. These are the turning points in your story. Make a big star next to each turning point on your list. I come back to them later when discussing structure and plot.

## Digging Deeper

Other top 10 lists are not so forthcoming. You may have to sit and puzzle over how or if the day when you were 10 years old and your father was killed in a car accident relates to your choice of a career as an airline pilot. If the connection is not clear but you suspect there might be one, it's important to allow your intuition to guide you.

As a follow-up exercise to writing your top 10 list, take two of the items on your list and free write about them—allow one word to follow another without a specific destination in mind. Try to put yourself back into your age and worldview from that time. Record your visual and other sense memories and the feelings that you experienced when it happened. This is when the magic of writing happens—when you're not planning it.

## The Least You Need to Know

- Knowing the purpose of your memoir will lead you to make other key decisions about focus, setting, other characters, and more.
- The memories that stick with you over time are the ones calling out for inclusion in your memoir.
- Sorting out memories for use in a memoir requires reflection, which requires self-knowledge and courage.
- Take one decision and one page at a time when writing a book-length memoir. Don't worry about the roughness of a rough draft or the total number of pages ahead.

# Truth Telling

## In This Chapter

- Making a pact with the truth
- How to think like a reporter
- Do's and don'ts of telling your true story
- Discovering the healing power of truth telling
- Seizing your golden nuggets

Writing a memoir is simple—we dredge up old memories; write them down; and move things around to give our story a nice beginning, middle, and end. If we have to make up a few things or add some people or events to create some sizzle or smooth out the rough edges, it's no big deal, right? Well no, I'm afraid it *is* a big deal. When you start inventing things or combining people in an otherwise "true story," you are writing fiction. When you put the word *memoir* on a book's cover, your readers have every right to believe that everything you've written is true. Truth is stranger than fiction, and it's more popular with readers, too. Any writer who puts a memoir out in front of the public has certain responsibilities. This chapter looks at those responsibilities, with some guidelines so you can honestly meet your readers' expectations.

# Fact Versus Fiction

For a fiction writer, every external event in a story, plus the internal thoughts and desires driving each character, are fair game, meaning these story elements can be whatever the writer wants them to be. The more imagination employed, the better.

In a memoir, this option of imaginatively making things up to create a more memorable "true" story is off the table—or it should be. Those of us who write memoir strive for something closer to journalism. It's not the same kind of journalism you read in a newspaper or magazine; it's more personal. But the rules for memoir are actually closer to journalism than they are to fiction. That's why I'll take a moment here and dip into the mindset of one intrepid (fictional) newspaperwoman to try out a reporter's point of view. Imagine you are none other than Lois Lane as she carries out her reporting duties at the *Daily Planet*.

Lois is at her desk when she gets a call from her editor. He tells her to run out to cover an accident scene at a railroad crossing where a train has collided with a car. As a trained reporter, Lois knows that in the course of the next hour she must quickly answer five questions.

# The Five *W*'s

In journalism these are referred to as the "five *W*'s," and they are always answered in the lead paragraph of any news story:

- Who?
- What?
- Where?
- When?
- Why?

To answer each of these *W* questions, Lois does two things: she looks at the scene and talks to witnesses. What can she tell from examining the physical impact of the train on the car? Perhaps she can determine the angle of the crash, which would reveal where it was when it was struck.

Then she finds and interviews any witnesses who saw the accident. Her goal is to reassemble the most likely version of what happened at the railroad crossing. Did the warning lights flash and the siren ring? Was the car attempting to speed through before the barrier came down? Was the driver on his cell phone when the crash happened? Did the train slow down and attempt to warn the driver?

In reality, even Lois Lane, whose stock in trade is reporting "just the facts," can only make her best surmise of what might have happened from eyewitness accounts of the train conductor, the driver of the car behind the one that was struck, survivors from the struck car, police at the scene, and so on. If two or more sources or witnesses report seeing the same thing, she can more reliably call their conclusion a fact. But even after getting such a corroboration, a reporter will not assert certainty. If there is a divergent point of view among her witnesses, she will include that, too, just in case. Her newspaper then has the right to bill Lois's story as "objective reporting." In fact, it is the closest thing to the truth available. Close, but not ironclad.

That is why eyewitness testimony in a courtroom is intensely cross-examined, and often dismembered. The dirty little secret about eyewitness accounts of anything is that everything we see is subjective—and another word for subjective is *biased*. We see things subjectively especially when there is a lot of emotional content in the events being remembered and when the stakes are high. Our subjectivity is shaped by who we are and everything we've lived to that moment—our culture, race, gender, social class, upbringing, and current circumstances, meaning what is at stake for us at any given time.

# Rules for Writing a True Story

The very common human problem of subjectivity in memory makes memoir, by definition, a problematic form. In a memoir, reality and imagination can, and often do, blur. Subjective remembering is more common than objective, and it's another human foible to forget that the way we see things is not necessarily the same as others. So what's a memoir writer to do? You are not going to put your memoirs in the *Daily Planet*. Where are the rules for you?

## Revealing Your Secrets

The rules for memoir boil down to one: keep no secrets from your readers. Get as close to the truth as you possibly can, and then tell it as it comes. If you must make a conjecture based on limited evidence, just tell your readers what you are doing. That way, after they give you their trust, they'll let you keep it. If you label things what they are—a fantasy, a dream, or a wish—readers can handle it.

Memoir lovers say that what draws them to personal nonfiction is the knowledge that these are true stories from people who are not so unlike them. Everyone, including every one of your readers, knows that the truth is subjective. But there is still a leap of faith involved based on an expectation that you have wrestled with the gods of truth and come out of it with your best assessment of what happened and why it matters. This then becomes a pact you form with your readers. From there, everything else flows.

> **QUICK PROMPT**
>
> Here's a counterintuitive exercise for this chapter on truth. Write two statements summing up your life. Make one truthful and the other a blatant lie. Read them over and over and then sit with each checking how your body feels and what emotions come forward. Which feels better?

The distinction between fact and fiction leads us to two cornerstone principles that apply specifically to memoirists and newspaper reporters but not to fiction writers:

- Do not add.
- Do not deceive.

Let's elaborate on each of these principles and see how they translate into guidelines for your writing.

## Do Not Add

Writers of memoir should not add to or include things that did not happen. If you were frightened by a drunken, ranting man while walking on a deserted street at night, this is quite different from your writing that this person lunged at you and took your purse. Even subtracting or omitting things can distort an event or a situation. If you passed this character in broad daylight with other people present on the sidewalk, it would probably not have been nearly as frightening. While subtraction of certain information about a situation may distort reality, the line between fact and fiction is more dangerously crossed when we invent or add facts, images, or sounds to a scene that we know were not there. The addition of invented material can change what you're writing entirely. Even when we add a quote that was never uttered, we cross the line into fiction. And we deceive the reader.

## Do Not Deceive

Memoirs should never mislead readers in reproducing events or conversations. The way the situation is represented on your pages is, to the best of your knowledge, the way it happened. Anything that intentionally fools the readers violates the pact you made with them. Thus, any exception you choose to make to this pact should be transparent, meaning disclosed by you in the pages of your memoir. For example, if you are writing about the day of your grandmother's funeral, you might honestly write, "I never knew what Grandpa was thinking...since he never spoke much. But here's what I guessed was going on for him that day...."

## Other Don'ts

**No composite scenes.** This would be if A happened on Monday and B happened on Friday, and rather than have two separate scenes you decide to put A and B together and call it a Wednesday.

**No composite characters.** Some well-known memoirists say they use composites in their memoirs to protect the privacy of people whose names they can't or won't use. Although it is acceptable and common to change the names of real people in a memoir for privacy purposes, that's very different from, for example, combining three friends into one and then writing as if what that "friend" did or said was pivotal to a life-changing decision you made.

Let's say, over the course of five years, three girlfriends of yours were divorced and in each case the woman told you her plan to leave her husband before she informed him. To simplify and heighten the drama in your memoir, you might write (falsely) that on the night before you told your own husband that you intended to file for divorce, you met this (composite) girlfriend at a bar. Your purpose, so you write, was to talk through your plan so that you could keep up your determination to go through with the plan to leave your husband the next day. You describe how you stayed out with this girlfriend until 1 A.M. to rehearse your lines. What was true here? In fact, you had been to that bar before and you had had this kind of conversation on the phone with each of the three girlfriends who divorced before you in the course of the last few years—meaning you'd practiced your lines in your head and with your friends many times before. Okay, so the scene at the bar the night before your break-up conversation never happened. You might wonder, aren't these two sequences of events more or less factually and emotionally the same? I'm afraid not.

The reality is that divorce is always dramatic and painful. There should be no need to invent scenes or conversations to increase its emotional difficulty and fallout for all involved, especially if children are involved. Your job as a memoirist is to dig deeper into the truth of your experience (and those around you) and describe what happened honestly. Believe me, the real drama is there if you're willing to really open up and tell us about it.

**No misstated chronology.** When I say don't change dates and sequence of events, I don't mean you have to tell your story in a linear fashion. You can jump around in time; just let the reader know what you're doing. There's no reason for prohibiting a writer from placing a Tuesday scene prior to a Monday scene, especially if you think readers should know how a situation turned out before hearing about how it developed.

It is easy to keep readers unconfused and undeceived just by letting them know what you're doing. While narrating a scene, you have the right to digress; in fact, this is often what makes personal writing engrossing. You might wish to quote comments made elsewhere or embed secondary scenes or personal memories. It is possible to do all these things faithfully, without blurring or misrepresenting what happened, where, and when, simply by explaining as you go along.

One way to establish a timeline for a memoir is to place your personal story against the backdrop of well-known public events: the assassination of a president, the Watergate hearings, the Iraq War, or during the height of popularity of a TV show or music act, for example. Then be sure that you have the accurate dates and any specific details of those larger events that you are using.

**No falsification of the proportion of events.** If you spent one hour in a jail holding cell, not a month in the county lock-up, say so. An hour can feel like a month to a first-timer; so play that hour as if it will never end. Just tell the truth.

**No invention of quotes.** Get as close as you can to what you remember. Don't completely make up conversations that never happened.

**No attribution of thoughts to people unless they've told you that they had those very thoughts.** This is the essence of the difference between memoir and fiction. It's also why memoir is closer to real life in certain respects than any other form of writing. In real life you don't get to take a tour of someone's inner thoughts. You must ask him to tell you how he feels. Or you can use your intuition and power to read other people's feelings and thoughts, as most of us do every day. In other words, you can make a guess based on a person's actions, comments, and expressions. Just call it that in your memoir: your best guess of what he was going through.

# Finding Your Emotional Truth

Memoir writers who try to justify a lie they tell in print will often say it (the lie) was their "emotional truth," as in, "the way I remembered it, so I wrote it like I felt it (even though it didn't exactly happen that way)." Some go so far as to call this type of confession "more true" than writing factually. But let's face facts—adding or combining are ways of stretching the truth. Instead of being creative with the truth, use your creative juices to remember and re-create what actually happened.

---

**QUICK PROMPT**

Write what you dare not say! On a sheet of paper, write down the scariest or angriest, or possibly even the most hateful, words that you wouldn't have the nerve to say to someone. Make it the person in your memoir who is causing your pain or with whom you're in conflict. Use these feelings to fuel your self-understanding and perhaps your internal dialogue or reflections in the memoir. (Don't write them as if they really were spoken.)

---

## Using Emotions Truthfully

Now you might be surprised to hear me say that there is great value in pursuing your emotional truth, even when you know it's exaggerated or dead wrong. For example, most children, psychologists say, believe they somehow caused their parents' divorce—even when their parents insist this is not so. What does that have to do with using your emotional truth? Let's say you are re-creating your feelings about the breakup of your family when you were nine years old. By all means, use those deep feelings to mine your childhood experience! Make yourself the center of the universe, as every young child believes she is. Just let the reader know that you're dipping into that childlike point of view. Introduce us to this break from your grown-up point of view with a sentence that begins, "The way it looked to me then was…." Then it's all smooth sailing from there; just don't forget to tell us when you've returned to the adult you.

## Realizations Create Suspense

Your parents might have ended their marriage for a reason you didn't know until you grew up. There is a good deal of potential for dramatic tension in framing a dramatic situation with realizations that don't arrive until later. After sharing your childlike point of view, you can conclude with the arrival of your a-ha moment of truth using phrases like "I wouldn't learn until much later that..." or "If only I'd known then that...I might have spared myself some of that guilt."

**TAKE IT TO HEART**

The gold standard of truth-telling in memoir, according to one veteran memoirist, is to be able to write the following at the start of your book: "This is a work of nonfiction; it contains nothing invented, no composite characters or scenes. I've used direct quotations only when I heard or saw (as in a letter) the words, and I paraphrased all other dialogues and statements—omitting quotation marks—once I was satisfied that these took place."

We might not choose to follow the gold standard of truth-telling in our own memoir, but if we depart these principles, it's best to tell our readers what we're doing and why.

# Painfully Personal

The stakes are highest when our interpretation of a set of facts has more personal meaning for us. Imagine a memoirist is resurrecting the sequence of events before the end of her marriage. As any divorce lawyer or family court judge will tell you, a husband and wife who are ending their marriage rarely see things the same way. Typically, there are at least two truths in this situation, his and hers.

Still, it's her memoir, not his, so she gets to say whatever she wants, right? Yes, to a point. But if she also wants her readers to trust her as a reliable narrator and find her sympathetic enough to keep reading, the memoirist still has to get as close to the truth as she possibly can. In a word, she has to be *believable*. If she was at fault in a past situation, it's nice to hear her say so, even if the realization didn't come until she started writing a memoir (as is often the case). We all have flaws. Admit them and readers will be on your side.

## Writing It Real

If the memoirist writing about her divorce wants to include an incident of cheating by her husband that she believed took place, but of which she has only suspicions, not proof, how can she go about it without violating the pact of trust she has with her readers?

Let's start with what may have happened in this suspicious incident: When the wife (our memoirist) answered the phone, a female caller asked for her husband but hung up abruptly after being asked to provide her name. The wife immediately suspected that it was the voice of a woman who, up until a few months ago, her husband mentioned frequently whenever he talked about the office, but now suddenly doesn't mention anymore. In her thinking, the wife put this call together with another time she picked up the phone by accident and heard the two of them speaking to get to her suspicion.

As is by now apparent, this writer is using her memoir to build a case against her ex in a blame game around her divorce. As such, she does not plan to collect competing points of view from her ex-husband or his new wife. Still, what would be a more honest way for her to write about this incident? She can identify her suspicions and lay out the evidence. Sure she can, but this is not *Divorce Court;* any memoirist worth her salt owes her readers more than that. In addition to hurling blame, they expect her to fess up to her fears and insecurities and dig deeper into what caused the breakup and breakdown of this marriage. As we all know, it takes two to tango.

## Dual Perspective Technique

In order to dig deeper and find your emotional truth in a highly charged situation, it is helpful to use two different points of view. But this time, they are both yours:

- Who you were when the incident occurred
- Who you are now

Using these dual points of view—and going back and forth between them—gives you emotional distance, which translates into perspective and reflection. Paradoxically, by first getting some emotional distance on what happened, you can then find your real emotional truth. Some teachers of memoir recommend that a writer wait 10 years after a particularly painful event before writing about it. For one thing, it helps get you out of the blame game.

Returning once more to the memoirist who is writing about the end of her marriage, let's think about what she could do differently. She could start by going beneath the surface and asking herself some pointed questions about the period when her marriage was breaking down. The suspicion she had about the phone call obviously came from somewhere. Was her husband traveling frequently during that period? Did they have money problems? Did she and her husband talk about things that mattered to each of them? How was their sex life at the time? Yes, these are intensely personal questions, but then she *is* writing about a very personal subject. That is usually what a memoir is—your most intimate and personal story.

> **TAKE IT TO HEART**
>
> Life must be understood backward, [even though] it is lived forward.
>
> —Philosopher Søren Kierkegaard

# Daring to Speak Your Truth

Psychotherapist Linda Joy Meyers, president of The National Memoir Writers Association and author of *The Power of Memoir: How to Write Your Healing Story*," said, "Forgiveness through writing can lead to a lightening of past burdens. This, of course, can be beneficial and healing for the writer."

In her book, Meyers observes that "re-membering" means to bring together different parts of ourselves to become whole. She offers these suggestions and inspirations for the process:

- Writing your deep truths frees you from the past and creates meaning out of chaos.

- Telling your truth frees you from shame and guilt.

- Your stories on the page will be different from the ones in your head.

- Writing a memoir can be a transformational and spiritual path.
- Creating a narrative where you are both the "I" character and the narrator can help integrate your past and the present.
- Writing and sharing your story breaks you out of isolation and connects you more deeply with others.
- Your story can help change your readers' lives for the better.

Once you start writing a memoir, particularly if you set a daily time and stick to it, the act of writing becomes a habit, which some writers further dignify by calling a *practice*. The benefits Meyers offers can multiply over the months and years of maintaining your practice.

## Allowing Discovery

As a memoirist who uses writing to identify and come to terms with unresolved feelings from my past, I can attest that it's a powerful process that can help you uncover previously unknown parts of yourself and other people. One way this happens is by entering the point of view of another person in your life and reliving an event that occurred involving the two of you. For example, I allowed myself to enter the point of view of the neighbor who had molested me when I was nine. It occurred in the attic of the house across the street from my own. Approaching the memory, I re-experienced my fear and confusion as I recalled the smell of alcohol on his breath and the coaxing tone of his voice. To my surprise, when I switched to my perpetrator's point of view, my feelings changed radically. I felt this man's self-disgust and weakness as a human being. My fear immediately turned into pity as I saw how pathetic this previously "scary" person really was. This breakthrough in my understanding allowed me to take the power away from him and give it to myself, something that occurred simply through the threefold process of remembering, switching my point of view, and writing about the experience.

## The Science of Healing Through Writing

Memoirists who write to find emotional healing now have science
on their side to demonstrate the effectiveness of this self-healing
technique. New research demonstrates that a life writing practice
can in fact bring improved physical and psychic health. Dr. James W.
Pennebaker, chair of the Department of Psychology at the University
of Texas, has performed experimental research to prove it. In one
study he found that college students who wrote expressively for 15
minutes a day over four days about matters of emotional significance
showed better vital signs and lower stress levels in hormonal tests
compared to the control group. The control group wrote daily, too,
but theirs were mundane assignments—for example, reminders and
to-do lists. The difference was that the experimental group used
their hearts and their heads, while the controls simply tapped the
latter.

**TAKE IT TO HEART**

The parts of our brain that control memory (hippocampus) and emotions (thalamus)—the limbic system—use the same neural circuits,
which is thought to explain why memories containing a strong emotional flavor tend to stick in our minds more than those less emotional
experiences.

# Seizing the Gold

If there's a single persistent memory that comes up frequently when
you look back at your life—a scene, a conversation, or an event that
simply won't go away—you should consider such a memory a golden
nugget. This recollection could be the one that's going to propel you
from just thinking about writing your memoir to actually writing it.

At 64, Pulitzer Prize–winning memoirist Frank McCourt wrote
*Angela's Ashes*, his account of an impoverished childhood in Ireland.
He says that readers often marvel at his ability to remember things
that happened to him as a very young child. The example one reader
used was McCourt's memory of being on the playground at age 10

and having a sore between his eyebrows. "How can you possibly remember that?" the reader asked. McCourt's answer was, "How can you not remember it? Just give yourself a chance."

## Creating a Golden Notebook

I would amend that to say give yourself a chance through preparation and by using the prompts that appear throughout this book. Now that you've begun brainstorming for your memoir, you'll need a dedicated notebook for recording the results of all this mental and emotional effort. I call it your "golden notebook" because if you apply the effort, your notebook will without a doubt contain innumerable gold nuggets, many of which will find a place in the pages of your memoir.

Your golden notebook should contain at least 200 blank pages, ideally with dividers for subcategories for different assignments and recordkeeping. For example, one subcategory could be dreams; many writers keep their notebooks on their bed stands so that they can jot down dreams and their first thoughts upon waking. These can contain some of your most fruitful ideas and inspirations for writing. Having a notebook nearby will serve as a reminder to get them down on paper before they're lost to the day's routines.

I urge you to use a paper notebook for this purpose, rather than an electronic device. Although you're probably going to do most of your writing on a computer, the act of putting pen to paper for the purpose of free writing helps loosen up the mind. Don't ask me how or why. I'm guessing there's an anatomical or central nervous system connection between the brain and the hand as it writes (unlike when the same hand types on a keyboard). Just believe me when I say the hand knows things that the keyboard doesn't.

One more thing: be sure that nothing else goes into your golden notebook—no grocery lists, phone messages, or directions, unless these tidbits are part of the story you wish to tell. Use your golden notebook to record responses to the quick prompts that appear in every chapter of this book.

# Mining for Nuggets

Here are some prompts focused on early childhood. Try each with
your golden notebook open, and be ready to record whatever nuggets—
golden or otherwise—might come up:

- When was the first birthday party for you that you can
  remember? Describe the scene, what you wore, who came,
  and what kind of icing was on your birthday cake. What was
  the best present? Were there party games (musical chairs,
  pin the tail on the donkey, Twister)? Did you win? What was
  your predominant feeling on this occasion?

- Write about your first best friend. Where did he live? What
  did you two do when you were alone? Re-create a typical
  conversation. Did you play pretend games? Was yours an
  outdoor adventure–filled friendship? How did that friendship
  end, if it did? Share your feelings about losing touch with
  this person.

- If you had an especially close grandparent, describe a perfect
  day with Grandma or Grandpa. Did she let you help cook
  pasta from scratch or bake a cake? Did your grandfather take
  you fishing or show you his coin collection?

- If you're old enough, where were you on the day President
  John F. Kennedy was assassinated? Or on 9/11? Who might
  have explained to you what happened and what it meant? Or
  choose any world event that occurred when you were a small
  child and describe the conversation you had with an adult
  about it.

- Write about someone in your early life who had a garden.
  Describe being in that garden and watching or helping weed,
  plant, or harvest. Remember and write about the feel of the
  dirt, the smells, and the colors.

- If you had a special prayer that you said aloud or silently
  daily or nightly, write out the words of that prayer. Then see
  what feelings come up around it and write those down, too.
  Was there something you prayed for that came to be? How
  did that make you feel?

- Pick the sibling (cousin or friend if you were an only child) who influenced you the most, positively or negatively or both, growing up. Describe an incident that exemplified that relationship. Put in all the anguish and joy that came up for you. Describe how you felt then compared to how you feel now looking back.

Those exercises should fill quite a few pages in your golden notebook. Leave room for going back and adding some more after you reread them later. Childhood is obviously a rich well of memories for your writing; for most people, it's the richest. So plan on going back there again and again to mine more gold as we continue in the chapters ahead.

## The Least You Need to Know

- Memoir readers highly value the fact that everything in your story is true.
- If you are making a conjecture, tell your readers what you're up to, provide your evidence, and make your best guess.
- Let your flaws show in even the most painful life experiences you write about. Don't be a victim; show your part in it.
- Writing about painful experiences can be healing, and there is now science to prove it.
- Create a golden notebook to record your memories and exercises for writing.

# Researching Your Memoir

## In This Chapter

- Sorting and file your artifacts for easy access
- How to scour vast databases for a missing piece of your story
- Learning how to make genealogy work for you
- Discovering interview techniques for loved ones
- Locating your answers in social history

Memories provide the bones of your memoir, but research gives it flesh and blood. You don't have to be a genealogist or a professional researcher to find the gold nuggets waiting for you from historical sources. There are many tried-and-true avenues of investigation available on your home computer and at your local public library. You can also make use of church, civic, and cultural organizations' archives. The biggest and best way to do all for your factual digging will, of course, be the Internet. The primary goal of the research stage of memoir writing is to assemble an accurate re-creation for the backdrop of your personal story. You're especially looking for clues to your story's setting, chronology, context, and texture. Sometimes we get lucky and personal research yields big surprises that shed light on the missing "why" behind events in our lives. Many memoirists find this stage of writing the most fun of all.

# Starting with What You Have

Every memoir writer starts with a treasure trove of basic information and artifacts, meaning objects of relevance to their stories. Some items might be useful solely as a way to jog your memory. Undoubtedly, you have photographs that can provide many details to fill out your personal memories. You also can use the diaries, letters, photographs, home movies and videos, e-mails, and perhaps other digital files available to you. There might also be a closet full of old clothes, a garage of tools, and a coin or stamp collection. That's a lot of stuff to manage, but I trust you've got the delicate items in a safe, dry place not far from your writing desk.

**QUICK PROMPT**

Choose a family heirloom. It can be a handmade quilt, a military medal, a vase, or something entirely unique to your family. Hold it in your hands, stroke it, smell it, rub it against your cheek. Then put it down and write for 10 minutes uninterrupted about this heirloom: what it is, who made or bought it, what does that person and the heirloom mean to you?

## Choose a Talisman

Sometimes, one object serves as a talisman during the time you're writing a memoir. A century-old, 2"×3" photograph of my Irish grandmother served as my talisman while writing my recent memoir, *A Lethal Inheritance, A Mother Uncovers the Science Behind Three Generations of Mental Illness.* Ellen Costello's photo was frayed at the edges and revealed a young woman's face with features and hair strikingly similar to my own. This one surviving photo of my grandmother, who died in her 30s, transported me to the brief life she lived as an immigrant in New York City during the first decade of the twentieth century.

**TAKE IT TO HEART**

As you sift through your photos and artifacts, see if one thing calls out to you as a suitable talisman for your memoir. You might put this item in a prominent place, on the wall above your desk, on a window sill, or in a top drawer, so you can return to it again and again for inspiration and focus.

Once you've assembled your photos, letters, and other items into categories, each dedicated to a certain time, place, or person, place each group of related items in its own file. Then store these memoir project files in a dedicated portable or standing file. Before you put everything away, be sure to create a master list indexing everything you have and how you've filed it. You never know when you'll want to return to one of these items in the course of your writing. And then it will not be convenient to have to look through everything again or, needless to say, climb up into the attic to search for it one more time.

## Make a Timeline

You might not choose to tell your personal story in chronological order. But you will absolutely need a linear chronology of the time period in your life that you're writing about. Make a note on this timeline of each major (and the occasional minor) event in your story. A strict timeline will help keep you sane while writing a long and winding narrative.

Such a chronology prominently placed in front of you and the reader also serves another purpose. Keeping to a single sequence of events over time is one of the ways a memoirist builds trust with his readers. If your timeline is shaky—that is, if in one chapter you write that your grandmother died in 1960, but in the next you're sitting on her lap watching President Kennedy's (1963) funeral on TV—you've lost track of time and you've also lost the confidence of a few of your more alert readers.

Some memoirists tape several pieces of paper together in a linear fashion and mark it up as a timeline to keep on the floor or a wall near where they write. You might also just keep your timeline handy on paper or in a computer file. Refer to it often, until your dates and places are locked into your mind.

## Sources and Methods

You might be wondering how to go about doing research when you occupy two prominent roles: as researcher and as subject of your research. One way to navigate this process of searching and sorting is to revisit the five *W*'s discussed in the last chapter. For example, to find out exactly *what* happened to you beyond the details you remember, you can interview other people who know something about these events. If there's no one left but you, you can access public archives and genealogical repositories to look for facts about family members who were present or connected in some way to what happened in the past. These family members may have lived as recently as 1 or as many as 10 generations ago.

Then, to establish the look and feel of the location *where* your story took place not now but *when* the events occurred, there are all kinds of historical collections at your disposal. From your library, you can get books with photographic and descriptive information on period architecture, interior design, clothing worn by various classes and cultures, as well as economic conditions and street scenes.

## Basic Historical Records

There are a myriad of public and private sources for facts about the lives of those who came before us. Among the best databases are

- Parish registries, which can include birth, baptism, marriage, and funeral records
- Social Security indexes
- Census details telling who and how many people lived at each address as well as their relationships to each other
- Wills
- Corporate and small business records of employees
- Old newspapers that are either digitized or on microfilm, which are often available at the main branch of a city's public library and contain old obituary notices

If you don't have personal online access at home, you can usually gain free access to these databases at your local public library.

## Ways to Narrow Down Your Search

This exciting field of personal family research is all about tracing the lives of your ancestors back over decades or centuries, on both sides of the family, until you've drawn a tree with many branches. You can elect to go back for a certain number of generations or trace your family line to a specific event, such as the Civil War.

In addition to the sources mentioned previously, you can find software programs and websites dedicated to helping the amateur genealogist wend her way through the thicket of relevant databases. One particularly rich avenue to pursue for genealogical information is to look into your family's ethnic heritage through organizations devoted to immigrants to the United States from Ireland, Italy, Germany, China, Mexico, and many other countries.

# Interviewing Family and Friends

By now, you've recorded some of your memories, you have some idea of your focus, and you've made a rough chronology of those events you want to cover. This might be an opportune time to obtain more details from your private circle of family and friends.

Some memoirists choose to interview family members and other central or peripheral characters in their lives before they start or while they're writing their memoirs. Older relatives, siblings, cousins, aunts, and uncles are all potential witnesses to the events you wish to re-create. And yet, approaching someone you know personally about sitting down for an interview usually requires that you tell him something about your intent. Are you ready to talk about your project yet?

The word *memoir* might frighten some people away from consenting to an interview. They can feel threatened about the fact that you've written or will write about them or another loved one. Family secrets are more the norm than the rarity. Family privacy will mean more to some relatives than others. Hearing discomfort articulated by someone you care about might put a real wrench in your creative process. As discussed in Chapter 2, we all tend to lose objectivity when the subject is us.

## A Safe Way to Begin

The person you want to interview might fear that she will inadvertently spill the beans or offend someone by her comments. One way to make it easier for a hesitant interview subject to say yes to your request is to describe what you're doing simply as a genealogy project. Eventually, if you do complete your memoir and decide to distribute it publicly, you'll need to get back to the people you interviewed to obtain permission to use their names and any direct quotes. (Written permissions are best if you name names in your memoir. They are less important if pseudonyms are used.)

As you prepare for an interview, you'll need to think carefully about the questions you plan to ask and how best to word them. Also important is your readiness to listen well. Either out of nervousness or passion for the project they're doing, the tendency of inexperienced interviewers is to talk over their interview subjects. They'll explain and offer their own points of view instead of letting the other person talk. The trick to getting a good interview is to disengage your inner commentator and editor and become absorbed in the story you are hearing.

Whenever you conduct an interview for your memoir, bring and use a tape recorder. You don't want to be scribbling notes instead of listening. That's a sure way to miss important things said. Set up the recorder on a surface directly in front of your subject and check it periodically to make sure it's still recording and that you haven't run out of audiotape or digital file space.

## Interviewing Tips

Here are some tips on how to conduct an interview, with an emphasis on listening well. Most of these tips also apply to people you might interview whom you don't know personally:

- **Prepare a list of questions about the story in advance—**
  You may never have to ask one of the questions, but listen for the answers. Make a mental note each time one of your questions is answered in the story.

- **Know your subject in advance**—This is not merely a matter of acquaintance. You should already know the historical context of your subject as much as possible before you begin your interview. When was he born, where did he live, who were his family members?

- **Don't interrupt unless the subject has strayed so far from the story that he can't get back**—Most people know their own stories and will return to the thread eventually. There are cases, however, when people lose track of what they were saying or become entangled in a web of memories that they can't escape. Use the most gentle reminders and questions to steer your subject back to the path.

- **Ask open-ended questions**—The object in an interview is to have the subject talk. If you ask, "Was it love at first sight?" you might simply get the answer, "No." Ask instead, "How did you first know you were in love?" Notice I didn't use the word *when* in that question because that might also lead to a monosyllabic answer.

Leave room to respond. Don't rush your subject. If you ask a question and then follow it up immediately with another question—even a clarifying question—your subject might become confused, not knowing which question he is supposed to answer. Chances are he is simply searching for the right answer or memory. Give him time to get there.

# Genealogy 101

I first learned the ropes of genealogy in the course of researching the lives of my Irish grandmother Ellen and her young husband, my grandfather Michael Costello. Although I'd never met either, they were central to the story I was writing in which I investigated three generations of my family around the theme of mental illness. When I set out, I knew that my father had become an orphan by his late childhood. I also knew there was some suspicion around Grandfather Michael's death. My mother had once told me the story of his having died "accidentally" on a New York City railroad track. This was said in a rushed, strained conversation with the unspoken inference left that his death had not really been an accident. But then it was never spoken about again. Twenty years later, when my teenage son started developing symptoms of a serious mental illness, it suddenly became important to know my family's mental health history. That's when I decided I had to track down as much as I could about my grandfather's life and death.

Being new to genealogy, I did the easy things first. On a lunch break, I went to the Ancestry.com website, a resource that I consider (in a positive way) the McDonald's of genealogical research. It's a user-friendly website that makes finding things easy and gives you the exhilarating feeling that you're just a click or two away from filling in a slew of blanks on your family tree—each oscillating leaf on the computer screen signaling another nugget of heretofore unknown information delivered to your personalized family tree home page. Victory feels imminent; that is, until you discover as I did the relatively small number of popular names used by any particular ethnic group in a single historical period.

Beyond offering a place to collect and share genealogical finds with other people, some of whom might be your long-lost relatives, Ancestry.com functions as a portal providing users access to dozens of public databases. Among these sources are government census rolls, birth and death registries, records of military service, and of course the kind of ship manifests where I eventually would find both of my grandparents.

## Peeling the Onion

If your family were immigrants to the United States who arrived at a port on the Eastern seaboard, as millions were, there is a wonderful resource available on the Ellis Island Museum website. It has an abundance of riches that can soon become overwhelming—I found steamships arriving monthly between 1900 and 1910 from Irish ports alone, each carrying more than 400 passengers with a dozen Michael Costello's often among them. I had to narrow my search, so I worked backward from my father's date of birth. I figured that in order for

Grandpa to get to America, marry, and have a baby by 1914, he'd have to have immigrated prior to 1910—maybe.

As I continued searching the Ellis Island database in this narrowed range, I quickly found a passenger named Michael Costello, 21 years old, arriving in May of 1906. *Hmmm. Don't get too excited*, I told myself. Checking August of the same year, I found another one. This Michael Costello was 19 years old, his ship the *SS Majestic*. I dutifully printed out the *Majestic* passenger list, stuck it in my file with all the other candidates and forgot about it. Here's what it said.

> Passenger name: Michael Costello. Age: 19.
>
> Nationality: British/Irish.
>
> Read/Write English: Yes.
>
> Marital status: Single.
>
> Last Place of Residence: Ballenstock, Tuam.
>
> Occupation: Farm laborer.
>
> Final destination: Jersey City, N.J.
>
> Relative: Sister, Mrs. P Fergus.
>
> Cash in pocket: Six dollars.

As part of my research, I took a trip to Ellis Island to walk through its halls and holding rooms in person. When I stopped and closed my eyes it was easy to picture the masses of immigrants who had passed through there—my own ancestors among them. I highly recommend it to anyone with a family history tying you to that place.

## Corroborating Evidence

The evidence to corroborate that this last record of a young man named Michael Costello arriving from Ireland in the summer of 1906 was indeed my grandfather surfaced three months later. It was found by my brother James in a paper bag full of memorabilia in his basement. That was where we found Grandpa's citizenship papers, which revealed his new address in Jersey City as the home of the sister named on his ship manifest. In the same pile of papers, we found Grandpa's marriage certificate to Ellen, which recorded their civil ceremony a month after Michael became a U.S. citizen. But then we were thrown for a loop when we came upon something else: A $40 receipt for the purchase of a 4'×6' burial plot, with room for two. The signature on the receipt was "Ellen Costello." It didn't say who, if anyone yet, had been buried there.

It was at this point that my brother and I had a sharp disagreement, not about what we'd found, but what it meant.

James looked perplexed. "Maybe they just wanted things set."

"Set?"

"You know, for the future."

"I don't know about you, but I'm 50 and I don't have a burial plot. $40. Think about it, James. They were dirt poor." He shrugged, clearly not getting my point.

I sat waiting for my brother to see the obvious gap in his logic. But he'd already turned his attention to the football game in the next room. My mind, however, was stuck on the St. Raymond's receipt.

Eventually more digging confirmed the fact that Grandpa was buried there at the age of 28, seven months before the birth of my father, his only child. No cause of death was given.

I offer this piece from my memoir, *A Lethal Inheritance*, as a sample of the process of discovery inherent to researching your own life and those of other family members to whom you are connected by blood and story. The notion of the darkness before the dawn is also an apt one for this process. Just when the researcher believes she has arrived at a dead end, the key to the story she's seeking can appear out of nowhere. This happened to me. The final piece of evidence I found in my grandfather's story proved to be the most significant and surprising of all.

# The Darkness Before the Dawn

Watching *CSI* on TV one night, it occurred to me that there were medical examiners and coroners in 1913, too. The next morning I thought I might be close to finding something when I came upon thousands of turn-of-the-century records already digitized and available to the public on the Westchester County website. I found lists of almshouse and jail residents, wills and judgments filed, and even autopsy records. But in a chillingly close call, I discovered that coroner's records were not saved until 1914, a year after Grandpa's death. I felt teased by my new proximity to Michael Costello's life, but still unable to locate anything other than a burial receipt to shed light on his premature death.

Finally it came: the letter from the New York State Department of Health, Vital Records Section. When I opened the letter, I was shocked to see an official copy of Michael J. Costello's death certificate, raised seal and all. I scanned down quickly searching for the area where it listed his cause of death. "Body found in the Hudson River, opposite Newburgh, New York." And then, under "Cause of Death," the words "Accidental Drowning."

There was no mention of a train accident. The only link to a train was under the deceased's occupation where it read "Fireman on the Erie Railroad." I learned later that this was the person who shoveled coal into the train's engine, not a fireman in today's sense. But the bigger issue was the recorded cause of Grandpa's death, not his occupation. *How could this be?* Mom told the story as if it were absolutely true, an irrefutable given. Perhaps she, too, had been given the lie and simply passed it on to me. Or maybe she'd made it up, perhaps to underscore the dangers of Grandpa's reputedly drunken, wild ways. Either way, it now struck me that this official document explaining Michael Costello's "accidental drowning" was no more reliable than if the State of New York had said he died in an "accident" with a train. People intentionally walk into bodies of water and step in front of trains every day. Most of these incidents are reported as accidents, whether they are or not.

In addition to demonstrating the types of sources that proved most helpful to me in researching my memoir, I hope this story also shows that the process of discovery can be a dramatic element in any memoir. There's a sleuthing quality to it that can work like any good detective story in drawing the reader in and holding him as the answers are doled out in pieces over the course of your story.

# Using Social History

At a certain point, a researcher of family history will reach the end of records that are particular to the ancestor she is seeking to learn about. But that does not mean there isn't still good material to be mined from public sources. When you've collected all that you can find about a specific person, you're at the point in your process when it's best to move on to the social history surrounding your subject.

## Re-creating Other Eras and Places

To get inside the Michael Costello of 1913, I allowed myself to ask the first of many "what if?" questions. What if Michael and Ellen's two-year-old marriage was buckling under financial and emotional strains? According to the *Majestic* manifest, Michael left Ireland as a farm laborer. In a listing for him and Ellen in the 1913 Manhattan phone directory, Michael's occupation is given simply as "laborer." On Ellen's death certificate, she is described as a widow and a house-keeper. Irish immigrants in East Coast American cities during the decades before and after the turn of the twentieth century were at the bottom of the social and economic heap. Signs reading "No Irish Need Apply" hung on fences around construction sites and ship-yards. Any family members to whom my grandparents might have turned for help would have been in the same fix as they were. The census records of 1910 and 1920 showed tenements in Manhattan and the Bronx typically filled with anywhere from 6 to 12 people, many with different last names, some identified as "boarders." It was not hard to get a feeling for the odds a young man might have felt were lining up against him, or the temptations of an escape.

**QUICK PROMPT**

Write about your great-grandfather (or grandmother or any other relative you never knew).

Take 15 minutes to describe this man as if you knew him. Include everything you discover through genealogical sources and anything gleaned through your study of the social history of his time and place. When you're not sure, use your gut instinct to imagine who he might have been.

## Family Secrets Show the Way

It seems that many, if not all, families have at least one secret. Usually it concerns a perceived scandal—an illegitimate child, a deserted spouse, a stolen inheritance, a crime committed but not reported, or a mentally ill family member who is banished from sight. A family secret is not necessarily something that is never spoken about. It can also be an alternate explanation for an event that is accepted as fact when most, if not all, concerned know it not to be true.

If the likely truth about my grandfather's death ever entered my conscious awareness before I decided to get to the bottom of it, I chased the impulse away like so many dark things in the night. It was part of an unspoken family decree: the importance of getting on with things at all costs. Since then, I've learned why this course is neither wise nor possible; it seems there's another rule with more sway over the human heart—and, if I can extend the metaphor, over the neuroscience of mental illness. It says whoever is denied his rightful place in a family will possess the hearts and minds of those left behind, unless and until he is acknowledged. For memoir writers, a family secret is like a lighthouse guiding a ship into a foggy port. This is where the gold nuggets lie for the finding.

Of course, unlike *CSI*, you might not complete your research process with all the facts tidily in place. You can still make a story from your journey of discovery. You can also use your intuition to come up with your best guess of what occurred, taking care to separate facts from hunches in what you write. That way, you allow your readers to join you in wondering about the parts that will remain unknowable. Everyone loves a mystery.

# Other Perspectives on Family History

One courtesy that some memoirists carry out as a matter of course in their writing process is to give family and friends who appear in their memoirs the option of reading a finished first draft before it is revised and completed. This gives these "characters" in your book a chance to be forewarned. It also can jar loose a valuable memory that you can then add to your story.

Among the things you might ask them after they've read some or all of your memoir are the following:

- If you have heard me tell the story before, what did I leave out that I usually say or that I should have said?

- What did I include in the story that made it confusing or wasn't really relevant or interesting?

- At what points did it not sound like me telling a story to family and friends? Where did I lose my voice?

- What are some other experiences you know I've had that you think I should write about?

These four questions will often generate positive feedback that will help you improve this and future memoirs.

This pre-reading by people who appear in your book is a brave and potentially valuable thing to do, but it is one that is entirely up to you. There is no golden rule that says you are ethically bound to let others read your memoir at any stage of your writing. See Chapter 19 to check into legal issues that might be involved in revealing certain private things about someone else in a book that will be seen by others.

## The Least You Need to Know

- Government and church records on births, deaths, marriages, and military service are the first stop for family researchers.

- Interviewing family members must be approached carefully and respectfully, with an emphasis on listening, not talking.

- Family secrets often cover the truth about a missing or banished person whose life can hold a key to your personal story.

- Clues to your family history can be gleaned from the social history of a people and place in time.

- Going back to get a family member's response to what you find through research can be a good way to double-check facts.

# The Mechanics of Memoirs

# Chapter
# 4

## In This Chapter

- Finding the best place and time to write
- Figuring out the best card or file system for you
- Embracing uncertainty in your creative process
- Learning the fictional techniques used in memoir

The three previous chapters gave you food for thought about what a memoir is and how to focus your personal story to write a good one. Now it's time to set up a writing practice that will enable you to manifest the finished product you have in mind. Like piano, painting, or dance, writing memoir involves both art and craft. Inspiration and talent fuel the artistry side of the process, but both of these elements are somewhat mysterious, thus hard to pin down. In contrast, the craft of writing is a set of skills that can be learned and practiced. This chapter will help you begin a solid, daily writing habit that will fill the pages of a memoir in whatever timetable you have set for yourself, with some inspiration from the masters added for good measure.

## A Memoirist's Tool Kit

There are some basic things you must have to write anything longer than a term paper. Right off, you'll need a "room of her own" as Virginia Woolf famously described a writer's space—either a dedicated room that is all your own or part of a larger space that you can section off as yours.

That said, more than a few writers find that the best place for them to write is a public location. With laptop in hand, they frequent coffee bars and public libraries where they find a version of solitude with other people around. One advantage of writing away from home is that it puts you farther away from the undone dishes and housework that may otherwise call out to you to get done and interrupt your writing.

Writers being a quirky bunch, there is some great lore about how certain famous ones went about doing their writing. Vladimir Nabokov, the author of *Lolita*, did all of his writing standing up. Truman Capote, who wrote *In Cold Blood*, claimed to be a "completely horizontal author." He said he had to write lying down, in bed or on a couch, with a cigarette and coffee. The coffee would switch to tea, then sherry, and then martinis, as the day wore on. He wrote his first and second drafts in longhand, in pencil. And even his third draft, done on a typewriter, would be done in bed—with the typewriter balanced on his knees.

## Organizing Your Time

What works best for most writers is to have a set time when they write. Short of a natural disaster or an illness, they go to the same place every day and begin writing at the same time. More writers seem to prefer early mornings, but I've heard from plenty who do their daily practice right after getting home from work or immediately after the kids are in bed.

There's some disagreement about whether a writing practice requires five, six, or seven days a week. It seems to depend on whether the writer feels a day off will replenish his spent energy or simply take him off track. If your goal is to produce a completed long-form (book-length) memoir within a year or two, nothing short of five days a week is likely to be sufficient. If you plan to give yourself a longer time to complete this project, you can adjust your writing schedule to fit that. Your memoir might take three or five or even seven years. Your deadline, whatever it is, is a self-imposed one.

**POTHOLE AHEAD!**

Don't make your time to write dependent on receiving an inspiration. If you do, every time you write becomes a brand-new start, and it takes too much energy. If writing is a practice you do on a regular basis, you just show up, sit down, and do it.

## Deadlines Are Your Friends

Even if your deadline is fake in that it comes only from you and there's no boss (or editor) looking over your shoulder, it's still a good idea to give yourself one. For one thing, it provides an interim goal for your writing practice. For some writers, that goal is a page count of three pages a day; for others, it's five pages a week.

In his book *On Writing*, Stephen King said that he writes 10 pages a day without fail, even on holidays. That's an exceptionally high daily page count for a writer. But then again, King is one of the most pro-lific authors of our time. In contrast, Ernest Hemingway wrote 500 words a day. Hemingway, like many other great authors, was famous for his alcoholism, but he swore he never wrote while drunk.

Joyce Carol Oates, another prolific writer who writes in longhand, says she prefers to work in the morning before breakfast. She's a cre-ative writing professor, and on the days she teaches, she says she writes for an hour before leaving to teach her first class. On days without teaching duties, when her writing is going well, Oates says she can work for hours without a break, and then she'll have break-fast at two or three in the afternoon. For most established writers, a daily writing practice is set and then changed as need be.

Writing is hard. Without deadlines, we flounder. The goal can't be "it would be nice if I finished this book...." You must trick yourself into taking a self-imposed deadline as seriously as you take April 15 as the drop-dead deadline for getting your taxes done. (But with no extensions!)

## Accessories: File Cards, Bulletin Boards, Software

In addition to how they sit or stand, and which writing instrument they favor, authors use a variety of systems to organize pieces of their writing as they amass enough material for a book. An old favorite method is the lowly index card system. On each card the author places one scene, partial scene, or story point. Nabokov, known for his impressionistic writing, reportedly used a card system so he could write scenes nonsequentially. He then rearranged his cards as he wished. He said that *Ada* took up more than 2,000 cards.

In recent years, a number of computer programs used by authors and screenwriters perform the same function as the index card method, but they do it electronically. Tidy storage is one big advantage of a computer system. When done by hand, the card system often requires a large table, bulletin board, or sectioned-off floor space so the writer can see all her cards at once. On the other hand, many writers swear that seeing the cards, being able to mosey over, mull them over, and move them around is key to their creative process.

# Get Practical, Embrace Uncertainty

The creativity at the heart of this process means that while it requires strict form with many conventions and rules, there's an equal amount of chaos and unpredictability to writing anything beyond a grocery list. If there is one prerequisite to being a good writer, it is an ability to embrace uncertainty. Another way to put it is that a writer, if he is going to produce anything beyond the mundane, has to accept the need for crappy first drafts. He also must be able to handle the shock of discovering that his best written sentence or chapter will often be the first to land on the chopping block. That's when, as a writer, you realize that this sentence or even first 100 pages was only the warm-up you needed to get to the real point of your story.

---

**TAKE IT TO HEART**

"When you write, you lay out a line of words. The line of words is a miner's pick, a woodcarver's gouge, a surgeon's probe. You wield it, and it digs a path you follow. Soon you will find yourself deep in a new territory. Is it a dead end, or have you located the real subject? You will know tomorrow, or this time next year."—Anne Dillard, *The Writing Life*

# Fictional Techniques in Memoir

Another prerequisite to being a good memoir writer is to be an avid reader of memoirs. In Appendix B, I list the classic memoirs that might inspire your writing. Some of these are excerpted in future chapters. Reading great novels is also important to the learning process. That's because memoirists borrow many techniques from novelists to craft a memoir. Here are some examples.

## Viewpoint Writing

This technique reveals everything that happens through the eyes of the memoirist. As the narrator and main character of her memoir, the writer puts herself in a re-created version of an event and experiences it just as it happened. The less distance, the better. The first person *I* is used to enhance this immediacy. Some memoir writers prefer to write the past in the present tense. "The sweet smell of jasmine intoxicates me and makes me forget that I shouldn't be there alone with him at night." The narrator's present-day opinion of what was going on in that moment, others' views of her behavior, and the outcome of that night and this encounter are saved for later. In the meantime, the writer crafts a scene that is a pivotal moment in her larger story. This is viewpoint writing.

## Action Writing

Active writing uses strong verbs to show how important events or actions happen. *Strode, balked,* and *cried out,* instead of *walked, stopped,* and *said.* Another thing to watch for is the difference between passive and active verbs. Whenever possible, use active verbs. It's the difference between:

| Passive | Active |
|---|---|
| "It has been decided." | "He decided." |
| "The dictation of her remarks was taken." | "She dictated her remarks." |
| "Her arm was broken." | "He broke her arm." |
| "It was rumored that Henry was having an affair." | "His best friend said that Henry had an affair." |

Passive verbs are used to avoid saying things that are difficult for someone to hear or that the speaker doesn't want to take responsibility for saying. They curtail responsibility for the action or recognition of the action.

## Description

Earnest Hemingway proudly declared that nary a single adverb appeared in his writing. No *silently, slowly, inadvertently, interestingly,* or the like. Many other writers swear them off, too. I find that position a little extreme, but it's a good idea to stop and question whether an adverb weakens rather than adds to a sentence. Compare these two:

> He silently strode across the room, opened the door with one excruciatingly difficult yank, looking like he might explode from the significant effort it took to contain his anger.

> He strode across the room and yanked open the door, looking like he might explode before getting the job done.

Besides being terribly over-written, the first sentence contains far too many unnecessary descriptors. Just say it, the reader thinks, while plodding through such a sentence.

Keep on the lookout for the following:

- **Unnecessary qualifiers**—Words like *nonetheless, relatively, significant,* and all those *thats.*

- **Unnecessary, redundant adjectives**—Such as *slow, tedious, and repetitive.*

- **Weak verbs versus strong verbs**—*said* is weaker than *shouted, pulled* sounds a bit lame when compared to *yanked.*

- **Bland versus interesting nouns**—*guards* are more generic than *sentries, tract houses* is vague compared to *cookie-cutter boxes, throw* sounds pedestrian when you can say *hurl.*

- **Avoid extra prepositions**—Especially look out for these when you don't need them: *pour in the cream* can be *pour the cream*; *use up the rest of the soap* can simply be *use up soap.*

You get the picture.

# Five Golden Rules of Good Writing

These are my favorite all-purpose guidelines for keeping your writing clean and honest:

1. Say it simply.
2. Mix up your sentences. Follow long with short, and vice versa.
3. Don't start every sentence with *I*.
4. Details are always better than generalities.
5. Begin every scene in the middle, not when and where the action started.

We'll return to these rules in the upcoming chapters to see how they work in specific situations.

# Unspoken Dialogue

In addition to the spoken word, inner dialogue (what you're thinking but not saying aloud) and reflection are two literary devices that are used in all types of writing but are tailor-made for memoirs.

Here is one such moment of effective inner dialogue from Simone de Beauvoir's *"A Very Dark Death*, a portrait of her mother. "I don't know why I was so shocked by my mother's death…. [When the funeral director announced her mother's name] Emotion seized me by the throat…. 'Francois de Beauvoir': the words brought her to life; they summed up her history, from birth to marriage to widowhood to the grave. Francois de Beauvoir—that retiring woman, so rarely named, became an important person."

What makes this passage so powerful? It's an effective use of repetition, where the reiteration of her mother's name slows time and gets across her sense of shock and loss. It locates the author's emotional response in her body—her throat. Her description of her mother's life as small and unheralded until her name is pronounced honors the importance of words to this esteemed author, and yet brings forward the ordinariness and profundity of the rite of passage of which she is writing—losing one's mother.

# Overcoming Writer's Block

Perfectionism is the enemy of good writing. Anyone who thinks Simone de Beauvoir got this paragraph on the first go around is fooling himself. Underneath the need to get things perfect (the first time) is the fear of making a mistake or sounding foolish. To whom exactly? is a good question to ask yourself when this show-stopper strikes you. I presume you are not writing in front of an audience. But that is what the perfectionist is inadvertently thinking when he tries to write it right the first time.

## Love Your Bad First Drafts

Anne Lamott called attention to the need for bad first drafts in her classic book *Bird by Bird, Some Instructions on Writing and Life.* In it she says, "The first draft is the child's draft, where you let it all pour out and then let it romp all over the place, knowing that no one is going to see it and you can fix it up later.... If one of the characters wants to say 'Well so what Mr. Poopy Pants,' you let her...because you may have something great in those six crazy pages that you would have never gotten to by more rational, grown up means."

Inside every one of us are the loose pieces of our personal memoir puzzle, searching for the perfect fit. We long for the puzzle to be complete, but sometimes the missing pieces can seem impossible to find. Sometimes we have to let the empty spaces remain empty until the right memory comes to fill it.

**TAKE IT TO HEART**

"What I try to do is write. I may write for two weeks 'the cat sat on the mat,' 'that is that, not a rat,' you know. And it might be the most boring and awful stuff. But I try. When I'm writing, I write. And then it's as if the muse is convinced I'm serious and says, 'Okay, okay. I'll come.'"

—Maya Angelou, author of the heralded memoir *I Know Why the Caged Bird Sings*

# Best Ways to Write It Away

What if you find yourself blocked and unable to continue what you were writing? To tackle the so-called "writer's block" head-on, write down the reasons you don't want to write—right now. Explain to yourself on the page why you feel you can't possibly write another word, and you will be amazed how much you have written. This exercise is a way to channel your aggression and anger about not being able to write into something useful. Sometimes that's all it takes to knock down your personal wall of self-sabotage.

**Get off the Internet.** For procrastinators, it's easy to get lost in cyberspace. What starts out as checking your e-mail and social network accounts can quickly turn into wasted hours surfing the Web. If browsing CNN.com, checking your Facebook account, and catching up on personal blogs are part of your daily routine, give yourself a time limit. As soon as your morning coffee is finished, so is your Internet surfing.

**Post your deadline above your desk.** The procrastination monster loves writers who don't give themselves a deadline. Don't make it so easy. Being part of a writer's group (in person or online) is an excellent way to hold yourself accountable and defeat the beast.

**Small steps are better than no steps.** Writing a memoir might be one of the hardest things you'll ever do. There's a good reason you haven't tackled it to date. Feeling overwhelmed comes with the territory, and avoiding writing is an easy way to listen to those pesky voices in our heads. When you feel that sinking feeling, remember that a memoir is simply a string of personal vignettes. Take small steps and focus on finishing one sentence, one paragraph, and one vignette at a time. Worry about threading the story together later. Your main focus right now is to break through your stalling and just get it all down.

**Borrow juice from other writers.** When I'm facing down a writer's block, I grab a book from my shelf. Particularly useful for me are anthologies of writerly inspiration, something to fit every flavor of my resistance. Reading someone else's excellent writing inspires the writer in me to get over myself and try some of my own. It doesn't all have to be profound. Here's a great bit from Amy Krouse's *An Encyclopedia of an Ordinary Life*, in which she organizes a series of brief vignettes alphabetically. Under "B for Brother" she writes, "My brother, who grew up with three sisters, was I won't say how old when he finally realized that he did not have to wrap the towel around his chest when he came out of the shower." Priceless. Inspiring in its ordinariness and spot-on humor.

**QUICK PROMPT**

Try Amy Krouse's technique. Select one incident or topic for each letter of the alphabet. Make *T* about your most terrifying childhood experience. For *I*, find an idyllic moment. And so on. If nothing else, you'll end up with 26 ideas for your memoir.

You know you have a story inside you busting to get out. It's up to you to find the way to break past fear and avoidance and start typing, one word, one memory at a time.

## The Least You Need to Know

- Picking one place and time of day for writing works best to set up a writing practice.
- Overcome writer's block by embracing uncertainty, writing without a goal, and loving your bad first drafts.
- Key elements from fiction writing used in memoir include point of view, action writing, and description.
- The unspoken, inner dialogue is tailor-made for memoirs.

# The Ingredients of Memoir

Like any good recipe, the best way to write a memoir contains clearly delineated steps that, if followed, are guaranteed to take you from page one to "The End." But there's also room to make your memoir a special creation unlike any other. This part introduces and explains the essential ingredients that must go into every memoir: voice, dialogue, character, scene, setting, and revisions.

I demystify and give you practice in writing dialogue that sounds like the way real people talk (hint: with very few completed sentences). You'll also learn the essential differences between two character roles you play as a memoirist—narrator and protagonist—and how to tell them apart in your head and on the page.

# Voices and Views

## In This Chapter

- How to play with time in memoir
- Wielding the power of *I*
- Defining your voice
- How to make use of your dual perspective
- When to make your narrator unreliable

This chapter is about time and perspective. Both concern *how* you will tell your story more than *what* it is about. Where you stand in time as you share your life gives you either a present or past tense for your writing. The vantage point you take to describe what happened decides which pronouns you will be using, *I* versus *she* or *he*, and much more.

# Point of View: Get a Perspective

Before you act or speak on the pages of your memoir, you must select a perspective or point of view (POV). Are you omnipotent? This was the perspective taken by Charles Dickens when he gave life to the small army of characters who populated the fictional life of *David Copperfield*. Dickens wrote his characters as if he could see and hear every one simultaneously. He made himself privy to each character's inner thoughts, hates, and loves. He was godlike.

More likely, you will tell your life story from the more limited perspective of first person. It's the most common POV taken in memoir, and it's exemplified by the use of the pronoun *I*. Never fear, from this perspective a whole world can be seen and a complete life story told. And like real life, you'll have to work hard to understand what your other characters were thinking and feeling when you describe what they did and said.

## Narrator and Main Character

There is a difference between the narrator and main character of a memoir, although the differences are sometimes subtle. Complicating matters, of course, is the fact that you as memoirist play both roles. The relationship between your narrator and you as main character is vital to think through as you begin to write your memoir.

As your memoir's main character, you experience everything directly; your eyes, ears, skin, taste, and smell are the reader's conduit to every action or conversation contained in your story. If it's hearsay you're using, something someone else said about an important event, you share with the reader how you interpreted it as a younger person. If your interpretation changed at some later point, the narrator will be the one to explain why.

As narrator, you guide, ruminate, and reflect. The narrator has more to do in the story than the main character. In addition to giving meaning to events, the narrator must direct the narrative, take the reader forward or backward in time, and jump seamlessly to different places in the same time period.

There is usually a difference in tone between these two roles and the voices attached to them. Unless yours is purposely or accidentally an unreliable narrator (more on that momentarily), a narrator is the responsible one in what can be a fraught relationship with the main character.

The main character can be silly and innocent, unaware of the consequences of her actions. The narrator is usually one step ahead of such antics. If you as narrator don't share everything you know immediately after an action takes place, the reader subtly understands that you are withholding knowledge. This can work for you to create suspense and drama for your narrative.

## You Then Versus You Now

As noted previously, there are dual and often multiple perspective(s) you must occupy to tell your life story depending on your age and life experience at the time of the vignettes. There's "you then" and "you now," and possibly one or more "you in-betweens." The tension and differences between these perspectives provide a useful framing device. However, jumping around to these different incarnations can get out of hand. It's the narrator's job to keep track and let the reader know which "you" is on the main stage at any given time in the story.

A passage from Jeannette Walls's *The Glass Castle* provides a wonderful example of blending together voices of an adult narrator and the main character as a child.

> I never believed in Santa Claus. None of us kids did. Mom and Dad refused to let us. They couldn't afford expensive presents, and they didn't want us to think we weren't as good as other kids who, on Christmas morning, found all sorts of fancy toys under their tree.

Walls goes on to explain how her parents encouraged them to pity other kids around holidays. Her mother says, "Try not to look down on those other children…. It's not their fault they've been brainwashed into believing silly myths."

Walls, as narrator, then continues in this vein, telling us about one Christmas when, with her father out of work, she knew there would be no present coming her way, not even the bag of marbles she'd gotten the year before. Then she switches to her perspective as a young child, using a sense of awe to describe how that same Christmas her father took her and her siblings into the desert, one at a time. Looking up at the night sky, he instructed each of them to select one star as their own.

"You can't give a star," I said. "No one owns stars."

"That's right," Dad said. "No one else owns them. You just have to claim it before anyone else does, like that Dago character Columbus claimed America for Queen Isabella."

I thought about it and realized Dad was right. He was always figuring out things like that.

This child's point of view is given even more poignancy when it is framed by the adult looking back in the introductory paragraphs.

## Are You a Reliable Narrator?

To inquire about your own reliability as the narrator of your own story is a wonderful question to ask oneself. The answer has as much to do with self-knowledge as the sophistication of your writing. The unreliable narrator is one who allows the main character to contradict herself without acknowledgement or consequence. She does this by saying one thing and having her actions betray the meaning or seriousness of her statement. For example, a female narrator saying "I was done with unavailable men" immediately before falling (as the main character) for another married man undermines her credibility as narrator. If the narrator had wished to relate the truth, she might have said instead: "I wish I could have resisted the playboys and lying cheaters and found a good guy to love."

There are different reasons for making your narrator unreliable. It can underscore all that you didn't know back then and wouldn't learn or take to heart until later. But there's a risk that you might alienate the reader who from this point will take the narrator's comments with a big grain of salt.

This doesn't mean a character can't have self-defeating contradictions; we all have them, and such traits can make characters relatable and sympathetic. The narrator becomes unreliable when she acts as if the contradiction wasn't even there.

# What Is Voice?

Voice in memoir is the real you. It's how you sound when you get together with your oldest friend over coffee and gossip or have a heart-to-heart talk.

Voice is first and foremost the personality of the narrator because, as narrator, you will be there throughout the story. As the main character, you also have a voice, but it can be different from one stage of life to another.

Voice is an interactive relationship between narrator and reader. How so? As a writer, you build your reader's developing sense of storyteller (you) in an ongoing process not unlike how you allow someone to get to know you incrementally in real life. You tell him a little about yourself, seeing how he reacts before sharing more. Even if a reader isn't familiar with the use of the word *voice* in literature, he is intimately familiar with the voices of his favorite authors and books. It's the emotional glue between writer and reader. As you go from the beginning into the guts of your story, you will usually deepen, broaden, and complicate your voice as narrator.

## Tone Gives You an Attitude

In memoir, a writer's personality comes across vividly in the tone he uses to narrate his own story. This is more so in memoir than in fiction where the author is giving voice to a fictionalized narrator and characters. Some memoirists write in voices that are soft, self-reflective, and intimate. Isabel Allende, who wrote of her experience as a mother during her adult daughter Paula's last year spent in a coma in *Paula: A Memoir,* is one such memoirist. Of Gore Vidal's memoir *Palimpsest*, one reviewer wrote, "His doubts are few and well disciplined," reflecting this author's larger-than-life personality and much-vaunted arrogance.

Elizabeth Gilbert's trip around the world in *Eat, Pray, Love* was enchanting not only because of its glimpses at Italian food, India's ashram culture, and the beaches of Bali. The single element that sent this book to bestseller heaven was the rueful, self-deprecating, and hysterically funny voice of Gilbert as narrator. *Eat, Pray, Love* also illustrates how the tension between the alternating perspectives of narrator and main character can work to add to the charm of a true story. The ironic tone of Gilbert's level-headed narrator nicely sets up situations where Gilbert as main character, an inveterate extrovert in the process of self-discovery, can make a fool of herself but still come across as likeably ditzy. Think about the scenes when she attempts to maintain silence in the ashram and resist the advances of her new boyfriend. They don't exactly go as planned. Guided by her reliable and patient narrator, we don't hold either "failure" against her. We laugh with her.

**TAKE IT TO HEART**

In William Zinsser's terrific book for memoirists *On Writing Well*, he suggests reading your work aloud and not committing anything to paper that you wouldn't actually say. He suggests you use a tape recorder. Then, as you read aloud, make a note of sentences that are uncomfortable, places where you want to say something different from what you've written. Play back your tape and note places where it sounded unlike you. After you have your feedback, set about the process of rewriting the story to make it sound more natural. Read it aloud again after you have rewritten it.

## Humor Takes the Edge Off

Humor plays a prominent role in memoirs, especially when the subject matter is dark. When writing about difficult or painful incidents in the past, a memoirist can effectively use an ironic or humorous tone to make the journey less uncomfortable for herself and her readers—if not when the worst of whatever it was is happening, then afterward. This shift in tone doesn't necessarily take away from the meaning of the event or dull its pain. It can serve to reassure readers that the author did in fact survive this difficult passage. It also establishes that the writer is in charge of telling her story. She is not a hapless victim of the worst events that took place in her life.

The use of humor as a leavening agent in a painful true-life story is a tacit acknowledgment that you've taken your readers into some hard-to-read material. After staying with you for such a journey, many a reader needs to take a break, or a breath. You're offering a respite from the intensity of what occurred and, like any good story-teller, paying respect to the rhythms and needs of your readers.

As you know, voice in real life or print is much more than speech. We navigate the world taking in not just the surface content of spoken information, but also unstated, subtextual emotional cues contained in a speaker's tone of voice. There are also huge differences in how each of us puts our words together.

## Diction, Your Choice of Words

Does he speak haltingly or with a dialect? Does she use consistent tone and pacing as she talks, demonstrating a sense of entitlement born of wealth? Or does she mumble, revealing her insecurity in the silences between sentences as she waits for either approval or scorn from her listeners? These questions address *diction*.

**DEFINITION**

There are two inseparable aspects of **diction.** First, it is the person's selection of words and how he combines them to make a sentence. Equally important is the style used to deliver them, including accent, inflection, intonation, and sound quality. A person's diction can be blunt and staccato, even and humorless, or lilting and poetic.

In addition to personality, information about someone's fleeting emotional states comes to us through his diction—especially his phrasing, tonal quality, and speed of speech. Without being told, we understand that a character is in an emotional state of fury, hysteria, despair, detachment, lightheartedness, confusion, ignorance, or authoritative confidence. These are just a few samples among many often-elusive emotional circumstances that determine the meaning of an event or conversation as surely as any list of concrete facts.

# Practicing Voice

As a memoirist, your work with voice will focus on developing and refining the voices of your narrator and your main character at different ages and stages. The act of creating and finding the nuances of voice while writing a memoir is not so different from the work done by a ventriloquist. It involves stepping back and then stepping into a character's head. Once you're in there, you've got to tell the rest of us what you find. Then tell us in the voice of the other person. Here are some exercises to get your ventriloquist muscles working.

Describe in no more than a paragraph each of the situations or characters listed here, but do it from the different points of view given, using the voice of each person:

- Describe your pretty sister "Tania" at age 13:

    1. you as her older sister

    2. you as her younger sister

    3. you as her father

- Describe your boss "Mr. T":

    1. to show your admiration

    2. to show your distain

- Describe your reaction to a Sunday sermon:

    1. you with a hangover

    2. you as a zealot

- Describe your blind date:

    1. you as interested

    2. you as not interested

    3. you comparing him to your last boyfriend

- You found a wallet with a $100 bill in it lying on the supermarket floor; you took the money and left the wallet, telling no one:

    1. you feeling guilty later

    2. you offering a defense later

This exercise demonstrates how our feelings, thoughts, and character traits are elicited in different situations. Actions speak louder than words, but words can show us the subtleties in our feelings.

# The Expository Voice

If your memoir was the same as real life, it would be a transcription of your days, trying the patience of even your most faithful reader. *Expository writing* is what transports your readers from point A to point B in your story without having to read about everything that happened in between those two points. This is the voice in memoir you use to tell and not show. Often described by memoirists as second best, telling has its place. Without it, you wouldn't be able to get from "Once upon a time" to "The end."

If the drama in your story occurred at the scene of a car crash on your way to the senior prom, we don't need long scenes about the day three months earlier when your date invited you, or how long it took for you to dress, what you wore, what he wore, and what your dad said to him on the way out the door. Unless these moments add suspense, irony, or drama to your story, they have no reason to be there. When you think the reader should know any of these things but you don't want to spend a lot of time doing it, telling is better than showing. You can impart this information in a nicely written narration using the expository voice. That will get us more quickly to the important stuff that deserves to be portrayed in real time—in other words, shown in a scene.

**DEFINITION**

**Expository writing** is a type of writing that informs, explains, or describes. It is the most frequently used type of writing by college students for term papers. Key words such as *first, after, next, then,* and *last* usually signal expository writing.

The expository voice is especially useful when you're covering years in a story when nothing particularly important happens. It moves things along in your story until you get to something you wish to draw attention to by the use of a scene. For example, you can write that yours was a completely normal high school experience until one day.... And then go into a scene to portray the heartbreak you felt after your boyfriend told you he was dumping you to go out with your best girlfriend. Why tell this one story? Include it only if the experience shaped you in some fundamental way.

Everything in your memoir, every sentence and scene, must serve a purpose. It must provide an essential piece of the story. Otherwise, it should go into the trash file.

# The Essential Reflective Voice

Anyone can make a list of the 10 or 20 most significant or traumatic events and people in his life. Most of us have experienced a broken heart, a layoff from a job, a friend we've lost track of, the death of a parent, and a win of some kind on some ball field. Only a skilled memoirist can tell us why that event mattered and how it shaped the rest of his life.

## So What?

A memoir without reflection is like a list. Perhaps it's a nicely written list, but it lacks the all-important answer to the question So what? Lots of amazing things happen to people. Why does yours matter? Not to other people, but to you.

One of the main reasons we write memoir is to give meaning to the random, harsh events in our lives. The reflections that come to you after the pain has eased a little bit are the best kind to include in your memoir. By all means, write down what's going on in the heat of the moment. But then allow yourself to reflect before you put it in a memoir for posterity.

## Exercises in Musing

Many memoir writers in workshops I've taught encounter trouble with the reflective voice. They find it audacious to render judgment on other people, or themselves. They don't feel they have the right to judge or generalize from the particulars to an overarching statement about their meaning, even in the privacy of their own memoir. If this is a stumbling block for you, here are some phrases that can help ease you into a reflective voice:

- There must have been...
- Only later did I realize...
- There was no way to know then...
- The way I see it now...
- It has taken me 10, 20, 30 years to understand that...

To sum up, a good memoir contains narration and scenes. Scene is where the action takes place. There are two types of narration: exposition, which summarizes, and reflection, where you muse on what happened and give it meaning. While many types of creative writing contain scene and summary, personal reflection is the special domain of memoir.

# Past or Present: Choosing a Time

Every language uses verb tenses to mark and divide time. The main divisions of time reflected in verb tenses are:

| | |
|---|---|
| Present | I walk; she walks |
| Past | I walked; she walked |
| Present Perfect | I have walked; she has walked |
| Past Perfect | I had walked; she had walked |

As a memoir writer, deciding on a primary verb tense of past versus present is best made early in the writing process. Choosing early will make it easier for you to keep track of your timeline and communicate it clearly to your readers. As noted previously, this doesn't oblige you to tell your story in a linear chronology. You are free to jump around in time as much as you wish. But if you do move from past to present and back again, you must be sure to match each time frame with the proper verb tense.

## When Is Now?

This might sound like more of a philosophical question than a practical one, but it is not. Defining "now" in your story is another necessary and important step to grounding it in a certain reality—even if it changes. There can only be one now in a story, whether it is in the present or at a certain point in the past. If you anchor your story in a clearly delineated now, your narrative can then freely move backward or forward. Now doesn't have to have an exact date attached to it; an approximate point in time, even as long as five years, will suffice. The purpose of selecting one point in time is to ground your story and give you a point from which to take off and fly.

The most common verb tense for memoir is the past tense. However, there are notable exceptions. Here is Frank McCourt talking about how he chose the tense for *Angela's Ashes* in William Zinsser's excellent book *Inventing the Truth*.

> I began by writing in the past tense about my parents meeting in New York and having me. Then suddenly—it's on page 19 in the book—I wrote a sentence that says: "I'm in a playground on Classon Avenue in Brooklyn with my brother Malachy. He's two. I'm three. We're on the seesaw." I meant it just as a note to myself for the next day: how to continue. But the next day I continued where I left off, in the present tense, in the voice of the child on the seesaw. I felt very comfortable with it and just kept going with it.

There is an appealing immediacy and intimacy that accompanies the combined use of the first person *I* with a present tense verb choice in memoir. However, when you write in present tense, things can get tricky when you move the present forward and backward from one time to another.

## It's Complicated

Let's look at how this might come up in practice. A memoirist is writing in the present tense, "When I'm eight years old, my father gets very ill and can't leave the house without his oxygen tank." But then she wants to write about a time before her father fell ill. She can write "A year before, he's teaching me how to dive into the lake," or, "A year before he taught me to dive into the lake." Another option would be "It was just a year earlier when he had taught me to dive into the lake." Okay, you're still following along just fine. But what if the writer wants to stay in that earlier scene at the lake for several pages? Does she switch over to present tense or stay in the past or past perfect tense? As you can see, it gets a bit complicated when you designate now as present tense. Not impossible, but this choice of tense requires vigilance to remain consistent throughout a longer story.

> **QUICK PROMPT**
>
> Write a vignette about a memorable event, your wedding or a childhood birthday, first in the present tense, and then using past tense to tell the same story. Make a note of any differences in their tone, their immediacy, or your ease of writing.

## Wondrous Would

One of the more flexible verb tenses in English (which not all grammar experts recognize as a "true" tense like past and present) is known as *conditional* or *helping* and involves the use of the words *would*, *could*, and *should* and, in the present tense, *will* and *won't*. This tense is conditional in that it refers to things that happened regularly or might happen in the future. Some examples follow:

* *Would* for imagined or unreal situations:

   I would *love to visit New Orleans.*
   *She* would *like to be a professional athlete.*
   I would *go, but I'm too lazy.*

* *Would* in conditional sentences:

   If I *won the lottery, I* would *buy my mother a house.*
   If I *had worked harder, I* would *have made the grade.*

- *Would* for habitual past actions

  *When I was young I* would *be home right after school.*
  *In the summer we* would *always go to the lake.*

Every memoir writer, particularly those who are new to the craft, will benefit by having a few good grammar books within arm's reach. Some of the best are listed in the Appendix A under Memoir Resources.

## The Least You Need to Know

- Use the voice of your narrator to showcase your personality.
- Differences between the voices of your narrator and main character produce a creative tension that can enhance your story.
- Expository writing summarizes, getting you from point A to point B quickly without telling everything that happened in between.
- Without the reflective voice, your memoir is nothing but a list of events. When you muse about what happened, you answer the question So what?
- The four verb tenses—present, past, present perfect, and past perfect—will all be used in writing your memoir, but your choice of whether it's primarily set in the past or present tense should be consistently observed.
- The words *would*, *will*, and *won't* reflect the conditional tense, connoting things that happened frequently under certain conditions or might happen under others.

# Believable Characters

**Chapter**

# 6

## In This Chapter

- Drawing characters from real life
- How to mix flaws and positive traits
- Showing, not telling, us who you are
- How to compose a character sketch

When you write a memoir, you don't actually create characters. Fiction writers do that. Still, there's an art involved in creating a lifelike characterization of a real person using only written words.

The craft of memoir involves many of the same creative skills used by novelists, and readers expect nothing less of the heroes, heroines, villains, and minor players in our stories than they do of the fictional characters they encounter in a novel. Perhaps they expect even more because they know from page one that these are real people. Therefore, a memoir writer's job is to make the characters in his true stories as rounded, edgy, flawed, heroic, annoying, inspirational, and complex as people really are.

# Ready for Your Close-Up?

The main character of your memoir is, of course, you. To tell your story, you will most likely employ a first-person point of view. You will filter everything that happens in your memoir. No matter what you've done or not done in your life, you are the hero or heroine of this true story. Another word for the main character or hero of a story is *protagonist*.

> **DEFINITION**
>
> The **protagonist** of a story, play, or literary work is the character through whose eyes readers see the world and everyone in it. The protagonist is the character the reader most empathizes with and roots for. Its opposite is the **antagonist,** or villain.

There's an inherent contradiction in telling a part of your own life story. You have to peel away the layers of your persona to portray the essential *you*, while maintaining a healthy perspective on yourself and the events that formed you. Only the real you can tell a sympathetic and believable story. No one wants to hear a phony toot his own horn, justify his actions, or tear someone else down.

Therefore, knowing yourself is step one in writing a good memoir—which I presume is the only kind you wish to write. You might have found out who you really are by reflecting on life's ups and downs. You may have a closet full of diaries and journals to lend valuable perspective. Or perhaps you have gotten to your core self by going to therapy for a decade or two. However you get to it, having self-knowledge is indispensible for writing a memoir.

## Then and Now

There's another interesting wrinkle to think through as the writer of your own story: the difference between who you are now and the person you were when the events you portray took place. This is a dichotomy that adds depth and texture to life writing. It provides the necessary writerly distance that allows you to answer these five essential questions about yourself, which will then guide the rest of your writing. In reference to the events you want to portray:

- What exactly happened?
- Why did it happen?
- How have you changed?

- What have you learned?
- Why should anyone else care?

## Character Matters

You take on a great deal of power and responsibility when you are the eyes and ears as well as the conscience for the readers who will come blindly to your story. As readers taking the time to delve into your life, they want to like you and they'll root for you to win against any and all odds. But that doesn't mean they expect you to always be a nice or perfect person. In fact, they'll hope you're not.

Our flaws are what make us interesting and likeable. Try to remember what you thought of the smartest, prettiest, and most well-behaved girl in fifth grade—you know, the one who went on to marry a banker, never to be heard from again. Then consider how you felt about the scruffy, funny kid from the wrong side of town who always got in trouble, dropped out of high school, and then became a stand-up comic. If you were to find out that both of these former classmates had written and published a memoir, whose would you want to read first?

Not all good or all bad, the protagonist of your memoir must at least always be interesting. It's also helpful if he's caught in an interesting situation and is sympathetic, meaning he displays some of the positive and negative traits that make us human—as long as he tries to be more good than bad.

The best way to find out what someone is made of in life (or in literature) is not to see him when everything is fine and dandy in his life. We get a much clearer lens on a person's true character when the chips are down.

# Ways to Reveal Character

A life story, whether it covers one day or several decades in your life, must show readers how you have changed over time. There are many tools in the memoirist's toolkit to let readers in on who you were at each stage of the story you tell.

## What You Were Up Against

Readers want to see their protagonists confront difficult obstacles and come out on the other side of these difficulties better, stronger people. Obstacles can be growing up dirt poor, surviving a car crash with severe injuries, battling cancer or mental illness, committing a crime and serving your time, losing the love of your life, or growing up with a wicked stepmother or stepfather who abused you. Bring it on. We want to see how this obstacle nearly destroyed you and how you put yourself back together again and, hopefully, triumphed.

Before they'll root for you, readers expect honesty and authenticity from you. It's the only way they can truly be on board for your journey. Through your eyes, ears, and skin, readers want to feel the fear you experience as if they were really there. They also want to exult in the victory of every twist and turn in your trip, especially if it took you to hell and back.

## External Challenges

Challenges are unavoidable in life, and they're necessary for making a plot work as the backbone of your memoir. If, as a main character, you meet no challenges, then your story just lies there. Its plot is too weak to move, let alone get up and scoot, skip, and dance as any good story should.

The way a protagonist meets a challenge tells a lot about her character. Does she deal with things straight on, or is she more reticent, an avoider? Perhaps she likes nothing better than a fight. Does that mean she's an optimist about her chances? Maybe she thinks about a confrontation for days or weeks before challenging an opponent. Or she could be the type who snaps right after she feels slighted.

## Internal Challenges

Challenges can also be internal. Internal obstacles usually arrive in the form of emotional conflicts. Responsibility clashes with avoidance. Love with fear. How someone deals with inner conflict tells a lot about what kind of a character he is.

Show how your main character changes because of the challenges he confronts, both externally and internally. Many of us grow as a result of our experiences in life. Some of us shrink. Rarely do we stay the same. As you think about the changes you or another character in your story have been through, look for external signs of such change. Show readers how your characters respond when everything goes wrong.

# Building Characters by Describing Them

Physical description is the fast track to creating character, but there's much more to portraying someone's appearance than simply recording her features. We might be tempted to let a photograph do all the talking for us. But opting for a visual image in lieu of writing a vivid description of an important person in your memoir is a missed opportunity. With words, you can focus on aspects of someone's personality that might be missed in a photograph. There's the way she sashays when she walks, his habit of closing his eyes before he speaks, her use of slang, his greasy hair. The list goes on and on.

It's important to use lots of details by tapping all your senses: What does she look like, sound like, smell like, feel like—and, if you kiss her, what does she taste like? Toothpaste? Licorice?

What does he smell like? If a strapping young man hadn't showered in days, his T-shirt might have smelled like sour milk.

What does he feel like? Did he have smooth hands? Was his handshake weak and barely there?

Offer specific details. Not just white shoes—white shoes with red laces and little heels. A subject didn't just shout—he shrieked as if facing his own ghost.

# Telling Details

Two American high school students might look identical to a Chinese visitor. But a fellow high schooler could instantly classify one as a neo-hippie and the other as a preppie. That classification, in turn, would lead the savvy observer to all sorts of conclusions about each student's values, attitudes, and behavior.

Individually, details are very important; but taken all together, they are even more important. They help you convey your characters not just at the level where they can be seen and heard and smelled and tasted. Taken all together, they convey and portray people at the level where they truly come to life.

> **TAKE IT TO HEART**
>
> Character details lift your characters off the page, but not all details are worth reporting or writing. Look for details that distinguish the character from everyone else. Does she like to cook? So do many women. If, on the other hand, she's passionate about cooking Chinese food but has never been to China or even met a Chinese person, we are curious about her favorite cuisine. It has become a telling detail.

Let's say you're writing about your eyeglasses. What distinguishes your glasses from everyone else's? Perhaps your rims are shocking pink with sparkles adorning them.

Don't use just distinguishing details; make them telling details. What are the particular qualities of your eyeglasses that tell readers something unique about you? Let's say your lenses are filthy. You can barely see through them. If you put that in a description together with something your husband might say—You're always bumping into things, or You're off in a dream world—then you have a telling set of details about you.

## Physical Attributes

Height, weight, eye and hair color, skin tone—each feature completes the picture you're painting of someone in your story. But be careful not to leave out your character's physical flaws. Classical beauty is easy on the eyes, but it can also be boring. Describing how a man proudly wears a beak nose and makes it the signature of his haughty personality can be fascinating, much more so than picturing the handsome face of a bland young fellow who is described as looking like he just walked off the cover of *GQ*. Without flaws and adversity, a character isn't memorable either in real life or on the page!

## Clothing and How It's Worn

She's standing on a crowded subway, wearing a Chanel suit, reading a romance novel. Her diamond engagement ring glistens in the fluorescent light. Dangling from the same wrist, she wears a hundred rubber bands. Okay, what are they for? Who is she really? The reader wants to know.

Clothes make the person and the character. Give your characters multilayered wardrobes.

## Mannerisms

Does she always put silverware, candlesticks, napkins, and placemats in the same precise sequence when setting the table? Or is she constantly reinventing her table settings to suit her mood? Does she quietly scrunch up her nose when she's upset, or is yelling her thing?

The word *eccentric* comes from the Greek word for *elliptical*, meaning a form with lines that don't always meet neatly—lines that surprise and take off in unique directions. Make your characters eccentric and elliptical to keep readers guessing and riveted to your story.

## Psychological Attributes

Your temperament is something you're born with. It makes you either a loner or a social butterfly. Other psychological attributes— for instance, phobias, fears, and fantasies—come later.

Don't forget to tell us what your characters do with these attributes. In other words, they're not good for much if we can't see how they show up in your character's real life. Which is better? To write that a dear friend was afraid of life or that he never left his room in daylight unless he was covered head-to-toe?

## Possessions

New journalism icon Tom Wolfe made a career out of carefully observing the things we wear, drive, and fill our houses with. It became his way of explaining social class and culture. We use things, he says, as symbols of where and how we fit into society, our place in the pecking order. He calls such things *status indicators*, and he wryly refers to the social structure they help create as the *statusphere*.

> **QUICK PROMPT**
>
> Get your purse, wallet, briefcase, backpack—whatever you use to carry all your "essentials"—and turn it upside down so that everything lands in a pile in clear view. List each item on a piece of paper. There's the usual stuff. But what about that parking voucher from your first date with a long-ago ex? And what's up with the new leather gloves you don't want your husband or wife to know you bought? And the brochure for a cruise that has been in there forever? And your old phone that no longer works? For each item you carry, write a sentence explaining why it's there and what it says about you.

# Actions and Speech

In our writing, we build characters by showing their external actions. Many feelings are best expressed through actions. If someone is angry, he picks up and opens the newspaper in a very different manner than when he's feeling calm and peaceful. It can snap in his hands as he opens it. Or it can glide onto his lap as he settles in for his favorite time of the day.

You can also develop character-building information by providing anecdotes and vignettes. Let's say you write, "My father was easygoing about religion." Right away, you should follow up by giving an example; share a vignette or an incident when he showed this trait. Did he stay home to read the Sunday paper one Easter morning, precipitating a major row with your mother? Or was it more subtle, like the way he'd go down to the nursery to visit the little ones in the middle of a sermon rather than stay in his pew and pray piously?

Focus on what makes your characters extraordinary. It's not the ordinary details that bring a character to life. It's the exceptional, remarkable ones that do it. Here are some examples:

- A lot of people talk slowly, but when my grandfather talked, you could watch grass grow.

- A lot of people sound nasal when they talk, but when Aunt Sally talks, it sounds like gravel rolling down a tin roof.

- A lot of people say *hell*. When he says *hell*, it has two syllables and sounds like he's talking about standing on blacktop in 105° heat.

On the page and in your mind, these characters are no longer so ordinary, are they? A speaker's tone isn't the only thing that reveals character; there's also the vocabulary, the syntax, the person's own approach to grammar and usage, and so on. Teenage talk often lays character bare because it's so distinctive. The vocabulary is always changing, too, which makes it an especially colorful brightener to any story that carries it in its authentic form. It all helps produce a package that reflects each speaker's unique character. Are characters soft-spoken? Do they drawl? Twang? Are they clear, or do they mumble? Consider the 12-year-old boy who misses his curfew and greets his distraught mother with "Yo, Mom. What did you think? I was dead or something?"

We'll cover much more about how speech and dialogue work in memoir in Chapter 7.

# Motivation: What Do You Want?

To build believable characters, you must know and show what they want in every scene. If there is no reason or burning motivation for an action to take place or for a comment to be spoken, then the plot of your story will fall flat. It will be a dull read.

Motivation reveals much about your characters. If your protagonist does something for one reason, then it says something about her character. If she does it for another reason, then it says something else about her character. And what if she does something different from what she says she believes? It might show that she's brave or cowardly, bold or shy, generous or selfish. It also shows that she's human.

# Antagonists: Real or Imagined

An antagonist is any person or thing that keeps you from getting what you want. Very often antagonists are the people who teach us our hardest lessons in life. When writing your memoir, you must be sure to build and portray your antagonist as fully as your protagonist. Why?

First, they provide contrast and conflict. You won't make your protagonist stand out by skimping on your antagonist. Without three-dimensional villains or impossible situations to challenge him, your hero can't help but look weak. If the Joker is a wimp, it's hard for Batman to strut his stuff. If your mean, nasty stepfather didn't make your childhood so miserable, you might not have grown up with the determination you have to survive and triumph over today's challenges.

They are also more believable that way. No one has just one dimension, especially not a villain. And no matter how awful this person's actions may have been or how much they might have hurt you, it's important when writing a memoir to give your villain's some sympathetic aspects, too.

## Why Be Kind to a Monster?

In my role as a memoir midwife, I coached a young woman who was having trouble writing the painful story of the years she spent being abused by someone she loved. Certainly, it was easy to feel sympathy for her. But this writer had a larger purpose for telling her story: she wanted readers to understand why someone in her position doesn't always tell on an abuser. Her challenge—the thing stopping her writing—was to figure out how to portray the person who had hurt her so badly as more than a monster. How could she pair the bad things with the loving, positive parts of their past relationship?

The first question we had to answer was why she should have to. The perpetrator in question was already paying a high price by serving 25 years in a state prison. So what's the point of sympathy? Here's what she came to: as painful as it was to remember and tell, if she didn't show the reader how much she loved and felt loved by this person, they would never be able to truly understand the depths of her betrayal and loss—and her triumph as a survivor.

## Readers Ask the Big Questions

As readers and as human beings, we have a burning curiosity to know *why* people do the things they do, especially the bad stuff. It's one of life's great mysteries. Why is there evil in the world, and what makes someone commit an evil act? Think about great villains in your favorite books. What kept you fascinated by Lady Macbeth? How about when you watch the news? Weren't you curious about how a serial killer like Ted Bundy turned into a killer? It's never the gory details of what they did that hold our attention, however entertaining they may be to read about—once.

We wonder, if I had the same troubled, abusive childhood or faced some other impossible circumstance, would I behave as a heroine or a villain? What innate character traits or soul mission do we bring into this world that keeps us either on track or sends us off the rails into evil?

These are the questions we all love to ponder and would never want completely answered—just freshly readdressed in each life and story. To remove the judge and simply shed light on the experience of confronting evil in ourselves or others and how we choose to respond is the job of writer. The reader then comes to his own conclusions, hopefully after putting himself in the other's shoes. So, by all means, as you write your memoir, do spend as much time understanding and portraying the good and bad aspects of character for the antagonist as well as the protagonist in your story.

# Life's Minor Characters

Sometimes the temptation is to give minor characters nothing but their names, ages, and genders. Other times the temptation is to use too much characterization, to build them too large. But then they're not minor characters anymore, and readers grow puzzled, even disappointed, when they don't do much or even disappear from the story. Sometimes all you need is a few brush strokes: some physical attributes, a mannerism, and maybe a dash of dialogue. A good way to handle a minor character is to characterize him through the eyes of a major character.

When a man who is a main character in your memoir describes a casual friend or acquaintance (a minor character) as seductive and having a long neck and silky hair, it's not a big leap for the reader to guess that he has a crush on her. In fact, the reader might know it before the character in your story does!

**POTHOLE AHEAD!**

Minor characters add much to your memoir, but they also pose many dangers. Give them enough attention to make them more than stereotypes, but not so much that readers are misled into thinking minor characters are major characters. They might be indelible to you, but readers can only keep track of so many characters at a time.

Too many characters can tax a memoir. If you're writing about your family of origin with six siblings, each two years apart, with you smack in the middle, it might be confusing and time-consuming to describe each brother and sister in depth. Instead, focus on the one or two with whom you confide and share key moments of action and dialogue. Alternatively, if you were an only child, it would be important to include another character from outside the immediate household, perhaps even an imaginary friend with whom you, as the main character, can interact. Everyone needs a buddy to talk things over with in a story. Who was your buddy?

# How to Do a Character Sketch

Your memoir will likely be chock-full of characters, some occupying a large role and others far smaller in size and story time. Each presents a valuable piece of your story and offers a unique reflection of you at key points in your life (if they don't do one of these things, they shouldn't be in there at all). With any character, even people you've known your whole life—and especially yourself—make sure you know every item on this character sketch or biography before you try to write them.

## The Basics

These include a character's age, height, weight, hair and eye color, skin tone, perhaps his educational background, marital status, the car he drives, and occupation. These are things commonly known about someone.

## Hidden Parts of Character

But then there are the really important things, stuff you can't necessarily see and not everyone knows, such as:

- Scars or handicaps (physical, mental, emotional)
- Other distinguishing traits (smells, tattoos, how she dances, whether she snores, does she shower daily or every other day?)
- Belief in God
- Marriages, divorces, lost loves
- Best friend, past and present
- Enemies (include why)
- Addictions, if any
- Parents (alive? status of the relationship?)
- Present problem (how does it get worse?)
- Greatest fear (where does it come from, or come up?)
- Strongest and weakest character traits
- Sees self as _____. Is seen by others as _____.
- Tells jokes, or has no sense of humor?
- Philosophy of life (include how it came to be)
- Idioms used, speech traits (such as "you know")
- The single most important thing to know about this character
- A one-line characterization of this character

## Five Things You Must Know

These are the key questions to answer about each character who plays an important role in your life story:

1. What trait will make this character come alive, and why?

2. Why is this character different from other similar characters?

3. Do I like/dislike this character, and why?

4. Will readers like/dislike this character for the same reasons?

5. For what will this character be remembered? Characters who are remembered are those who are strong in some way—saints, sinners, or a combination.

## The Least You Need to Know

- By revealing your flaws and unfulfilled yearnings, you increase the authenticity of your memoir and draw readers to you.

- The things that drew you into an intimate relationship with someone who becomes the villain in your story are as important to portray as the things that made you leave it.

- Everyone in your life can't be in your memoir. Pick minor characters carefully. Each should reveal something new about you in that time period or situation.

- A character sketch should serve as an encyclopedic inventory of everything about that person.

# How to Write Like People Talk

## In This Chapter

- Re-creating decades-old conversations in your memoir
- How to remember lines and fill in the gist
- Learning the rules for writing dialogue
- Finding out when *he said* is better than *he blasted*

I'm not going to mince words. Memoir writers make up dialogue. They have to. It's impossible to remember a conversation verbatim from morning until evening, let alone from one or two decades ago. But that's very different from creating an entire conversation that never happened. Or putting in a grand tell-off speech that you thought but never actually said aloud. How does a writer remember enough to re-create a conversation years later? Unless you have an incredible memory, usually there are only one or two lines from any important conversation that stick with you. Memoirists then fill in what came before and after, while staying true to the characters' voices and personalities. Most readers of memoir don't focus on this issue as much as beginning memoirists and a few critics do. In this chapter, we work within the parameters that dialogue in memoir recaptures the gist of what was actually said, not every word. Dialogue in memoir is a crucial ingredient—leaving it out is like omitting sugar from a cookie recipe.

# The Art of Listening

Most writers are introverts, not extroverts. This comes in handy when it's time to write dialogue. While other people are chattering away, writers are usually the ones listening and, more often than not, taking mental note of what they hear. In that sense, we're eavesdroppers and scavengers. Whatever we hear is fair game. With parents, siblings, friends, enemies, and lovers, we store what they say and how they say it. When the time comes to write a memoir, it's all there waiting to be tapped. For the people who know and love us, it's a not-so-wonderful fact of life that goes with living with or around a writer.

Eavesdropping is particularly valuable for writers. Without any responsibility for holding up one end of a conversation, listening in on others allows us to focus on how people actually speak; and how long (or not) they go without being interrupted by the other person.

What you'll soon notice is that most dialogue is a series of bursts, each interrupted by another speaker who then gets her turn to speak and be interrupted. If you write it like it is, many em dashes (—) will be employed.

Pay attention to your own speech when you talk to people with whom you're intimately acquainted, and you'll discover something else new writers often miss. Rarely do we use the other person's formal first name. There's Mom and Dad, Granny and Grandpa, of course. But when it comes to spouses, siblings, and friends, more often than not there's a nickname or a term of endearment used. It's Tess for Teresa; Pip for Phillip; and Honey, Sweetie, and Baby for spouses. Writing it otherwise won't ring true. The exceptions to this rule are people whose cultures or individual personalities tend to be more formal.

# Why Dialogue in Memoir?

Dialogue brings your memoir alive. Unless you are a master wordsmith, a life story without scenes and dialogue will become monotonous. Dialogue, done well, serves several purposes at once:

- It allows you to show, not tell, what happened.

- It helps to dramatize the story.

- It helps you re-create what really happened.

- It changes the flow or pace of the narrative.

- It provides texture and gives your characters layers.

- It lets a reader judge your character's personality.

- It helps set a mood.

- It conveys information concisely.

- It adds rhythm and color.

Most of all, dialogue plays a critically important role in character development. Without dialogue, the reader has to take your descriptive words as truth for every character trait. With dialogue, the reader gets to see the evidence and particulars behind your general statements about other people.

Before addressing more of the craft involved with writing dialogue in memoir, let's return to and (hopefully) finish with the issue of truth raised at the beginning of this chapter.

# Not Verbatim

Dinty Moore, in his terrific book *The Truth of the Matter: Art and Craft in Creative Nonfiction*, gives the example of a student writer in his class who was wrestling with the re-creation of a conversation that occurred years ago with her grandmother.

This is what Moore said to help his student get past the hurdle of a sketchy memory:

> The first rule is, don't fake it. Don't put words that you know are entirely fictional into your grandmother's mouth simply to make her seem more warm and generous than she actually was, or to make her seem more disagreeable. Your obligation to the reader is to capture this woman's speech as accurately as possible. The reader will understand that you are not perfect in your recollection.

Moore encouraged the student to dig deeper in order to find whole lines of dialogue as well as the gist of how and what words her grandmother spoke:

> If you spend time sorting through your memory bank, if you really try to go back into time and into your thoughts and feelings, you will likely find that you can remember the way your grandmother often spoke—her inflections, some of her favorite expressions, the way she lifted her cup of tea and glanced up toward her bedroom window whenever she referred to your late grandfather. The more you try to remember, the more you will find remaining in your memory. You can offer the reader an accurate summary of what you know was spoken about that afternoon, and a few snippets of how she spoke, to bring her character to life.

As noted, a well-written scene of dialogue can make a memoir come to life for the reader. A memoirist might understand this, but he might also feel torn about whether the dialogue he is writing reaches the bar of being sufficiently true to life. Is he being fair to the other person (or persons), or is the conversation being distorted by time? Some writers address this issue by not using quotation marks around dialogue. Other memoir writers choose to openly acknowledge a lack of perfect recall by offering a proviso such as this:

> These events are distant, but what I'm recording here is the truth of what remains in my memory.

Another writer might say it somewhat differently, especially if he is concerned about the reactions of people who appear in his memoir:

> It's quite possible, even probable, that others who were there at the time won't agree with my memory of this event. However, to the best of my recollection, this is how it happened....

It is perfectly fine to admit to such failures of memory within the writing itself. Readers will appreciate your honesty.

Mary Karr, author of two celebrated memoirs, described how she sent the manuscript of *The Liar's Club* to all the major characters in her family to fact-check her memory. Karr also emphasized that no honest writer, or reader, expected a memoir to reflect anything other than the author's inevitably slanted view on the truth. There's a kind of recursive loop in memoir, she said. Imagination informs memory, and memory informs imagination. People are concerned that the events are fabricated when what's most lethal is the slant you put on it.

## Going to the Source

If the person whose speech you're re-creating is still around and willing to be involved in checking what you've written, then one solution is to ask her to read the work. There are, however, risks involved with this approach. First, doing this doesn't guarantee that the fixed conversation will be any more correct than your first draft. Often the other person has no recollection of what was said because it wasn't as important a moment to her as it was to you. Sometimes she'll disagree with what has been written, perhaps feeling that she hasn't been represented fairly, or she'll remember it quite differently. In fact, another person will usually remember any event in a radically different way. It's good to think through these possibilities and the best responses ahead of time.

**QUICK PROMPT**

Play telephone. Get your writers' group to devote 10 minutes to this party game, which begins with a phrase written down on a piece of paper. Something like *Her father gave Suzy $10 to go buy a new hat and get an ice cream cone.* Hand it to the first person in line, who then whispers it into the ear of the person on her left, and so on down the line. What comes out of the mouth of the last person will inevitably be a sentence with a very different meaning. *Dad wanted Suzy to bring back ice cream, but she spent the money on a new hat instead* uses many of the same words as the original sentence but has a very different meaning. So it is with memory.

To prod the memory of those with whom you had a long-ago conversation, you might want to try writing the remembered dialogue like a play, just focusing on the dialogue. Let's say the conversation involved three people: the author of the memoir and two others, Stan and June. The author writes down as much as he can remember of what he said or what the others said and then passes it on to the others to fill in their parts. They can also edit what the author has written, if they remember things differently. The author rewrites the scene, including all the details of the setting, what people were wearing, and so on, and sends it back to Stan and June for a final read-through. This exercise works best with people who have remained personally close to you.

If someone disagrees vehemently with what you've written in your memoir, you always have the option to simply tell rather than show what happened and make it clear that this is your impression of what was said.

# Strategies for Remembering

Authors have developed certain strategies to help them recall and write conversations from deep in their past. These strategies won't solve the problem completely, but in most cases they enable the writer to write the scene and get on with her writing.

## Focusing On the Circumstances

When trying to recall a conversation from long ago, close your eyes and picture the scene, trying to engage all your senses in the process of remembering. Open your ears and hear what was said. Recall the smells of the meal you might have been eating. If it was a Thanksgiving dinner conversation—always rich for family conflict—try to remember whether the turkey meat was moist or dry. What other sounds were present at the table besides the other person's voice? There's usually commotion around getting food out of the kitchen and lots of cross-talk at any large group dinners. If it was a crowded table, did you feel uncomfortable being squeezed between Uncle Bob and your little cousin fidgeting in her chair? How stuffed did you feel halfway through? And how much more did you eat after that? Remember the pies you ate, and whether you had to loosen a belt to breathe at the end of the meal. What happened next? Did you go watch a football game, take a walk, or help with the dishes?

## Blending Conversation with Guesswork

Start by writing down any words or sentences that come clearly to mind. When memory fails, leave a blank. Now think about the general content and tone of the conversation. What words were probably said? What might fill the gap reasonably accurately? The writer of the memoir can try explaining to readers how she felt and what she thought, to fill in the gaps.

Here's an example: "I clearly remember my sister Rita saying to me at a dinner long after our parents had passed on, 'You were always getting the best Christmas presents when we were kids. Mom and Dad liked you best.' And I remember then how she laughed as if it didn't matter to her."

Perhaps the writer was shocked to hear this because she always felt her prettier younger sister got all the attention growing up. The rest of that conversation is a blur. But she can still remember her sudden stomach cramp and the realization that Rita was jealous of how much she had now (a husband, children, and a nice home), while Rita was still single, losing her looks, and struggling financially. The writer remembers not sharing that realization with her sister at the table but saying simply, "You had plenty of chances," and the look of anger she got from her sister before someone changed the subject.

# Using Indirect Dialogue

Another way to use fragmented memories of conversations in a memoir is through indirect dialogue. It involves writing around bits of speech and contextualizing them with descriptive language. These sentences are usually introduced by the word *that*: "My grandmother said [that] Grandpa died on the first day of WWII" is an example of indirect dialogue. "My grandmother said, 'Grandpa died on the first day of WWII,'" is direct dialogue.

Indirect dialogue is often used when you don't recall the exact wording of a conversation or when you are reluctant to attribute specific words to an individual.

With indirect dialogue, you lose immediacy and impact. Because of this, indirect dialogue is often a second choice after direct dialogue. But it is a useful device when you don't want to, or can't honestly, place specific words directly in someone's mouth. With indirect dialogue, you get across the flavor of the person's speech and give the reader a kernel of your conversation without attempting a complete re-creation.

# Putting Dialogue to Work

Believable dialogue results from a memoirist knowing his character. Who were you then? Did this conversation take place after your mother lost her verve, or was it while she still had hope for her own happiness? If your character is five, his vocabulary is that of a five-year-old. If the character is uneducated, his vocabulary is more limited; he may use slang, and his diction might be less complicated. If your character is a lawyer, she may allow legalese (lawyer speak) or legal terms to seep into her everyday speech. If your character is from Ireland, he might have a sing-song lilt to his speech. How can that be integrated in writing the way he talked? He may begin many a sentence with *Say lad*, and, when speaking of the dead, throw in a *God rest his soul*.

Here are a few more how-to's for writing authentic sounding dialogue:

- Use contractions for most characters. Only the more formal speaker will say *I am* versus *I'm*. They also say *don't, shouldn't, we've, she'd, they're, they'd*, and so on.

- If it fits your character, use slang (*yeah, naw, gonna, shoulda, yo, ain't* and so forth).

- Whether to use profanities depends on your sense of propriety. But if it's a noteworthy characteristic of someone in your story, you might want to include the occasional expletive. Don't overuse them, though.

## What to Put In and Leave Out

Like many memoirists, I usually write a first draft of a scene, sometimes an entire chapter, without dialogue. This way I get an overview in one stretch of writing. I then go back and add dialogue later where I think it belongs.

To figure out where dialogue should go, I look first at sequences where I've written a lot of narration about what people said to each other. I then ask myself whether the points I've made with narration could be gotten across more vividly if I translated them into a scene with dialogue. If so, I adapt it. My characters now say what I had previously described using expository language.

Dialogue doesn't belong everywhere. It should be used to convey drama, not to download factual information. Your characters don't have to give their addresses and describe the weather over breakfast. Dialogue should reveal both the surface and the subtext of the relationship between two people. Since much memoir is about an interpersonal conflict, your dialogue should delve into this tension between people and the feelings that swirl around it for each person.

When you use dialogue in memoir, you have to cut and shape it to emphasize important moments in time and leave out the uninteresting and unimportant parts. You are after the kernel of an exchange, not an encyclopedic rendering of an entire conversation. The exception might be if you are trying to establish that a certain character rarely if ever shut up. Then you might re-create one of his long, insufferable monologues as closely as you can.

Otherwise, you can spare the habitual and humdrum "What's for dinner? Fish sticks and peas" type of exchange between people. Instead, you can cut to Dad's explosion upon seeing you (at age six) not eating your dinner. You'll write, "Sit there until every pea is gone, you ungrateful brat," if that's what Dad said. And you'll describe the tense silence at the table while you fought back tears and ate a spoonful of cold peas.

If your dialogue involves members of your family of origin, a reader should be able to hear how your dad says something differently than someone else's dad says it. We should know if your brother was a jock or socially awkward. We should be able to guess the extroverts and the introverts in your household.

## Using Silences

As much as people interrupt each other, real-life conversations are also marked by stretches of silence. Sometimes it's a comfortable silence, as when two people are happy to be in each other's company and feel no need to talk. In others, silences are covering up intense unspoken feelings.

When I was writing about my mother's baffling explanations for the strange circumstances surrounding my grandfather's death, I was helped by what I read in an interview with playwright Harold Pinter about his play *The Homecoming*. Addressing how he used silences in his often pointed family dramas, Pinter said, "The speech we hear is an indication of what we don't hear....It is a necessary avoidance, a violent, sly, anguished or mocking smoke screen which keeps the other in its place."

Of course, because you are writing a memoir, not staging a play, you will find descriptive language to convey the facial expressions and other body language during the silences in your speech.

## Gestures

You can add gestures to your dialogue either while you're writing a verbal exchange or after you've finished with the words. Gestures include facial moves and muscular responses, as well as how a body is situated and moves within a scene. Gestures are ideally woven into dialogue, not standing apart. Catherine doesn't just speak. When

Jesse says something that irritates her, she scrunches her nose and raises an eyebrow to express her displeasure.

Many people use their arms and hands to express themselves when they talk. By adding gestures to speech, your readers can visualize the characters talking and learn more about them. Gestures and expressions are not always easy to write when you know people well. It could be that you're so accustomed to them that you no longer even notice their physical quirks. That's why you have to step back and remember that your readers don't know about Grandpa's funny way of clearing his throat before speaking, Mom's pursed lips when she's angry, or your husband's crooked smile when he's holding back telling you something so he can build excitement. View your characters as strangers, and then tell us what you see. Describe how your brother-in-law habitually looks askance before he talks. After knowing him for years, you understand that when he casts his eyes down he's just weighing his words carefully. But when you first met him, this shifty-eyed gesture made you wonder if he was being evasive or, worse, about to tell a lie.

## To Clean Up or Not

England's King George VI was a notorious stutterer. And yet many treatments of his life prior to the book and movie *The King's Speech* omitted this central trait from their depictions of him. Other writers and filmmakers might have thought they were being kind to the king. It could be that they weren't up to the challenge of writing a stutterer's difficult speech patterns—it may have been easier to write it cleaned up.

In a story from National Public Radio, the same issue came up. NPR reporter Howard Berkes once interviewed a man who stuttered badly, and the story was not about speech impediments. How would you feel, Berkes asked the man, if I edited the tape to make you not stutter? The man was delighted, and the tape was edited to clean up his speech. Was this the creation of a fiction? Were listeners deceived? Or was it the marriage of courtesy (for the speaker) and concern for the audience's ability to hear and understand him?

> **TAKE IT TO HEART**
>
> Mark Twain, who masterfully used dialect in *Huckleberry Finn*, offered this advice in the *Atlantic Monthly*, back in 1880: "Listen. Study. Practice. Master. What is known as 'dialect' writing looks simple and easy, but is not. It is exceedingly difficult; it has rarely been done well."

The same dilemma can come up in memoir when you are writing the dialogue of someone with a dialect. There's no right or wrong; it comes down to the writer's choice.

# Rules for Writing Dialogue

Dialogue writing has its own conventions that can be confusing for a new memoirist. Here's a primer of do's and don'ts.

Dialogue is constructed using four elements:

- Quotation marks
- The verbal message, which includes the sounds or words spoken
- A tag or speaker attribution, such as *he said* or *she said* (note this always includes a verb, usually, *say, says, said, had said,* and so on)
- A gesture, a pause, and body language—She paused, and looked away.

Let's look at some examples for each.

## Quotation Marks

Like fiction writers and journalists, memoirists also include quotation marks to delineate lines of dialogue. The double quotation mark, word, word, word..., double quotation mark is the convention. When you include a quote within another quote, the inner quote is marked with single quotation marks.

Two other forms of punctuation frequently employed in dialogue are ellipses (...) and em dashes (—). Use ellipses when your character says something that fades away or trails off. Use em dashes when someone is interrupted by another character's dialogue or sudden action, or when they interrupt themselves. Don't include any spaces between the last word spoken and either an ellipses or an em dash.

## Dialogue Tags

Tags identify your characters. They tell you who is speaking. Tags like *he said* and *she said* are the most commonly used—for good reason. Since *said* is so commonplace as a dialogue tag, readers often don't even notice it's there. In other words, its use makes written speech sound natural.

Tags using verbs such as *mumbled, muttered, whispered, grumbled, replied, quipped, responded, demanded, retorted, commanded, shouted, hollered, cried,* and so on should be used sparingly.

Tags can be placed before, in the middle, or after a section of dialogue. If you insert a tag between two or more sentences, the tag always goes after the first sentence.

*Right and preferred:* "I'll keep the car window open so I don't fall asleep while driving," Gerry said.

*Also right:* "I'll keep the car window open," he said. "So I don't fall asleep driving."

*Also right:* He said, "I'll keep the car window open. So I don't fall asleep driving."

*Not wrong, but awkward:* "I'll keep the car window open. So I don't fall asleep driving," he said.

The general rule of placement is that it is always best to put a tag after a sentence of dialogue. If you use tags before, use them very sparingly. It is the dialogue that you want to stand out.

## When to Leave Out Tags

You don't need a tag or a gesture to identify your speaker as long as it's obvious which character is speaking. If it's not obvious, use a single verb like *said, asked, demanded, muttered,* and so forth.

If more than two people are talking, tags are usually needed for the reader to keep track of who's saying what.

## Verbs and Adverbs with Dialogue Tags

Words like *laughed, chuckled, scowled, sighed,* and *grimaced* are physical actions and should not be used as tags.

Use them to insert pauses after *he said.*

*"That's gross," he said with a grimace.*

*"I know," she said, laughing.*

*He scowled. "Then why are you still doing it?"*

Adverbs (*he said loudly*) should be used sparingly. Whenever possible, use the stronger verb (*he shouted*). Never use *he shouted loudly.* Use adverbs only when the dialogue or tag does not give enough information to the reader.

*Back away from the door.*

*"Back away from the door," she said quickly.* (Here we get a sense of urgency.)

Using adverbs correctly in a tag takes special care. Look for every adverb, in narrative and dialogue, and ask yourself: If I delete it, will the sentence still have the same impact? Delete the ones you don't need. If your dialogue is written correctly, it will usually tell the reader what the tone is.

## Internal Dialogue

The purpose of internal dialogue is to reveal a character's unspoken thoughts, showing us something that isn't revealed by either expository narration or dialogue. But this ability to muse and reflect only belongs to your narrator. It's logical for the narrator to reveal the thoughts of the *I* character. But even the narrator cannot read another character's thoughts.

Inner dialogue can be written and used effectively within a conversation. Instead of simply noting a silence, you may choose to say in an aside what you were thinking during a tense or emotional moment while no one was speaking. In this internal dialogue, you can also think about another situation, perhaps an incident that resonates with the one you were first writing about. As the narrator of your own story, you are a lot like the conductor of an orchestra. Use the power of *I* to dig deeply and give a full account in your memoir.

## The Least You Need to Know

- Memoirists don't claim to remember conversations verbatim; neither do they make up exchanges that never took place or change someone's character by making him sound nicer or meaner.
- Your objective in writing dialogue is to write naturally as people speak, just without all the boring parts left in.
- Save dialogue for scenes with conflict or drama; don't use dialogue to download factual information.
- Dialogue tags such as *he said/she said* tell the reader who is talking.
- Inner dialogue, the thoughts of the narrator, can effectively fill in the silences that occur in conversations.

# Plot and Structure

## In This Chapter

- Learning the difference between situation and story
- Finding the deeper desire under a surface want
- Building a plot using the central conflict
- Making smart use of time in your memoir

Plot, eek! This is the point where many new (and experienced) memoir writers become nervous. The very mention of the word *structure* as it relates to story brings to mind a labyrinth of plot twists a la James Bond; and this notion feels completely alien to the intimate journey they're writing about. Relax and breathe. Our exploration of plot and structure is not designed to teach you how to create the next thriller or murder mystery. Instead, it will help you find the best structural framework for your personal story. Even if your memoir is about an inner journey, it needs a framework on which to hang. Without one, your life experiences will meander in every direction, losing definition and meaning. Sometimes writing a life story can be overwhelming. Understanding structure is one way to gain control of the chaos. Structure and plot are synonymous and have only one purpose: to serve the needs of your story.

# Situation and Story: Not the Same

Vivian Gornick wrote a fabulous book for memoirists titled *The Situation and the Story*. In it, she differentiates between the situation and the story, explaining, "The situation is the context or circumstance...the story is the emotional experience that preoccupies the writer: the insight, the wisdom, the thing she has come to say."

Gornick uses St. Augustine's *Confessions*, a book written in 398 C.E., which many consider Western literature's first memoir, as an example. Augustine's conversion to Christianity, she writes, is the situation or plot of his book. His story is the journey he took from idle self-indulgence to purpose—in other words, from ignorance to truth.

Another jewel from Gornick is her definition of *personal narrative* (she prefers this term to *memoir*) as a writing process centered on self-definition. What makes your personal narrative different from every other, she says, is the way in which you engage with the world (your situation) to arrive at the accumulated wisdom (your story) that you share with the reader by the end of your essay or book.

Gornick's point puts a useful spotlight on specific experiences, meaning whatever life events pushed us to go from one state to another—for example, from innocence to a wiser state of being. If you apply this formula to your own life, you should begin to see the emergence of the situation (plot structure) that will best carry your tale forward to its natural conclusion (story).

# Protagonist + Antagonist = Plot

As noted previously, every memoir (like every novel) includes a protagonist, except that in memoir the protagonist is you. In addition, every true or made-up story needs an antagonist that is a person, a circumstance, or an internal obstacle keeping the protagonist from reaching her goal. It's pretty easy for a memoirist to see herself as the sympathetic main character of her own life story. It's harder sometimes to identify the antagonist(s) who has been central in your situation. If you're having trouble finding that piece of the puzzle, it may be because you haven't yet answered the essential question that precedes it: what does your protagonist really and truly want?

## Desire as Beacon

Think about any stage of your life and what you wanted most back then. In grade school, maybe you longed for the teacher to like you. As an adolescent the object of your affection no doubt switched to the opposite sex. You also might have decided early on that you wanted to be a doctor. After making that decision, everything fell into place around it, including where to work during summer vacations (hospital versus fast food joint), where to send college applications (the best schools for premed), and the content of your daydreams.

**TAKE IT TO HEART**

"Penetrating the familiar is by no means a given. On the contrary, it is hard, hard work."

—Vivian Gornick

Much later in life, a decision to divorce may have signified several different desires converging at once: your changing preferences in a mate, an identity crisis, a long-submerged need to become or do something different. Each of these examples potentially sheds light on your desire. But do they tell the whole story?

## Matching Surface Wants and Deep Desires

Your task as a memoirist is to look at the things you wanted at different stages in your life and go deeper into each to find the unmet need that may have been hiding beneath a surface want. Through this process of reflection, it might occur to you that getting your teacher to like you in second grade was actually a gambit to get your emotionally distant father's approval. Your unmet need to feel loved and adored may have been what made you such an outrageous flirt in high school. Your medical ambition might have been part of you wanting to feel needed.

There's nothing wrong with any of these surface wants. What's important is to identify the want that drove you during the time in your life you're writing about, and connect it with a deeper desire you might not have recognized until much later.

## Following Desires to Obstacles

Perchance did you, like many of us, discover that your original life goal didn't turn out to be your ultimate desire? The old saying "Be careful what you wish for" can be pertinent. Sometimes the only way to learn about a deeper desire is by getting something and not wanting it anymore.

If you didn't achieve your goal, the important question is what stopped you? Very often, the obstacle keeping us from fulfilling a desire is an internal flaw—for example, a lack of self-confidence that keeps someone from seeking love or the career path he always wanted. In both cases, the person might stop trying rather than risk failure. There are many other self-sabotaging strategies that might have blocked your fulfillment. Were you always a people pleaser? This flaw brings many rewards but can also leave a person feeling overextended and underappreciated.

Then there are the villains, both literal and figurative, in our lives. An external antagonist is an obstacle that comes at you from the outside—for example, the car accident that took away your ability to walk or the authoritarian father who dictated the way things would be, never asking what you wanted. It might have been a prejudice that held you back or a lack of money to pay for the formal education you were qualified for. If you correctly identify the deeper desire beneath your surface want and put it head-to-head with your chief antagonist, you should be looking directly at the situation and story of your life.

# A Container for Your Conflict

Okay, you say, I know what I wanted and I've identified my main obstacle. Now what do I do? Your next step is to take this conflict of desire and obstacle and put it into a narrative framework with a beginning, middle, and end.

Let's say you're using a search for true love as the central through line of your story. One memoir tells the story of a single relationship over time, from the first blush of romance, through marriage and family, and then perhaps to betrayal and divorce. Another memoir strings together several episodes involving different romantic partners, each beginning with great promise and ending in loneliness and despair.

Either of these plots can get you from a situation of conflict between lovers to a story about self love as the essential prerequisite to loving another human being. An example of this situation and story working together in a single unified relationship plot is Julie Metz's *Perfection: A Memoir of Betrayal and Renewal*, in which the author discovers her husband's double life and eventually a deeper sense of self only after his death. An episodic treatment of the same story is used in *Falling into Manholes* by Wendy Merrill, a comedic treatment of the same essential story.

**POTHOLE AHEAD!**

A common problem in memoirs is their lack of a steadily building through line of conflict to hold a reader's interest. Your protagonist's desire should butt up against an obstacle early on; the conflict between protagonist and antagonist should then grow more intense until a climax is reached and the conflict resolved.

And though these can look and read like very different stories, their plotting relies on the same ancient storytelling framework that we will now study in depth: the three-act structure.

# Building a Structure

One plot structure is used as the dominant framework for the stories told in most of the movies you watch and the majority of novels and memoirs you read. It's called the three-act structure because the action of the story moves in three distinct stages. This story structure is found in every culture, in every part of the world. Hmmm. What does that tell us about ourselves? Let's see what light psychology can shed on the question.

## Meaning in Chaos

Psychologists say we like stories with rising complications and high stakes leading to a crisis, climax, and resolution because this structure responds to a fundamental human psychological need. What is that need? It is our strong desire to order reality so that cause and effect are put to good use. We need assurance that internal and external conflicts can be resolved by confronting a challenge. When a crisis comes, it leads to big trouble but ultimately ends in a resolution reflecting a new level of self-understanding and a positive external change. We use stories to give meaning to seemingly random, painful events in our lives.

Another way to look at this need is that we are reassured by knowing that our human suffering is not for naught. A school of psychological thought known as *narrative* or *life story psychology*, best articulated by psychological researcher Dan P. McAdams of Northwestern University, says that the specific stories we tell about our lives reflect our core personalities and levels of life adjustment. McAdams has done research showing that midlife adults who are more "generative," meaning they are personally and socially committed to others, often tell a life story with a strong theme of redemption.

At the center of the redemption story line is the storyteller's belief that he was born with an advantage, perhaps being the favorite child. This then, according to McAdams's research, gives such an individual the inner resolve to confront a grave obstacle—for example, racial prejudice—which he sees in retrospect as having made him a stronger person. In turn, this experience leads him to give back to others. In contrast, individuals who have fewer social ties tell life stories where challenging events are seen in much more negative terms. For such individuals, the research says, one bad thing leads to more bad things. There is no point or redemption.

## Self-Understanding for Writing

Applied therapeutically, a therapist using a narrative psychology approach might help such a client identify and change his life narrative to help him bring a positive resolution to an underlying conflict. Someone who believes he will never find love because his mother never loved him might create a new story for his life. In this story, he is the seeker in a quest to overcome the obstacle of being a "motherless son." The external crisis that might have begun as a series of marriages and divorces may climax with his loss of a high-flying job on Wall Street. In the new and improved story line, just as all appears lost, the seeker breaks through and finds his feminine side. This broader self-understanding might manifest in a new career giving financial advice to nonprofits and his first emotionally open relationship.

## Character Driven

The phrase *character driven* is often used to describe memoir precisely because the plot typically emanates from an internal conflict in the main character. The opposite of character driven is *plot driven*, in which the narrative details what happened and not so much how the protagonist changed as a result of events. Examples of plot-driven stories abound in fiction and film; take *Jurassic Park* and *The da Vinci Code* as two examples. But there are also plot-driven memoirs, especially in the true adventure and war genres, including *A Long Way Gone: Memoirs of a Boy Soldier* by Ishmael Beah and *Left for Dead: My Journey Home from Everest* by Beck Weathers.

Even within the category of the character-driven memoir are subcategories in which a different slice of life is emphasized. Each emphasis then suggests slightly different plots and storylines, such as:

- Romance
- Journey
- Business Success
- Inspirational

The romance plot keeps the focus on you and the object of your affection, suggesting more scenes between you and your lover/spouse at different points in your love story.

Inspirational memoirs employ more internal dialogue as the struggle is very much an internal one. The challenge with a spiritual quest or plot line is to find an externalization for this through line in the material world.

# Putting Your Story into Plot

Now is the time to put the situation and story in your memoir into this classic narrative structure. Note that act two is usually much longer than either act one or act three. I'll use two hypothesized real-life situations as examples for our exploration of plotting: one affecting a young female, another involving a young male.

## Act One—Characters and Conflict

In act one, you introduce your protagonist, along with a chief antagonist and the conflict or situation of your story. This is where you show us what the protagonist wants and how the antagonist is keeping her from getting it.

Act one should include an inciting incident, an event that sets up this conflict. After that set-up, the protagonist's situation becomes increasingly complicated, as a result of her own continuing self-defeating actions and/or due to further obstacles entering the narrative. Complications continue to build. By the end of act one, the protagonist is forced to enter a new world.

If an underage female protagonist's inciting incident was a decision to have unprotected sex with her boyfriend, the new world she enters by the end of act one is pregnancy. The inner flaw that might have gotten her to this place was an insecurity that led her to cave in to sexual pressure from her boyfriend. An external antagonist may be the boyfriend's callous reaction or her parents' insistence that she give the baby up for adoption.

## Act Two—What Have I Gotten Into?

In this second act, the protagonist, a stranger in a strange land, faces complications and ultimately a crisis that calls something fundamental about him into question.

If the inciting incident for a young male antagonist was to drop out of college and backpack alone through Turkey, by the end of act one he is stranded in Istanbul without money. The inner flaw that got him into this fix might have been his recklessness and inability to ask for help.

At first, act two can show the protagonist coping and growing in his new world. The young man makes friends. But his antagonist is still present—perhaps he refuses to let his parents know where he is. Then an external antagonist enters the story. He's arrested for selling drugs. Does his pride permit him to contact his parents and ask for help? This is when the conflict and the protagonist's stakes escalate to the highest peak of your story. The reader sees exactly what the protagonist is facing, experiences his increasing discomfort, and viscerally feels his inner and outer pain. As a result, by the middle of act two your protagonist faces an even bigger crisis than the one that ended act one.

This is the event that brings the protagonist to his knees. It's the breakdown that leads to his breakthrough. If his own flaw is keeping him from what he wants, this is when he can no longer blame other people. He must face his own self-undoing.

If it's an external antagonist, this is when the protagonist commits to the confrontation against him or it. However, while the protagonist commits to the fight, his antagonist is also hanging in there. The conflict between them reaches a peak.

Act two ends with the protagonist reassessing his life. He sees that he must change if he is to survive, but he isn't sure how.

## Act Three—Climax and Resolution

This final act brings the climax and resolution of the protagonist's confrontation with her antagonist. It is when the main character gets knocked down and considers quitting the fight before getting back on her feet for another round.

In this sequence of the three-act narrative plot, the protagonist is stripped of all illusions and must rebuild using new, hard-earned self-knowledge. As a memoirist, you must reveal to your reader the impact of how you changed by showing us that one thing you can do now that you couldn't previously. Perhaps now you are capable of giving unconditional love because you love yourself. Or you realize that you have strengths and talents, and this allows you to use them to help others. In some major way, you are the polar opposite of the person you were at the beginning of your story.

For the hypothetical story of the pregnant girl, a story climax might be reuniting with the child she gave up for adoption, in spite of resistance from her parents and current husband. For the young man in jail in Turkey, his story might climax with a realization of the advantages he's taken for granted after encountering real suffering and charity among his fellow prisoners. This could lead to reconciliation with his parents and a new life purpose.

# A Plotting Exercise

Memoirist Adair Lara, in her latest collection of essays and writing exercises titled *Naked, Drunk and Writing*, offers an outline prompt for writers seeking structure for their stories.

Fill in the following blanks with your story elements as prompted.

- I wanted _____ (surface want).
- I wanted it because _____ (deeper desire).
- To get it, I _____ (actions taken).
- However, something got in my way: _____ (antagonist).
- I had to try something different, so I _____ (actions and complications).
- All the time I was thinking that _____.
- The turning point came when _____.
- When that happened, I realized _____ (when the point of the story and your realization are the same thing).
- Resolution: After that, I _____ (what you did as a result of your realization).

Lara suggests that essayists and memoirists begin by figuring out the turning point in their story and then working backward from there. She explains that once writers realize the important revelation they came to in their story, what Vivian Gornick called "accumulated wisdom," they'll instinctively know where to start.

Lara's book contains many other useful exercises like this one. The best-selling memoir she wrote about the difficult relationship she had with her teenage daughter, *Hold Me Close, Let Me Go*, is a classic in the mother-daughter genre.

**TAKE IT TO HEART**

Imitation is flattery. As a new writer, if you resonate with a published memoir, try using its structure as a model for your own story.

# Time and Plot

You might be wondering how a memoirist can work a nonchrono-logical narrative into this basic three-act plot. You can definitely still use this structure for stories that are nonlinear; just be sure to accurately depict the content and impact of your turning points, not just when they occurred. It might be that your *character arc* was not a straight line. Perhaps your protagonist took two steps forward and one step back. Well, join the club. That's how most human change occurs.

**DEFINITION**

**Character arc** refers to the literal or figurative distance traveled by the protagonist; the steps she took to get from point B and achieve her goal. Often the arc in memoir culminates in a new level of self-understanding and/or reconciliation.

It also might be that you knew something important as a young child that you then forgot until many years later. This nugget of wisdom may have returned after an incident occurred and brought it back when you were in your 20s. To depict this process of knowing something important and then forgetting until you remembered it around a significant event would suggest a nonlinear narrative timeline.

## Traumatic Memory as Inciting Incident

Because so much memoir writing involves a process of stitching together fragments of memories, the presentation of time is a crucial factor. When a memoirist begins her story with part of a traumatic experience—for example, a violent action or threat against her as a child—we know that the rest of the memoir will be the process she went through to understand how this event turned her into the woman she is today.

In her memoir *Liar's Club*, Mary Karr begins with a terrifying memory at age seven when she is being examined by a family doctor who's inspecting her body for injuries. The doctor says, "Show me the marks." But Karr as a child freezes, unable to tell the doctor what happened. This state of being frozen, unable to remember, persists for much of the book that follows. As Karr writes it, "It took three decades for that instant to unfreeze." Mimicking the slippery process of remembering and forgetting again, the rest of *Liar's Club* skips on the surface of this one traumatic memory, with this tension providing much of the suspense that holds the reader in place, waiting to finally find out what happened. The reader finally does get this pay-off after the revelation of another family secret dislodges Karr's memory and precipitates an emotional catharsis with her emotionally erratic mother.

# Using the Gaps

It's a given that your memoir will leave out major chunks of your life story. These gaps can be used effectively in your plot structure to build suspense and drive home important turning points. When the memoirist puts himself in a scene reflecting who he was then as opposed to the man he has become, the reader is given a pointed look at the essential psychological and emotional changes that have taken place in between. Sometimes just showing the difference makes a vivid statement.

When the memoirist is telling a story of estrangement and reconciliation—say, with a parent or adult child—the absent years when there was no or little contact become an important presence in the story. As Sven Birkerts writes in *The Art of Time in Memoir:*

> The push to reconciliation is powerful in all of us. In the memoirist it often proves to be both the instigating impulse and the sustaining force.... The writing is in every case propelled by the need to find closure in the self, to make pattern from contingency, and to enact the drama of claiming a self from the chaos of possibility. For this reason, inescapably, memoir requires that a balance be struck between then and now, event and understanding. The manipulation of perspectives is but the means for achieving this. It reflects the restless search for sense that is universal, but which achieves its most realized expression in the memoir.

Birkerts closes by pointing out that even if the reader realizes that the memoirist has emerged intact from a harrowing experience, it doesn't take away from the suspense and empathy felt when reading such a story.

# Jumping Time

There are a myriad of literary devices for getting around within the narrative framework of your story. In defining how these techniques work, remember that in memoir there must be one "now," a point in time from which you can then move. Among the most useful are

- **Flashback**—Commonly, this is a jump backward to show cause in a cause-and-effect sequence relevant to the present.

- **Flash forward**—This is sometimes used as a sneak peek at the implications of an event.

- **Stretching and condensing**—Describing long passages of time without scenes usually handled in narration.

- **Foreshadowing**—Hinting at what is to come, creating anticipation and thus suspense.

- **Cliffhanger**—Again a suspense-building technique usually put at the end of a chapter to keep the reader turning pages.

These techniques are borrowed from fiction to bring the same full reading experience to the memoir form. Narrative is told in chronological order, but you can move within the narrative without disrupting a reader's sense of the overall chronology. Knowing when to break from a linear storyline helps. It also helps to know that you can have parallel tracks of narrative—maybe alternating, maybe not completely balanced, but two stories that move forward in time in different places and with different characters. At some point the two come together.

## Finding *the* Moment

Identifying the turning point that produced that one fundamental shift in your life is the most useful step you can take to plot your memoir. As Lara suggests, you can then back up and create the sequence of events that got you there. One of the biggest criticisms of today's memoirs is that they lack this natural build-up of conflict. They can cover too many years filled with thematically unrelated events. With nothing to build to, your story collapses into episodic moments. Your task then is to identify *the* moment, and the change that came about because of it.

## The Elegance of Simplicity

The majority of published memoirs don't make use of multiple plots or wildly fluctuating timelines. They begin early in the writer's life and move in a chronological fashion to a crisis, climax, and resolution. This still provides plenty of opportunity for a rich story, just not a complex one. In fact, there can be a real elegance to such storytelling simplicity. Examples of memoirs that move beautifully in this way through their authors' lives include Jeannette Walls's *The Glass Castle*, Tobias Wolf's *This Boy's Life*, and Barack Obama's *Dreams from My Father*. Once again, it bears noting that the story itself should dictate the right structure for your memoir, not vice versa.

## The Least You Need to Know

- *Situation* refers to the conflict in your narrative; *story* is the accumulated wisdom that allowed you to resolve it.
- By determining what you wanted and who or what prevented you from getting it, you should arrive at your central conflict.
- The three-act structure is a universal storytelling framework used in memoir to carry a protagonist from desire to complications and, ultimately, to a climax that results in a deeper self-understanding.
- Time can move forward, backward, or sideways in your memoir; all are effective ways of moving through the narrative in a three-act plot structure.

# Creating a Scene

## In This Chapter

- Finding out when to show and tell
- Discovering the five essential ingredients of a scene
- Knowing your purpose in every scene
- Learning how to think in pictures

Think of the scenes in your story as the precious stones interspersed with other, less glittery items—beads, shells, and polished glass—on a long necklace. Scenes are where the dramatic action in your story takes place. They are the sapphires, jades, and onyx of your necklace. Therefore, their placement is very important to create an overall effect. Bring your creative ability to visualize to this chapter where your memoir will take a cinematic turn.

# Putting Your Life into Scenes

When you translate something in your memoir from a couple of sentences of description into a full-fledged scene, you've decided that this is a part of the story that is important and thus will be better shown than told. On the other hand, some story points should not be scenes; they work better told. Which is which?

## When to Tell

Whenever a sentence is there simply to move your story from point A to point B in a timeline or to change locations, using a summary sentence from your narrator's point of view will be your best bet. You'll also use narration when you muse on the meaning of things that have happened to you. Unless they're on a literal or figurative pulpit, most people don't share their inner reflections on the meaning of life by speaking them aloud to friends and acquaintances.

Dates and times, weather, and *backstory* are also best told via narration—that is, if they are important enough to be there, and then they should be used sparingly.

**DEFINITION**

**Backstory** is everything that happened before the first sentence of your story. What the protagonist and other characters did, felt, and said at some point in time *before* the main action of your story is the backstory for your memoir.

Summaries cover and abridge long spans of time. They stitch scenes together, transporting the reader from one scene to the next. The summary is usually shorter than a scene. In that sense, it can be more efficient for story points that don't hold strong emotional content or meaningful interactions. Summary is less specific, more general and global. It fills the reader in on stuff he needs to know but doesn't necessarily need to see in detail. If you have a minor event that leads up to an important scene, use summary for the first event and then let the important event be a scene.

## When to Show

For centuries, writers of nonfiction have borrowed the tools of their fiction writing counterparts to reveal truths that could be rendered in no better way. They do this by placing characters in scenes and settings and having them talk with each other. The way writers have their characters do these things is possible only by putting them in scenes: they reveal a single point of view and show the feelings behind the words told through body language, expressions, and silences.

Scenes are where your action takes place and your plot unfolds. You write a story point as a scene when the scene will reveal something new or changed in the character arc of your protagonist, or in a conflict between the protagonist and antagonist. You don't put things in a scene that could be better told in a single sentence of narration. That's because a scene slows down narrative time and approximates real life.

**QUICK PROMPT**

Consider this one story point: you got caught by your boss stealing office supplies. She chewed you out for it so badly in front of co-workers that you felt humiliated and quit on the spot. Now write this two different ways: first as summary, and then as scene. Read both aloud. How does the experience differ as a writer and as a reader?

## Five Scene Must-Haves

Here are the five essential elements for any scene:

- **A place or setting**—Place refers to location, which can refer to your family home, travel destination, nature, and so on. Be sure to include the time and location where the event or experience took place. It gives your story context and makes your story real.

- **Concrete and specific details of place and characters**—Details are sensory images that appeal to the reader's sense of sight, hearing, smell, taste, and touch. Example: "Walking in the snow, the wind howling, the cold biting my face, I could see the trail to the road and the lake in the distance. I was hungry, exhausted, and my body ached from two hours of cross-country skiing through the woods. During the summer months, I would walk this same trail to get to the lake where I swam. Now, it was January and the bitter cold clipped short my memory of those sunny warm days. I wanted to get home to a cup of hot cocoa, sit in front of the fireplace, and relax in my rocking chair."

- **Action**—You can write about your own or another person's behavior. Your goal is to include action that is important or significant, that is related to the event or events of your story.

- **Time passing**—Time can refer to clock time, the time of day, the season of the year, or the time it takes for an event to occur.

- **Dialogue revealing something important**—A dramatic scene includes the comments you make or the conversations between two or more people. A dramatic scene requires dialogue that reveals character or advances the narrative.

If you don't have every one of these five elements present and accounted for, you don't have a scene. But a scene can also include other elements such as your thoughts, feelings, and opinions. For instance, as the event or experience takes place, you can tell the reader how you felt or what you were thinking. After the experience, you can provide the reader with your own viewpoint.

# Thinking in Pictures

In a scene, you want the reader to feel like he's right there with your characters. Scenes contain tension and detail. They should unfold moment by moment. When writing a scene, it's helpful to think in terms of making a movie or putting on a play: the curtain rises, the scene begins, your characters walk onto center stage, and there's action. They move through the scene, talking, fighting, eating, and expressing or not expressing feelings. The curtain goes down, and the scene is over. The curtain rises, and a new scene begins.

As noted previously, not all story points deserve to be written in scenes. You certainly can write a narrative that is one long scene, and if you're working on a shorter narrative, that might be appropriate. But for book-length memoirs, it's more common to write a series of scenes tied together by summary in the form of narration. As you map out the story, there are a lot of things for you to consider: the overall shape of the story, the pacing and purpose of each scene and how the scenes play off each other, the climactic moment and how you lead up to it, and how much you tell afterward.

> **POTHOLE AHEAD!**
>
> When you render too much of your story in narration and don't create scenes for the important turning points, you end up with a beige-colored and flat-feeling memoir. No important turning point should be denied a scene in your book.

## Why Summary Alone Doesn't Work

It's not ideal for a long memoir, but as I just wrote, it might work to put your entire story into the form of a scene. However—and I will state this unequivocally—the opposite is rarely if ever true. For the vast majority of book-length memoirs, it simply doesn't work to write everything in the form of summary. Readers like and expect to feel that they are there with you in the story. The only way to achieve this is by re-creating key story points in scenes.

If you're just starting out as a writer, you might need to work with the fine points of these distinctions. Try the Quick Prompt writing exercise in which you write about being humiliated by your boss for stealing office supplies. Then try the same exercise with a story point from your own memoir. How does scene feel different from summary?

Once you get the hang of scene, you might go the other direction, making everything a scene, laying everything out in endless detail, well beyond what the story warrants.

Your job is to figure out when to use scene and when to use summary. You have to be judicious; only the significant moments in your story belong in scenes.

## Writing from a Point of View

Point of view is your perspective on a scene; on a physical level, point of view describes what you see from a particular location. Are you in the corner watching at an angle, on the ceiling looking down, or hiding behind the sofa and only able to make out the feet of those speaking? In an emotional context, point of view is how you see what occurs based on your previous experiences and the feelings you bring to the situation. This would reflect what you wanted then from the characters who were with you at that time in that scene.

To make a scene vivid, ideally take off your writer's hat and put yourself in the role of a moviemaker. Don't try to describe everything; aim your camera. What do you want to zoom in on? Do you want to focus on one character with a close-up? To get inside that character's thoughts and feelings, you slow down and build tension by staying on her, watching carefully for pursed lips; a tightening jaw; and, of course, anything said aloud.

Or do you want to pull back, show more sweep, use a wider camera angle, so to speak? If you're walking on a crowded street with your fiancée when she says she can't go through with the wedding, where would the camera be? A close-up zooms in on instant reactions. A wider shot could signify your inability to comprehend what you just heard.

Keep in mind that as a writer you have a tool that moviemakers don't have. Except for the rare instances when they use voice-over narration, movies and TV shows are exclusively made up of scenes. Scene is their only tool because they rely completely on what can be shown through images and sound. You, on the other hand, can get inside your main character's head. It's a tremendous advantage that can be exploited fully in a scene by keying in on what she's seeing, hearing, saying, smelling, touching, and feeling.

## Using Details

Even when you're going moment-by-moment within a scene, you're still choosing which details you want to include in your writing of it. Make sure these details have meaning. You want *telling* details, not random ones.

To capture a sense of place in a scene, use all your senses, not just sight. But you don't want big hunks of description dropped into the middle of a scene, slowing the action to a stop and depriving the reader of the sense of immediacy you were after when you opted to put that story point into a scene. You want to fold the description into the action.

If a scene in a memoir is about meeting a charming old flame, you need to describe how the old flame looks. You must also show, and not tell, how that charm manifests itself. You must capture that charm through describing how the person dresses, his particular mannerisms, and other behaviors, and through dialogue. At the same time, you could use both the charmer's behavior and dialogue to reveal other, underlying aspects of his character and foreshadow future events. Readers will then feel compelled to find out what happens next.

# Giving Every Scene Purpose

Just as you figured out the burning desire that motivates your protagonist to go through the arc of change that is at the heart of your story, you will do the same for every scene. Yes, you read that right. In every single scene your protagonist wants something. The purpose of the scene is to show him going for it, encountering an obstacle and either succeeding or failing to get around it to reach a goal. This goal can represent one small step toward a larger goal: taking your buddy out for a beer in order to get him to introduce you to his gorgeous sister, who you'd like to date; combing through every box in the attic to find the death certificate for the great-grandfather whose story you're hoping to tell; calling the father you haven't seen in over a decade in an attempt at reconciliation.

Martha Beck wrote an unusual and touching parent-child memoir titled *Expecting Adam: A True Story of Birth, Rebirth, and Everyday Magic*. She and her husband John are an intellectually oriented Harvard couple. Despite everything they know about themselves and their belief system, when Martha accidentally gets pregnant and the fetus is discovered to have Down's syndrome, the Becks find that they cannot even consider abortion. The presence of the fetus that they each, privately, believe is a familiar being named Adam is too strong.

As Martha's difficult pregnancy progresses, odd coincidences begin to occur for both of them, though for months they don't share them with each other. Martha's pregnancy and Adam (once born) become the catalyst for enormous life changes for the Becks. In the end, Beck's story is as much an account of opening up to paranormal and spiritual experiences as it is about becoming the parent of a special needs child.

In one scene from Beck's memoir, she and her husband are in a hospital examination room, waiting for a nurse to conduct a test. While they are waiting, John fingers some equipment and idly pushes buttons.

> "This must be the ultrasound thing," he said, picking up the metal detector. It had a plastic handle, which was attached to a flat metal disk. John held the disk to his ear, then rubbed it along his forearm. "Put that down," I said. "You're going to break it." "No I'm not." He poked the buttons on the keyboard.

This scene continues with casual repartee between the two of them. The ordinariness of their exchange in the context of the larger story does several things that can only be accomplished in such a scene:

- **It offers a glimpse of their relationship**—We see how John uses humor to distract his wife from the tension they are both feeling.

- **It provides pacing**—The episode takes place right before she has her amniocentesis, and since the book is about her baby's genetic defect, the reader knows the medical procedure will be important in setting up their decision about whether to go through with the pregnancy. But instead of jumping ahead to the test and its result, Beck slows down her story and brings us into the examination room with her. It's an effective pacing technique.

- **It shows the physical surroundings where much of the story plays out**—The high-tech obstetrics wing of a hospital grounds the story in reality, which is particularly important as paranormal incidents begin to occur.

• **It provides details on a technical fact that will be new to most readers**—When the technician looks at the ultrasound screen and points out to Martha and John how the fetus is positioned, she marks an X on Martha's abdomen at the spot where the needle can be safely inserted. This detail also provides a sense of the delicacy of Martha's situation and that of her fetus.

These are only some of the reasons for putting a story point in scene. But they are indicative of the ways in which using scenes brings a memoir alive on the page.

# Beginnings and Endings

Most teachers will advise new writers to resist the urge to tell everything in a scene. But some go so far as to recommend starting dead center in the middle of the action in any scene you undertake to write. As movie watchers and readers, we've become a very sophisticated bunch. We no longer need to see the heroine open the door, walk up the unlit front steps, and creep down the hallway before discovering the dead body. Give us a few seconds of dark steps and some scary music and, boom—we're there, inches from the bloody corpse. We can use our imaginations and our experience as readers and viewers to fill in what took place before this scene and the transition between this one and the next.

As to how to end a scene, there has to be a sense of completion, but you don't want it to feel too complete; you want the reader to keep reading.

## Pacing the Action

You don't want all of your scenes to move at the same steady pace. You don't want to give every fact and action the same emphasis as all the other facts and actions. Slow down for crucial and dramatic moments. Let the moment unfold with some tension.

In the plotting of a story, it's important to regularly take a step back from your story and get a sense of the overview. This will give you a better perspective on pacing. Is there too much reflecting going on in act one when we should be getting to know the main character in scenes? Or do the scenes unfold too closely together? That's when you have to be concerned about overwhelming the reader with action and details. She might not know what to do with all of it because you haven't mused sufficiently about the meaning of what has already transpired. Another way to put it is that you haven't yet established the stakes for your protagonist.

## Using an Outline

This is a good time to talk about outlines. Should you write one? When? What's the best way to go about it? These are topics writers love to fret about. Some say they assiduously avoid doing outlines. Others swear by them. So what's the point of an outline?

When you are writing a book-length memoir, the main purpose of an outline is to help you get a big-picture view of the whole story—beginning, middle, and end. You can break the pages down by acts and note all the scenes within each act. You can note who appears in the scenes with your protagonist, when they return, and what's left unresolved. You can see where you're offering reflection on what's already occurred and where you raise questions, express surface wants, get or lose what you wanted, and reveal other important story points.

Your outline should include

- The introduction of each new character and setting

- Any change in time frame

- Every scene in the book

- Each major reflection in narration

- Lots of blank spaces

What's with the blank spaces? Rarely will you have all the answers to even the questions posed in the previous paragraph until well into the writing process. But the presence of blank spaces on an outline will remind you what still needs to be filled in as you write and revise.

# A Master at Work

At a certain point, the only way to learn how to write well in any form is to study its masters. Here is a wondrous and revelatory scene that takes place in the final pages of Vivian Gornick's *Fierce Attachments*. She is with her elderly mother with whom she has a complicated love-hate relationship, primarily, the author admits, because they are so alike.

> Tonight I'm hanging on by my fingernails, barely able to hold it together. I sit at my mother's kitchen table, drinking coffee. We have just eaten dinner. She stands at the sink washing her dishes. We are both edgy tonight. "It's the heat," she says. The apartment is air-conditioner cool, but we both love real air too much. We have turned off the machine and opened the window....

Notice how Gornick does several things to make this scene work:

- She writes the past in the present tense, to establish immediacy.
- She uses simple descriptions to establish the setting and place.
- She uses indirect bits of dialogue to suggest the essential action in back-and-forth interactions, both verbal and nonverbal.

## Using Inner Thoughts in Dialogue

Gornick then dips into her inner thoughts to highlight the backstory between mother and daughter, from the daughter's point of view (POV).

My mother is conversant with all that is on my mind. She is also familiar with the usual order of my litany of complaint: work, friends, money. This evening yesterday's conversation in Paley's Park seems to drift in the window on the sexy summer air, and to my surprise I find myself saying, "It would be nice to have a little love right now."

I expect my mother to laugh and say, "What's with you tonight?" Instead, not even looking up from the dishes, she goes on automatic and says to me, "Well now perhaps you can have a little sympathy for me."

I look up slowly at her. "What?" I say. I'm not sure I have heard right. "What was that you said?"

"I said maybe you can understand now what my life was like when Papa died...."

## The Use of Rising Tension

Tension rises as the scene and the conflict escalate, too, until Gornick is raging at her mother. She accomplishes this dramatic tension using a delicate interweaving of summary, reflection, and dialogue. Her mother insists that, unlike her daughter who has satisfying work and her travels, her husband's love was all she had. Finally, Gornick says the thing she's been holding back for years.

But heartbreak was not our style. "That's not good enough, Ma," I say. "You were forty-six when he died. You could have gone on with your life...."

Gornick finishes the interaction with her mother by reverting to Yiddish, what the author calls "the language of irony and defiance," to say, "You'll write down here on my tombstone: 'From the very beginning, it was all water under the bridge.'"

In these bits of scene interspersed with summary and inner dialogue, Vivian Gornick shows and tells us everything we need to know about the difficult relationship she has had with her mother. There is no less drama (maybe more) in this scene of two people talking than can be found in any equivalent length scene in a thriller.

## The Least You Need to Know

- Putting characters in a scene shows the immediate impact of events and other characters' actions.

- Summary and inner dialogue—telling rather than showing—is best used to abbreviate story and offer your protagonist's reflections.

- Thinking in pictures allows the memoirist to re-create the sensory experiences of what took place so as to better establish place in a scene.

- Effective pacing includes interspersing summary and scene and starting scenes in the middle of the action rather than before any bit of action starts.

- Every scene in a memoir should have a clear purpose, reflecting an action taken by the protagonist to reach her goal.

# Make a Setting Come Alive

# Chapter 10

## In This Chapter

- How a strongly rendered setting adds authenticity
- Finding the most powerful nouns and verbs to render setting
- Using vivid details to evoke and write memories
- How to use alternate realities in your memoir

Every story has a setting, meaning a specific time and place when and where your story occurred. Setting establishes the backdrop and context for everything that happens to your protagonist. A novelist deliberately creates a particular setting to reveal character, create a metaphor, set up a conflict, and create a mood. In contrast, the memoirist re-creates a setting from the past, but he does it no less thoughtfully. In this chapter, we zero in on how to re-create the real time and place to provide a backdrop for your memoir that makes each memory come fully alive on the page.

## What's a Setting For?

A setting does more than provide a backdrop. It contributes to the believability of your story. Ironically, even though events in your story are true, they might not be easily believed. If the reader cannot visualize where and when your story took place through your careful rendering of both, your memoir will suffer. Your task is to convincingly re-create every place in which your characters walk and talk. You also must establish a specific time span. A conversation, for example, usually happens in a shorter time—an hour, a few hours, or perhaps it stops and starts over the course of a few days. A significant relationship, on the other hand, spans years.

Sometimes a life story takes place within a particular context: social, political, economic, or historical. The memoirist must re-create a setting that allows the reader to see long-ago and far-away events in her mind's eye. If it is a specific period—for example, during World War II or 9/11—you'll offer specific days, months, and years when any major event occurred.

## The Backdrop

A well-rendered setting grounds your memoir in a specific reality that the reader can see in his mind's eye. With vivid descriptions and sense imagery, a writer creates authenticity and immediacy, which make a story more compelling. Think about a story without a setting. The events could have happened anywhere at any time. I think you'll agree that it will be inherently less interesting than a story playing out in one or more identifiable places and times. In a specific place, readers get to go somewhere new. Even if it's a familiar location, readers see it anew through your eyes, filtered by your experiences.

Sometimes, setting adds to the conflict of a story by stressing the tension between the main character's desire and the tough odds he faces to achieve it. For instance, in Frank McCourt's *Angela's Ashes*, young Frank's impoverished setting provides a stark contrast to his desire for safety.

Setting also adds an atmosphere and mood. A writer can create a particular mood to help the reader feel the psychological state of the main character. A memoir set in a war zone or a prison gains immeasurably from the immediate danger and inhospitality inherent in its setting.

Setting can act as a motive in a story. This is especially the case when the protagonist longs for a place that either has never existed or that he has not seen for a long time.

## Location and More

The way you write about a location can add meaning to a memoir. Place can be an event in your story. If you are writing a travel memoir, you will spend much of your book describing the place you are visiting. You'll write about the culture, language, values, morals, beliefs, customs, cuisine, traditions, and way of life of the people who live there.

In a coming-of-age story, you will take note of any and all physical attributes of the place where you grew up, using the strong emotions of adolescence to render these images with special intensity. Here is an example from Jennifer Lauck's *Blackbird*, a memoir about growing up in foster care:

> L.A. is hot and gray and dirty. Look up and it's smog. Look down and it's black and brown stains on concrete. Who knows what's on this sidewalk and how it got there.

Place is also about the socioeconomic attributes of a setting. Some places are populated by the poor, while others are reserved for the wealthy. Some places have high unemployment, while others have an abundance of employment opportunities. Some places have schools and hospitals, while other places have rudimentary housing and run-down public buildings. Again from Lauck's depiction of L.A., here's an example of place as embodied by a stranger:

> An old man walks up to us and he has on a long coat, a dirty face, a sunburned nose, and he carries two bags full of shoes. He stops in front of Deb and he smells like trash and pee.

In memoir, more often than not, the place where a story unfolded holds significant meaning for the writer. It can be a catalyst for memories of childhood, adulthood, and unique experiences. It can hold a mood. These moods and emotions can be used and, as exemplified by Lauck's evocative writing, integrated into the physical descriptions of a place.

# Place as Character

Some memoirists view place as a significant character in their stories, right up there with Mom and Dad and Sis. Similar to developing a character, place then needs to be developed. The writer can use personification to develop the place. It can become nurturing, menacing, foreboding, and so on.

In writing *Eat, Pray, Love*, place had a powerful meaning for Elizabeth Gilbert. After her divorce and a mid-life crisis, Gilbert decided to travel for a year by herself in an effort to restore balance and meaning to her life. Her memoir chronicles the three places she visited: Rome, India, and Bali. Each of these places had significant impact on her. They also had distinctive moods and meanings to her life. It's hard to imagine Gilbert achieving the same effect if she'd had similar experiences in her own backyard of New York City and its environs.

**POTHOLE AHEAD!**

Don't be vague in your rendering of place. Concrete nouns and specific details convey a place more vividly than abstract nouns. Compare "honeybees hopping across a bed of violet petals" to "a beautiful garden."

## Places Tied to Memories

We can associate a particular place with good memories or bad memories, as being a happy place or sad place, as being a relaxing place or stressful place. In our memories, place and formative experiences are often intertwined. Use your evocation of memories to visualize the places where they occurred. Then do the same process in reverse: use your visual and other sense memories of place to resurrect memories of events that happened there.

If you do a good job of describing a location—by using all five senses to place the reader there—your story can come remarkably alive. So bring us there: describe the scents of the first flowers that bloomed every spring (jasmine, honeysuckle, or roses), the cold linoleum floor under your feet in the winter, or the soft wet grass beneath your small body as you searched for constellations in the night sky. Other memories are likely to pop up and surprise you.

As Judith Barrington writes in her classic guide *Writing the Memoir:*

> Memory resides in specific sensory details, not in abstract notions like "beautiful" or "angry" (ask yourself, in what particular way was she beautiful? or what did the angry dog sound like?). If we capture and name the smell of the wax polish in that long ago house, then other memories seem to follow.

Scientists say that smell is the first sense that a baby develops while in the mother's womb. Perhaps that's why it has such a powerful effect on memory.

## Lost Places

Of course, as real and meaningful as a particular place might have been in your life, so, too, can be your yearning for a place that you've lost or one you dreamed about but never actually had. These yearnings can be important characters that change and grow in the course of a memoir, helping to ground your story in a figurative place.

 **TAKE IT TO HEART**

Memoir writers often find it useful to draw the physical layout of their childhood home on a piece of paper while they write. Try it: count the steps from your bedroom to the kitchen, and recount where the sun came in at different times of the day. These are the telling details of your characters' lives.

# Components of Place

Often the setting for your memoir is a childhood home in a formative period of your life. But it can also be a distant country where you served as a solider or a Peace Corps volunteer. Or it might be the vacation spot where you had a memorable love affair. Grounding the events of your memoir using all the idiosyncratic details of a real place helps add to the drama and meaning of a memoir.

In writing about place, consider including any or all of the following:

- **Name**—Where did the name of the place originate? What is the history of the name? Who were its native inhabitants? How does their presence continue today? Do you have any awareness of this history while you are in this place?

- **Location**—Where is it in relationship to where you live now? What large city or landmark is it near? How does the location of this place affect you in your story?

- **Physical attributes**—Consider the important features and physical attributes of place. Is it a walk-friendly place or a driving metropolis? Hilly, flat, dry, moist, trees, desert? How do these characteristics shape you or your moods?

- **Home as place**—In memoirs of childhood, place is most often the home of your family of origin. This gives place a significant meaning in your story. Home is supposed to be a place of comfort, protection, love, stability, and permanence. Did your childhood home contain any of those qualities to you? What good and bad memories do you have about this place? For some children, home was a transient place. If that was your experience, what was it like to move many times and experience different schools and neighborhoods as a child?

- **Nature as place**—In writing about place, you can also consider it in relation to nature. In his memoir, *Walden*, Henry David Thoreau viewed nature, wildlife, and the woods as being a spiritual place. As a transcendentalist, Thoreau believed that God was actively present in nature. When you write about nature as place, does nature embody larger forces?

- **Travel as place**—In writing about place as a traveler, don't write what everyone else has written. Find a unique angle on the place and its people. To create a travel piece that is more than just about transcribing the experience, you need to consider a larger theme.

- **Meaning**—When writing about a particular location, you ought to consider what special meaning the place has for you. Ask yourself: What do I like or dislike about this place? What favorite memories do I have here?

# Tips for Writing a Place

When writing about place, your top priority is to put your personality into the perspective you take. Your experience of the place is inherently different from others'. Tell us why. Be original by doing the following:

- Describe the place as if it is a character in your story. What is its appearance and behavior? What is the place saying to you?

- Use literary devices to describe the place, such as metaphors, personification, and simile.

- Describe the physical attributes of the place using sensory images. How does the place smell, sound, taste, feel, and look to you?

- Write about the meaning of the place to you then and now. Do you have fond or troubled memories of the place? How have you transposed those positive or negative feelings to the environment itself? Does it hold a universal truth for you?

- Use concrete and specific details. Remember as many significant details about the place as you can. Don't use clichés or trite expressions to describe a place.

**QUICK PROMPT**

Write about the places where you have lived for any length of time. Think about what was unique about each and reflect upon your life at the time. How did place shape your life at that time?

# Foraging for Details

The quality of detail the writer uses to describe a setting (like character) are where his memoir succeeds or fails. It's not just finding the right adjectives or using a lot of them that matters. "It's a searing, bubbling blacktop," versus "a hot, black pavement."

## Landscapes as Setting

Readers base their impressions of your characters in large part on where you place them. Here is a piece of vivid description from Dorothy Allison's *Two or Three Things I Know for Sure:*

> Where I was born—Greenville, South Carolina—smelled like nowhere else I've ever been. Cut wet grass, split green apples, baby shit and beer bottles, cheap makeup, and motor oil. Everything was ripe, everything was rotting. …It is the country of my dreams and the country of my nightmares: a pure pink and blue sky, red dirt, white clay and all that endless green—willows and dogwoods and firs going on for miles.

Even if the reader never steps foot in rural South Carolina, she has an indelible image of the place after reading this paragraph.

## Historical Settings

Here the Russian writer Vladimir Nabokov renders an interior/ exterior location and historical setting in stunning detail in his memoir *Speak, Memory*. The word *oriel* used in this paragraph refers to a bay window:

> My mother's boudoir had a convenient oriel for looking out on the Morskaya in the direction of the Maria Square. With lips pressed against the thin fabric that veiled the window-pane I would gradually taste the cold of the glass through the gauze. From that oriel, several years later, at the outbreak of the Revolution, I watched various engagements and saw my first dead man: he was being carried away on a stretcher,

> and from one dangling leg an ill-shod comrade kept trying
> to pull off the boot despite pushes and pulls from the
> stretchermen—all this at a goodish trot.

His childhood point of view and the use of distinct details adds to
the power of the setting and scene. In the introduction to *Speak,
Memory*, Nabokov describes the process of remembering such details,
writing:

> I discovered that sometimes, by means of intense concentra-
> tion, the neutral smudge might be forced to come into
> beautiful focus so that the sudden view could be identified....

What a lovely description of how memory and setting exist in a
symbiotic relationship for the memoirist.

# When Place Is an Alternate Reality

Some pivotal experiences in people's lives take place entirely within
the confines of their own minds. These experiences are spawned by
mental or physical illnesses, accidents, drug taking, and confinement,
among other causes. Is there a place for these highly personal altered
realities in memoir? Without question, yes; in fact, there's a long
tradition of memoirs written in what can be called *alternate realities*.

## Life or Afterlife?

A large proportion of these memoirs are authored by people who
believe they once tiptoed into the afterlife and then, for one reason
or another, returned to an earthly existence to write about it. Such
a journey might have occurred after an accident when the individual
lost consciousness; perhaps she fell into a coma during a grave illness. Many people who have near-death experiences report seeing
the same physical attributes in this nonphysical place that they
frequently identify as Heaven: a bright light, a feeling of total calm,
a lightness, and a sense of floating in air. Their memoirs are often

written with a Christian slant. In this category, you'll find *Embraced by the Light* by Betty J. Eadie and *Flight to Heaven: A Plane Crash...A Lone Survivor...A Journey to Heaven and Back*, a true story told by a pilot named Capt. Dale Black.

## Parallel Realities

There are also some highly regarded literary treatments of an alternate reality in the memoir form. These books tend to frame the author's story as a temporary insanity resulting from an extreme experience such as the sudden loss of a loved one or a mental illness. Two excellent examples are William Styron's *Darkness Visible, A Memoir of Madness* and *The Year of Magical Thinking* by Joan Didion.

In Didion's book, considered by many the best grief memoir ever written, the author allows her usually very rational protagonist to travel in a distinctly irrational time and space for the year following her husband's sudden death and her adult daughter's grave illness. Didion shows us how she is pushed from her logical state of mind into a mindset of skewed logic, or no logic, exemplified by her recurrent belief that her husband will be back by her side when she wakes up in the morning. The reader stays with Didion as she struggles to make sense of this state she finds herself in; her difficulties made no easier by her awareness that the special rules bestowed by her magical thinking are not possible in the real world to which she knows she'll eventually return.

An alternate reality can also be the setting for part of a memoir in which the majority of the story takes place in a more mundane place and time. A child's imaginary world and an adult's fantasy life are two examples.

## Special Rules

In an alternate reality memoir or a passage employing an alternate reality, memoirists have an even greater task when it comes to establishing the settings in which their characters dwell. They must describe any special rules regarding time and space that apply to their protagonist's experiences in the private realities they're writing about.

Readers are quite willing to go with an author to a "strange" place, as long as they eventually understand exactly where they are. After setting is properly established, character development and scene writing rules that apply to standard realities are equally applicable to these alternate realities.

## The Least You Need to Know

- Setting consists of a specific location and time period as backdrop for a story. The memoirist's re-creation of a real place and time is very different from a novelist's creation of a setting suitable to a fictional set of characters and story.

- Place can be a character in a memoir if it contains special meaning as a symbol, metaphor, or destination.

- The symbiotic relationship between the vivid details belonging to a setting and their power to evoke memories can be tapped to aid a memoirist's creative process.

- If a memoirist chooses to include an alternate reality as a setting, he must clearly establish the rules governing this place and time, lest he cast the reader into confusion and frustration.

# The Rules for Revisions

## In This Chapter

- Finding the right time to revise
- How to revise for voice, coherence, pacing, and more
- When in doubt, draw or act out scenes you've written
- What to expect from a writer's critique group

Some writers believe that rewriting or revising is where their work actually takes form, and any sentences they put down before a first or second revision are just free writing, or playing around. Revisions should provide an airtight container for your creative inspiration. Without revisions you risk losing any pearls of wisdom you've worked so hard to accumulate along with almost everything else that's good in your story. They're washed away in an ocean of over-written prose. Fortunately, legions of writers before you have come up with some tried-and-true rules to help you hang on to the good, and let go of the no longer necessary.

## First Drafts Are Terrible

First drafts have every reason to be awful. They are the terrible two's of your writing process, ignorant of the basic rules of behavior. But you cheat yourself as a writer if you don't indulge in the sorts of flights of fancy that so many first drafts contain. These are the authorial tangents that can be so abominable that you cringe when you read them the next day when it occurs to you that this dreck could have been written by a third-grader—but that would be unfair to most third-graders who surely write better than this!

Or, miraculously, one such tangent of free writing, a rebellious sentence that begins with no clear destination, leads you to a wonderful new place. One thing is certain: you would never have reached this unfamiliar territory unless you'd been absolutely sure that the pages in question were for your eyes only. That's why you have to let your first drafts be terrible. So they can also be wonderful...once in a blue moon.

# When to Revise

Before we delve into the fine points of how to revise, we must enter the fray of another writerly controversy. As with the question of when to write (morning or night) and whether you should let others read what you've written as you go along, this is an issue on which writers have very strong opinions—which they feel compelled to share with new writers. You might never have considered the question, or you might have a clear preference already. Either way, it's time to hear what the fuss is about. There are the two basic strategies employed and endlessly debated about making revisions.

## Waiting to Revise

This is the contingent that says you should allow the energy driving the writing of your first draft to flow uninterrupted from beginning to end without stopping. These writers say it's of vital importance not to muck up your creative juices with the persnickety demands of grammar, word choice, and punctuation. In other words, don't stop for any reason other than to remember where you left off. Write, write, write...until you have what feels like a reasonably full first draft, until you write "The End" for the first time.

## Revising as You Go

The other camp, of which I am a member, believes that by returning to what we've written the day before and fiddling with it, we launch the next stage of our writing on better footing. We get a serious boost of energy by tidying up and at times beautifying the ragged things we left on paper or on the hard drive when we last ran out of juice. We also get the opportunity to delete things we really hate because leaving them there is depressing. They are so bad they drain energy from us by merely existing. Plus, by getting rid of such clunkers, we know exactly what weak story point we have to readdress in our thinking because its first incarnation is already in the trash.

There's no right or wrong way. You might in fact employ a little of both strategies. Write a full chapter and go back only after you have 10 or 20 solid pages and see how you feel about them. Or just keep driving until the end. I must confess I've never been able to not revise as I go along. I know plenty of writers who religiously do just the opposite of me. Having said that, I wholeheartedly believe that we gain an invaluable new perspective by taking a step back from our writing and returning to it fresh after a few days, weeks, or months. Even if you revise daily, returning to the whole later is essential.

# Ten Ways to Revise Your Memoir

Some writers (again, count me as one) love the process of making revisions. We prefer it to facing a blank page (especially a first page) and having to create something out of whole cloth. There are different perspectives to bring to revising, depending on your mood or sense of what's wrong with what you have:

1. **Revise for voice**—Perhaps you're not happy with the voice of your narrator. It's inconsistent; one way in act one, another in the middle, still another in act three. The personality of your narrator is a reflection of you and who you are in this piece of writing. Aim for consistency (unless your character arc demands a change in narrative voice). Should it be more conversational, informal, reserved, or distant? Explore different options until you find the right voice.

2. **Revise for tone**—What is the tone of your memoir as a whole, including protagonist, narration, and scene? Is it humorous, dire, ponderous, cynical, or optimistic? Make sure your tone matches content.

3. **Revise for tense**—In what tense is your memoir told? Does the narrator look back from the present or take the reader into the past through the present tense? Find the single tense or combination that fits your story.

4. **Revise for meaning**—Does everything in your memoir mean what you intend it to mean? Go through your piece and look for sources of confusion. Is there a premature realization on page 50 that doesn't fit with where you are on page 60?

5. **Revise for conflict**—Does your memoir contain a central conflict that drives the action throughout the story? If not, go back and identify a missing desire and/or what's stopping your narrator from getting what he wants.

6. **Revise for description**—Is your memoir descriptive enough? Does it invite the reader to experience your memories? Is it too descriptive? Does your memoir get bogged down with too many adjectives and not enough nouns and verbs?

7. **Revise for the process of discovery**—Does the protagonist discover something new? How about the reader?

8. **Revise for who is reading**—Identify your audience and make sure your memoir speaks directly to that type of person: age, gender, culture, and so on (no one reads everything out there).

9. **Revise for surprise**—Does your memoir surprise the reader? Or is it completely predictable?

10. **Revise for resolution**—Do you have a strong ending? Does it resolve the original conflict? Does the protagonist change? Or is the reader left hanging?

# What Should Stay and Go?

Sometimes the verbiage that needs to go into the trash is glaringly obvious immediately after you return to a first draft. Be thankful when that happens. Other times it's not so easy. You might have a sinking feeling that a page or passage doesn't work, meaning it serves no real purpose and even slows down a vortex of action or emotion, but you can't bring yourself to cut it. It is one of your pearls. Sometimes these gems are the first things we write. Maybe you wrote it as a poem years ago, knowing it deserved a prominent place in your memoir, if and when you ever got around to writing one.

It might have served you as a beacon when you began writing your memoir, helping you, for example, find the deep desire beneath a surface want. But now if you're honest with yourself, it's superfluous. You've already gone deeper into the essence of what it said in other passages. You feel guilty thinking this way about your pearls. If it helps, know that what you're going through is typical and necessary. The point is to let go of your pearls. It's a sign of your growth as a writer.

**TAKE IT TO HEART**

"Aim for the chopping block. If you aim for the wood, you will have nothing. Aim past the wood, aim through the wood; aim for the chopping block."

—Ann Dillard, *The Writing Life*

The essence of revising is deciding what to leave in and out. Many times, the less we say, the more we communicate.

## Some Guidelines for Big Chops

When you go back to the beginning of your first draft and read all the way through, you might immediately feel that parts of it are simply "wrong." Certain whole pages shouldn't be there and something else should be, although you're not sure what it is. Here are some questions to help you zero in on where to do a major chop or place a whole new piece of wood:

- Where are you in this story?
- What is happening inside you?
- What did you learn from this event?
- What changed as a result of this event?
- What do you want people to know about you at this stage in the story?
- What does the story thus far say about who you are as a person?
- Where does this experience fit in relation to the larger character arc your protagonist must traverse?

Answers to these questions should point you in the right direction. But you might simply need to try many different options until you land on what feels right. Writing is a very intuitive process.

## Another Point of View

Sometimes the thing that's missing is someone else's perspective on what happened in your story. This can sound contradictory to your right to tell it like it was for you. But adding another point of view (POV) can actually help underscore your perspective. This is especially true if you were a young child when the event took place and if the other person was someone who hurt you. As readers, we want to understand why people do bad things. If we find out, for example, that your abusive father had been abused himself as a child, we end up learning much more about you, too. We also acquire a unique understanding of a larger universal truth about how a cycle of violence tends to repeat in families.

## Saying the Same Thing Better

The revision process, whether draft two, three, or four, more often than not gives birth to the "perfect" word, light years better than the placeholder you had there before. Be thankful both for the placeholder and the new and improved occupant of that space. The reason these better words pop out in such large numbers during a revision is that at this point your thinking is much more precise about what it is you're trying to say. It wasn't just cloudy that day; the sky was hung over and in a dark mood. Your mother's lips weren't pursed; they were twisted into a pretzel. The same goes for sentences: you'll look at one with 10 words and see how it can be 3; the right words are clamoring for your attention, demanding that you jettison their slacker neighbors.

# Reading Aloud and Other Tricks

Reading your work aloud to yourself is probably the single most valuable step you can take in the revising process. It is mindboggling how many words and whole paragraphs suddenly sound useless when you give voice to them. For reasons not entirely clear, when we write silently off by ourselves we can get very redundant, wordy, vague, and worse. We write in a way we would never talk. When read aloud, such passages sound as tasteless, pompous, and self-indulgent as they actually are.

**POTHOLE AHEAD!**

A caveat to the "if you hate it, throw it out" rule: don't let fear lead you to destroy something that may in fact be precious just because it's radically different for you. If you're torn about whether something you've written is terrible or great, take that doubt as a clue that it could easily be either. Make another copy of the same sequence and give yourself a choice between the two versions on another day.

When you return to your keyboard after reading them aloud, wordy first drafts invariably become shorter and better second drafts.

Here are more tricks:

- **Draw a section**—If you like to draw, try making a sketch of part of your memoir. You can create a single picture or draw a series of scenes as if they were a comic strip, which are also called *storyboards* when used by movie directors to visualize a scene before turning on the camera. When you're done drawing, consider whether you have a complete picture. Try adding things to your writing, but do it visually first. Then go back to your draft to turn these images into language.

- **Act out a section**—This is like reading aloud on steroids! Get together with a partner or small group and act out some of your memoir as if it is a play. Make it a section that has some dialogue and action, or else there's nothing to act out! Ask someone else to play you. You might try playing the antagonist. Ask others to play any other characters. See if the performance comes close to what you thought you were writing. If not, revise your writing to make it come closer to what you had in mind. Your partners might have some great ideas for how to improve the scene.

- **Make a detailed outline of a problematic section**—Try mapping out a section or major chunk of your memoir using the outline format. Move the chunk you currently have at the end up to the beginning (this is easier to do on a computer than on paper, of course). Move what is currently in the middle to the end, and so on. Think about how reorganizing the sections would change the draft, and be open to finding a new and better way to organize the major parts of your draft.

**TAKE IT TO HEART**

Write at least five different beginnings to your memoir; then choose which one you like best. See how your memoir would change with each of those possible beginnings.

- **Retell your memoir from the imagined perspective of another character in your story**—What changes about the story? What remains the same? How can you incorporate what you've learned from this exercise into your own perspective?

As you can see, most of these exercises are designed to help you take a step back from your own writing and gain a different perspective. One of the best ways to do this is by joining a writer's group.

# Why Every Writer Needs a Critique Group

A group of writers getting together one afternoon or evening every month to share and critique each other's creative writing can be a rewarding and productive process. It is being done online with chat rooms and message boards, but, trust me, the experience is a thousand times more powerful when you meet with your fellow writers face-to-face.

Think of it as a book group only with your name on the cover of "tonight's book." It will move your writing forward in leaps and bounds. However, writing groups are not for the faint of heart. Because the pages you've toiled over are like your babies, sometimes it can feel as if you're throwing your flesh and blood to a pack of hungry wolves. Tough criticism can hurt and make you doubt yourself. But your fellow writers would not be doing you any favors by lying and telling you that every word you've written is wonderful. Toughen up, and you'll be very happy you did.

Among memoir writers, a critique group is an especially intense experience because the subject matter is so intimate. Everyone in the group is well aware that each submission is not just a story; it often contains some of the most intimate and toughest moments of your life. Many such groups meet for years, their members becoming the closest of friends. Others keep their contact strictly for writing and don't mix it up socially.

## Giving and Getting Feedback

No matter what else you do or don't do together, the time writing group members spend together to work on each other's writing should consist of equal parts constructive criticism and warm encouragement. To ensure this, a common set of rules has developed for writer's critique groups. Many have been developed by writing instructors teaching in one of the thousands of MFA writing programs now operating in the United States. Here are some of the most tried and true:

- The writer whose work is going to be critiqued the next time the group meets hands out or e-mails copies to her fellow writers at or soon after the prior meeting.

- Members spend each group meeting focused on one or two pieces of writing so that every writer gets a large dose of group attention and feedback.

- Within the time period of a meeting, the writer whose work is being discussed does not talk. She listens and takes notes. She does not debate or argue specific points of criticism.

- When offering feedback, the person critiquing always offers positive feedback about the writing first. Hearing an onslaught of negative feedback makes any writer shut down and go into a defensive posture. (Have I mentioned that all writers are incredibly sensitive about their work, no matter how experienced or how many times they've been published?) So don't make it worse. Give the good news first. It softens the bad.

- Here are some of the usual points of criticism covered by each person offering critique:

  - What did the reader think this piece of writing was about, in as few words as possible?

    - In general, what worked and what didn't work (for her) in the writing?

  - Was the narrator reliable?

  - What was the reader's response to the main character?

  - What about the antagonist? Was he clearly depicted?

  - Where did the writing slow down, get vague, or become redundant?

- Each reader in the group offers most of her criticism uninterrupted, taking up to 10–15 minutes to do so. Then, the next reader is up and so on around the circle.

- After all critiques have been given, the writer gets to speak. This is a time to ask for clarification on individual points of criticism and ask for suggestions. Again, it is not the time to argue or defend one's writing.

By the end of a critique session, the writer in the spotlight can feel wrung out, even by positive feedback. It's best to let what you heard sink in over a few days before attempting to apply anything that was said.

## Using Criticism Wisely

Very often the group member whose writing is critiqued hears clear, actionable feedback from the group. For example, when the same thing is said by several readers. At those times, the writer knows immediately what to do with her memoir and wants nothing more than to make the suggested changes. Other times a writer vehemently disagrees with a particular criticism.

Ultimately, it's your life story and you must be satisfied with the final pages above anyone else. Simply know that if you received certain criticisms from readers at this stage and choose not to clarify the sections that caused confusion, you risk having that reaction again from many more readers who will be reading the pages with far less care than your writing group members are giving them. Often, these are the parts of a manuscript best left to sit for days, weeks, or months before tackling again. Time away often provides more clarity.

**TAKE IT TO HEART**

If only one person in your critique group expressed a negative reaction to something in your memoir, take it with a grain of salt. If you don't agree, then don't change it. However, if two or more readers comment on the same issue, then you really need to take a hard look at why they felt that way and try changing it. If they say something you wrote was vague, think about how you might rewrite it with more specificity.

# Checking Beginnings and Endings

The first five pages and the last five pages of your memoir are the ones you are probably going to revise the most. And that is as it should be. You must capture your reader in the first five pages. You do that by drawing him close to your protagonist. Readers need to care what happens to her; otherwise, they are less likely to continue reading. The protagonist must be seen as facing a struggle to get something she doesn't yet have but really needs or wants. This goal should involve a matter of emotional or physical survival.

Similarly, in the last five pages, your protagonist must be seen as a new person, changed in some fundamental way for having made an arduous journey over the previous hundred or so pages. It often takes many consecutive reiterations of beginnings and endings to make sure you've delivered on the implicit promise you made with your readers when you invited them to join you for this journey.

And yet, sometimes a memoirist doesn't know the ending of his story until he has nearly arrived at the final five pages of his first draft. It might be that he didn't previously realize the significance of the wisdom he had acquired through the experiences he has written about. This meaning has emerged from the writing itself. This is an exciting experience when it happens—one that should be savored. Don't rush the writing of your realization. Free write your immediate thoughts and feelings. Take a long walk, and then attempt to put it into crystalline form.

# The Final Proof

A good grammar handbook is essential to have on your desk at all times while you're writing. (Some good ones are listed in Appendix A.) Don't rely on software to tell you whether your sentence or spelling is right or wrong. We've all faced the situation where the spelling of a word depended on its usage, such as "their," "they're," and "there." As a soon-to-be-published author, you're way beyond relying on your word processing program's spelling or grammar check.

**TAKE IT TO HEART**

Beware of too many or too few commas! If you are weak in grammar or spelling, you might want to bring your completed memoir draft to a professional copyeditor (for paragraph and sentence construction) and/ or proofreader (for more of the details, especially punctuation) for a once-over. The money spent will be well worth it.

# Revision Checklist

Use the following checklist to evaluate your memoir as you move between drafts. You might also find it handy when you're reading and reviewing memoirs written by others, published or not.

### Revision Checklist for Memoir

- ☐ Is the beginning engaging?
- ☐ Does it start with action (dialogue, interpersonal interactions)?
- ☐ Does it tell a story, with a clear beginning, middle, and end?
- ☐ Do flashbacks (if there are any) make sense? Do they provide context for the story being told?
- ☐ Can you find sensory details?
- ☐ Do you feel transported to the place and time where the story is happening?
- ☐ Does it include dialogue?
- ☐ Do you feel that you know the characters? Do you care about each of them?
- ☐ Does the author reflect on the significance of the story?
- ☐ Does the protagonist (*I*) learn something from the experience described in the story?
- ☐ Does the author use varied sentence structures?
- ☐ Does the author pace scenes and narration?
- ☐ Does the author use strong, specific, and active verbs?
- ☐ Is the writing free from grammatical and spelling errors?
- ☐ Does the ending provide a sense of closure?

There are many other tips and suggested rules from earlier chapters to check for as you revise. Be on the lookout for the emotion that feels trumped up or overwrought, and the reflection that's too pat, sentimental, or vague. When in doubt, dig deeper and find specific words. Don't reuse the same adjectives, verbs, or nouns. Make a list of alternatives; create your own dictionary of synonyms. And keep writing!

## The Least You Need to Know

- Some writers prefer to revise as they go along. Others swear by getting all the way to "The End" before touching a word. You have to decide what works best for you.

- Revise many times, each turn using a different point of focus for improvements: voice, pacing, consistency, meaning, and so on.

- A writer's critique group is a great antidote for the isolation of the writer's life. Any group should follow certain ground rules: the most important of these is to balance positive and negative criticism of any piece of work.

- Revising inevitably makes a piece of writing shorter. A sure method for finding extraneous words is to read your first draft aloud to yourself.

- In some instances, consistency of tone and plot are a problem. Taking a step back and reconsidering the order of things, even moving big chunks around, can help you find the right sequence of events for your story and reflections.

# The Bigger Picture: Theme and Genre

Every memoir tells readers about a journey the author has taken toward self-definition. How you did it, and against what odds, will help you fit your memoir into a specific category or genre. With the huge popularity of memoirs today, there are now several major genres to be found among them. Each genre has slightly different rules and gives its readers certain expectations. By reading other memoirs in your category and focusing on how their authors solved certain problems, you'll acquire guidance for writing your own. In this part, I break them down into the most popular genres, including coming of age, relationships, overcoming adversity, travel and adventure, and business memoirs. Lastly, I dissect the themes of different memoirs. By knowing your theme, you'll be able to better summarize the wisdom you've acquired on your journey and then share it on the pages of your book.

# Theme Blossoms

# Chapter 12

## In This Chapter

- Finding one word or phrase to sum up your life story
- Discovering theme through psychology
- Seeing the themes in fairy tales
- Differentiating between plot and theme
- Searching out particulars in the universal

Every story—be it a novel, memoir, myth, fairy tale, or even a song—has a theme. If a book doesn't have a theme, as readers we might nod off after reaching the middle. Theme is not as obvious as plot, or the "what" in a story. Theme answers the questions why? and so what? It represents the writer's and reader's hard-earned wisdom at the end of a long journey. It's not unusual for theme to fully materialize to you as a writer only after completing act two; when you survive your climax and finally slide into the resolution where theme arrives as a three-dimensional picture staring you in the face. When that happens, your sense of self-discovery makes you sit up straighter in your chair. Hopefully it also permeates your pages and dazzles your readers. Readers will be as satisfied as you were to arrive at this point because you fulfilled a promise made on page one: that you would make a necessary change in your life (story)— and then faithfully tell them all about it.

# Theme in a Word or Few

One way to identify theme is to ask yourself what one word (or brief phrase) conveys what your story is about. *Ambition. Survival in the wild. Addiction. Love is eternal. Abuse. Woman in a man's world. Against all odds. Rags to riches. A Cinderella or Horatio Alger story.* These are only a few possibilities. Theme takes in the physical reality of what happened to you, as well as the psychological and spiritual dimension of where you have been and gone. In every case, theme describes how you changed, grew, lost, or triumphed and became a different person than when you started.

## Returning to Purpose

Your theme should be a mirror reflection of your purpose in writing a memoir. Are you describing a hardscrabble childhood and how it shaped you into a young adult? Then you are telling a coming-of-age story. Still, a story in this genre can have many different themes. It can illustrate the theme of surviving poverty through sheer grit. Or it can address the theme of a mother's love conquers all.

Similarly, if your purpose is to memorialize a three-decade-long marriage, once again your purpose and theme can go any one of a number of ways, such as betrayal or the timeless love of soul mates.

## Not the Same as Plot

Although theme arises from conflict, and conflict equates with plot, theme should never be confused with the plot of your memoir. Theme is bigger than plot. Plot is the means to the end, which is theme. Theme is the thread that ties together your plot—particularly if your memoir jumps around in time and includes many vignettes only partially interconnected by plot. Then theme is the link between these episodes in your story. Theme can also help the writer go back and sharpen the plot or storyline in a memoir.

> **TAKE IT TO HEART**
>
> First-time memoirist Lalita Tademy, who told the story of her previously unknown slave ancestors in *Cane River,* submitted her manuscript to dozens of agents before finding one who took it on. One agent who rejected it said, "Slavery's been done too many times." The best-selling success of Tademy's memoir shows us that tried-and-true themes can be recycled in countless ways and proves that readers love discovering the particulars in a universal theme.

# Recycling Themes

The stories people tell involve a limited number of favorite themes. Not just within a single culture, but, as anthropologist Joseph Campbell revealed in *The Power of Myth*, the same human themes cross cultures, continents, and millennia. Campbell used *myth* to describe any universal story motif that reappears in different cultures. He applied the term to diverse cultural forms including oral and written stories, dance, and even masks. Among the classic mythical themes transcending time and geography that Campbell discovered in his survey of world cultures were these:

- **The hero's adventure**—Stories of man or woman vying against the forces of nature or fellow man.

- **The creation myth**—These are stories of the birth of a child, a home, a work of art, or a business.

- **Love and the goddess**—Stories of love or Eros as the spark of erotica and romance coming into being or flaming out; the things that the goddess represents: fertility, renewal, marriage, and motherhood.

- **Sacrifice and bliss**—These stories are about someone giving up something (such as possessions or life) for a greater cause. The bliss that comes can involve transcendence of worldly desires or reward in the afterlife.

- **The journey inward**—Stories of traveling on a spiritual path are as old as mankind.

If you find the theme of your memoir on or overlapping with a mythical topic on this list, then your theme is universal. At the same time, as Campbell and other mythologists point out, it is the particular flavors of a culture and the circumstances in an individual's life that make every story different. As storytellers and readers, we look for both the universal and the particular in the stories we gravitate to. Then, as is our human way, we love to hear them over and over.

**TAKE IT TO HEART**

By finding a universal theme, you can purposely mine its resonance by asking yourself questions that have been asked and answered countless times before. For example, does life's gravest danger come in the most familiar form? Does every young man have to leave his mother behind in order to "become a man"? And, to add a modern twist, if the boy must leave his mother, what should Mom do about it? Clearly, many memoirists believe she should reinvent herself for a fabulous second act!

## Finding Themes in Fairy Tales

As a fun exercise to help you recognize themes, fill in the thematic messages or morals in the classic fairy tales and modern children's favorites listed here. Choose among the following themes:

- There's no place like home.
- Danger comes in familiar forms.
- Use your wits to survive bad things.
- Time to leave childhood behind.
- Darkness (emotions) can be overcome.
- Betrayal brings down a kingdom.
- The quest for truth will out.
- Persistence brings rewards.
- The hero's journey is to the heart.
- True love will always win (in the end).
- Vengeance is sweet.

1. *Cinderella* _____.
2. *Little Red Riding Hood* _____.
3. Percival _____.
4. King Arthur, Lancelot, Guinevere _____.
5. *Where the Wild Things Are* _____.
6. *The Wizard of Oz* _____.
7. "Jack and the Beanstalk" _____.
8. "Hansel and Gretel" _____.
9. *Peter Pan* _____.
10. *Horton Hatches the Egg* _____.

As you recall or reread these stories, it will become evident that more than one theme can fit a particular tale. For example, "Hansel and Gretel" is as much about Gretel using her wits to push the witch into the oven and survive as it is about vengeance being sweet, like a gingerbread house. Peter Pan must grow up, but fighting pirates and winning helps him do it. And so on. The useful part of the exercise is figuring out which theme fits the nugget of wisdom grasped by each protagonist at story's end.

**POTHOLE AHEAD!**

Don't confuse theme with setting, character or plot. A memoir can be set in the roaring '20s, but it must be about something deeper than an interesting time and place. Its plot might concern the conflict between two brothers who loved the same woman, but its theme would be betrayal or true love winning against all odds. Theme is bigger than any of these other story elements.

## Theme Informs Plot

When your memoir touches a universal theme, such as the profound wisdom about living that can come from a grave illness, look to the specific ways in which you drew lessons from your experience in order to strengthen the plot of your memoir. Go back and chart your darkest moment, the darkness before the dawn that led you to the personal breakthrough that in turn got you to the figurative place you had to find to understand the lesson. In an illness narrative, the backbone of a memoir's plot often correlates with the diagnosis, treatment, and outcome of the disease, be it cancer or a mental illness. In some cases, the wisdom comes not in remission or even survival, but in accepting death as a natural part of life. This lesson can be for the dying person and/or the caretaker—for example, a spouse, a parent, or an adult child.

# The Psychology of a Theme

In so much as your memoir tells a story of self-definition, it might reflect a particular time or passage in your life that was marked by a high degree of struggle. The founders of psychology, particularly Sigmund Freud and his heir Erik Erikson, were the first to delineate these struggles in the form of a sequence of normal development as a person grows up. You might find clues to your memoir's conflict and theme in the stages they came up with.

In his seminal work *Childhood and Society*, Erikson identified eight distinct stages of maturation from birth through the end of a person's life. From this work, Erikson coined the term *identity crisis* to refer to the conflict and resolution that occurs in each stage of life. Like Freud, Erikson emphasized the benefits of successfully resolving the conflict presented in one stage as preparation for the next one.

In each life stage, Erikson identified the central conflict a child or an adult confronts as a struggle between two opposite qualities. He also pointed to the strength that comes from successfully navigating each of these crises.

In Erikson's view, the opposite of each quality in the second column (role confusion, isolation) represents the downfall that might result if a person doesn't successfully get through each of these normal identity crises. For example, if you don't figure out how to be intimate with another human being in young adulthood, there will be a lack of love later in your life. This lack of resolution can in fact be one of the reasons this struggle pops up as a theme in your memoir.

I return to Erikson's insights in Chapter 13, when I discuss coming-of-age memoirs.

## Erikson's Stages of Psychosocial Development

| Age | Stage | Strength Developed |
|---|---|---|
| 0–1 yr. | Trust vs. mistrust | Hope |
| 2–3 yrs. | Autonomy vs. shame | Will power and doubt |
| 4–5 yrs. | Initiative vs. guilt | Purpose |
| 6–12 yrs. | Industry vs. inferiority | Competence |
| Adolescence | Identity vs. role confusion | Fidelity |
| Young adulthood | Intimacy vs. isolation | Love |
| Middle age | Generativity vs. stagnation | Care |
| Old age | Ego integration vs. despair | Wisdom |

# Do Themes Ever Change?

Themes for life stories reflect universal motifs that undergo only cosmetic changes when they are put in modern trappings. For example:

- The theme of war making men out of boys (women out of girls) and, for some, the futility of war, as applied to the high-tech, post–9/11 wars in Iraq and Afghanistan.

- Coping with a physical illness or mental challenge, now with the advances of modern medicine and therapies making survival possible where it never was before.

- Recovering from a self-imposed adversity—for example, addiction. These stories have been around for as long as people told stories. But now they're told with a level of nitty-gritty detail reflecting a publicly confessional culture.

- Leaving family and/or everything that's familiar in midlife to go to an exotic place and begin life anew is a universal theme. What's different today is that women are doing it as much or more often than men and then writing about in their memoirs. The underlying theme of such stories is an outer quest to answer an inner need for self-realization.

So the history of human storytelling is a history of recycling themes. The same themes (and plots) with only slight alterations have been present since the cave paintings of Lascaux depicted stories of Neanderthals surviving the imminent threats of wild beasts, hunger, and the cold. Taking a long perspective on the limited number of themes that pertain to the human experience is of particular relevance to the writer of true human stories.

## Mining the Particulars

The successful memoirist uses the particulars in a universal experience to make his story unique. One editor at a New York publishing house who edits many memoirs said, "Part of the gift of the memoirist is to be able to find the extraordinary in the ordinary, to create meaning through seeing a pattern in a life, and to be able to convey both the meaning and the story."

Lest we forget, meaning in literature is synonymous with theme.

Writing your life story as memoir allows you to create order out of chaos using whatever facts you have and acknowledging what you don't know.

An example of an addiction theme where the author restored order to decades of chaos is the bestselling *Lit* by Mary Karr. This third volume of her memoir trilogy tells of her descent into and her recovery from alcoholism by finding God and becoming a Roman Catholic. *Lit* covers other important things in Karr's life, too—her breakthrough as a published writer, her difficult marriage, her failings as a mother to her son, and the friends in AA who helped her survive and thrive. It also reflects further on her difficult relationship with her mother and deeper reflections on incidents she wrote about in *The Liar's Club*. But the character arc and conflict of the story take us from Karr being hopelessly out of control and under the influence of alcohol to becoming sober and finding herself again through religion. Another way to frame the theme of *Lit* is as a quest because most seekers in narratives end up finding God even if their original goal was something far more material.

## Finding Meaning in the Missing

In *Growing Up*, Russell Baker finds meaning in the particulars of his family's struggles during the Great Depression, although his discovery of the theme of mothers and sons for his memoir didn't come quickly or easily. His first draft of *Growing Up* was, he confessed, disastrous; consisting of over 400 pages, which he eventually tossed in the trash can. A newspaperman by trade, Russell had written a meticulously researched depiction of the social history of that time, only to realize that the manuscript lacked an emotional core. He then saw that the vital missing element of the story could only come from his family's highly personal experience of that time—specifically his mother's.

Baker's hesitation in including personal matters, such as his mother's pregnancy (with him) before his parents' marriage, had been twofold. First, there was the potential besmirching of his mother's memory. Second, he lamented the details he didn't know and couldn't ask anyone about. Not having his five "Ws" accounted for, Baker felt insecure in calling his story a memoir. Writing in William Zinsser's *Inventing the Truth*, Baker explains:

> I decided that nobody's life makes sense, if you're going to make a book out of it, you might as well make it into a story. I remember saying to my wife, "I am now going upstairs to invent the story of my life." And I started writing....

Theme helps you fill in around missing facts because it focuses your attention on you and what you wanted in a particular situation or from someone in your life, regardless of whether you got it. For example, if you were adopted and, despite decades of searching, were unable to locate your birth mother, your desire for a missing mother (and father) as well as knowledge of your personal roots shapes the plot and theme of your memoir. If you understand and maximize that theme, your memoir has the best chance of resonating with readers, many of whose lives contain similar themes—whether they were adopted or not.

## The Least You Need to Know

- Themes are bigger than the plot, setting, or character in a story. They can often be summed up in one word or a brief phrase.
- Erik Erikson's eight stages of man can help a memoirist discover a theme based on the originating point of the central conflict in his life story.
- The history of humankind has been told using the same few, constantly recycled plots and themes.
- Theme can fill in for what's missing in plot by turning the spotlight on what a protagonist wanted and perhaps never got.
- Themes change cosmetically over time, but their essence remains the same.

# Passages

## In This Chapter

- Digging into coming-of-age as a rich source of memoir
- Locating the driving event in a turning point
- Why you should wait before writing about tough times
- Discovering surprising themes in universal passages

The ways we handle key rites of passage shape our personalities and adult lives. In that sense we should welcome and not fear the identity crises in our lives, those times when all hell breaks loose and we're brought both figuratively and literally to our knees. As memoirists, we apply a close-up lens to these turning points, taking them apart and re-creating how we got through the tough times.

When a writer reads what he has written, he often wonders if he captured the internal and external strife that sent him down path A instead of path B. Can readers viscerally feel how stressful it was and how the author patched together a resolution? In this chapter, we look at how some published memoirists have written about their most challenging passages and turning points. Then we evaluate what their finished products can teach us as we write our own.

## The Points of Change

Millions of readers defined their lives through Gail Sheehy's land-mark best seller *Passages*, published in 1989 and named by a Library of Congress survey as one of the most influential books of our time.

The four passages that Sheehy described in her book provide a useful framework as we focus on how to depict turning points in our lives. In Sheehy's hierarchy, a typical life lays out as follows:

- The "trying 20s," when the safety of home is left behind, when we begin trying on life's uniforms and possible partners in search of the perfect fit.

- The "catch 30s," when illusions are shaken and it's the time to make, break, or deepen life commitments.

- The "forlorn 40s," which are the dangerous years when the dreams of youth demand reassessment, when men and women switch characteristics, and when sexual panic is common.

- The "refreshed or resigned 50s," when "the greatest opportunity for self-discovery awaits;" the best of life arrives for those who let go of old roles and find a renewal of purpose.

Can you relate your experiences thus far to these passages? Millions around the world do. How appropriate, then, as the popularity of memoirs took off in the decades following Sheehy's book, that the passages she named were the primary stuff from which memoirs were made.

### TAKE IT TO HEART

"The power to animate all of life's seasons is a power that resides in each of us."

—Gail Sheehy, *Passages*

# Coming of Age

This is one of the richest life passages mined by memoirists, no doubt because so many adolescents find they have to come apart in order to put themselves back together between the ages of 13 and 18.

## What's Going On?

According to psychiatrist Erik Erikson, the teen years represent the culmination of each of the earlier conflicts that, if resolved, have resulted in a teenager acquiring trust, autonomy, initiative, and industry. Even so, Erikson said, the teenager might have to "re-fight" these earlier battles to integrate the different aspects of self together into a new self-identity.

According to Erikson, it is vital that this self-identity work for the teenager in the context of her social milieu. How does a teenager acquire a coherent self-identity? In Erikson's view, self-identity gains real strength only from "wholehearted and consistent recognition of real accomplishments." These he described as "achievements that have meaning in their culture." An accomplishment might be high grades, making the basketball team, building a home for Habitat for Humanity, or all of the above.

If avenues of expression and recognition are denied, Erikson warned, a teenager "will resist with the astonishing strength encountered in animals who are suddenly forced to defend their lives." This thwarted drive to belong and succeed, he said, is what creates the cliques and gangs of America's cities and fiercely nationalistic movements in other societies. Erikson saw negative adolescent behaviors such as intolerance for differences among their peers, even acts of cruelty, as a defense against all that inner turmoil. In the face of so many body changes and a self-identity in flux, it is difficult for a teenager to be tolerant of others and herself.

That's a lot of drama and, to be sure, it fills many a memoir.

## How Have You Grown?

Memoirists writing a coming-of-age story are detailing the end of childhood and the beginning of adult responsibilities, perspectives, and relationships. In the best of these stories, one pivotal situation forces the shift in these conflicts from latency to active expression. In Tobias Wolff's *This Boy's Life*, his single mother loves him but can't protect him or herself from her abusive husband. In the rural Washington State setting of the 1960s where they live, young Tobias, acting out the trouble at home, repeatedly gets into fights and skips school. Here he describes an emerging, conflict-laden sense of himself:

> I was subject to fits of feeling myself unworthy.... It didn't take much to bring this sensation to life, along with the certainty that everybody but my mother saw through me and did not like what they saw.

Ultimately, the violence at home and his troubles in town force young Tobias to prematurely make the leap into adulthood. He falsifies an application to attend a prestigious East Coast prep school and succeeds in getting there, only to fail and face expulsion after two years of less-than-stellar classroom performance. Wolff, shaped by his early life into the quintessential survivor, then goes off to fight in Vietnam and emerges intact to attend Oxford University. In this excerpt, he captures the sense of invincibility that appears to rule so many young men at this age:

> When we are green, still half-created, we believe that our dreams are rights...and that falling and dying are for quitters. We live on the innocent and monstrous assurance that we...have a special arrangement whereby we will be allowed to stay green forever....

In this excerpt from *This Boy's Life*, we hear the reflective voice of the narrator, now aware of the risks accompanying his earlier actions in a way he was not before. How might this voice have been different if the memoir had been written closer to the age Wolff was when the events took place?

Clearly the narrator-protagonist was almost ready to leave home before he took things into his own hands, but, as this memoir makes clear, that young man was forever shaped by the explosive forces that pushed him out the door.

# Between Parents and Children

Stories of conflicted and loving relationships between parents and children are the bread and butter of memoir. A parent writing about a child's birth, illness, rebellion, or addiction, along with the safe return of a child from a dangerous precipice, probably fill more memoir shelves than any other single category. As more Baby Boomers lose aging parents, still more memoirs record the loaded experience of becoming a parentless adult. The fact that so many of these stories reach bookstore shelves is a testimony to the unlimited number of unique angles being found to address these experiences.

## The Ten-Year Rule

A few years ago I took a nonfiction writers' workshop given by memoirist Adair Lara. It took place at the all-female Mills College, so most of the workshop participants were college-age women and all were English majors. On the first day of class, Lara stunned the group when she expressed the view that a decade is the minimum amount of time an author should let pass between the experience of a traumatic event and any attempt to write a memoir depicting that event. She immediately drew fierce objections from several students who had already begun excoriating their last boyfriends and break-ups on the pages of their newly christened memoirs.

Lara's point was that perspective requires distance. Without sufficient time to reflect, a memoirist might deliver plenty of drama, but her writing will lack heart and the essential reflective voice. To underscore her point, Lara used her own experience in writing

*Hold Me Close, Let Me Go,* her story of raising a rebellious daughter. She explained that since she had been a newspaper columnist writing personal essays throughout the period when the events in her memoir occurred, she was in the habit of recording her life on a daily basis. But when she then tried to convert these entries into a longer memoir, Lara found that the writing lacked depth. Her realization: she wasn't ready to write about her struggles until the soap opera playing out in her life had moved to another, calmer stage.

## Turning the Tables

Ten years later, she was ready. In *Hold Me Close, Let Me Go,* Lara writes episodically about her daughter's terrifying progress through adolescence, from drinking beer in a public park at the age of 13 ("having a thirteen-year-old was like having your own personal brick wall"), to the terrible day three years later when Lara sits in a hospital waiting room, ticking off in her head the potential teenage problems parents dread most: "cutting class, failing grades, smoking, drinking, early sex, drugs, running away, stealing, pregnancy," and realizes that with the exception of running away, her daughter Morgan has dragged herself and her family through all of them.

Throughout the memoir, Lara shares the incremental dawning of perspective she gains as a parent experiencing trial by fire, using a reflective voice doled out in dribs and drabs while the action proceeds apace. In this way she mimics the way such nuggets of wisdom arrive in real life as parents struggle to keep an unruly adolescent alive in spite of herself.

> Not having control was an awful feeling. When she talked on the phone for hours, and I knew she had a math test the next day, I was not enraged because she was in danger of not knowing any math. I was enraged because she wasn't minding me, because she was standing in my house and not doing what I wanted her to do. Sometimes the books advised me to use humor. "Don't give them the reactions they're after," they said. It struck me that my sense of humor had been the first thing to go. Where was the mom who used to drop on all fours? All of a sudden, parenting had become deadly serious.

Ultimately, Lara's memoir is about several passages involving parents and children: her own as a mother to Morgan; Morgan's hurried-up transition to adulthood by way of becoming a young mother; and then, in a twist, Adair Lara's unfinished business with her own father who shows up seeking forgiveness after abandoning his wife and seven children many years before. With an intricate weaving of the stories of father and daughter and mother and daughter, Lara's memoir packs a double wallop as she shows us the transformative power and universality of the parent-child experience.

**POTHOLE AHEAD!**

If you are going to permit your child read and veto power over a part of your memoir that includes the child's experiences, choose a time when you are alone and unrushed. Give him time to read alone, and let him know that your relationship is more important than the book. Giving him the option to take something out will often make it easier for him to say you can leave it in. Choice and an assurance of the primacy of your relationship are what matters in these situations. But if he says it must go, it goes.

## Do You Need Your Kid's Permission?

The ethics of writing about intimate events involving one's children is a hotly debated issue among memoirists. Is it an invasion of privacy to share their coming-of-age struggles when they're too young to object? When a child is under the age of 18, the parent faces no legal consequences by including the child's story in a published work of nonfiction. However, after children "come of age," they have the right to legally object to having their lives in print. An adult child can sue the parent to stop such a book from being published. So, for both ethical and legal reasons, her permission should be sought prior to publication. To get that permission recorded, the same release form recommended when a writer uses an adult's story in her book (see Appendix C) can be used to obtain permission from a grown son or daughter.

Many memoirists in this situation permit their teenage or adult children to read the manuscript before anyone else sees it. They then remove any portions of the manuscript that the child finds objectionable. Other writers solve the problem by sharing royalties from the sales of a published memoir with their adult children.

# Surprising Themes in Passages

Memoirs dealing with adoption as told by adoptive parents and their adopted children, as well as birth mothers, can include multiple variations on the themes of parenting, families, and coming of age. But in some memoirs, the experience of adoption can illuminate other themes that have nothing to do with parenting.

In Peggy Orenstein's *Waiting for Daisy*, we have the perspective of a professional woman in her late 30s who believes she doesn't want motherhood, but then, when she marries and finds conception and pregnancy do not come easily, decides she desperately wants it. Orenstein's six-year saga is encapsulated in the subtitle of her best-selling memoir: "A Tale of Two Continents, Three Religions, Five Fertility Doctors, an Oscar, an Atomic Bomb, a Romantic Night, and One Woman's Quest to Become a Mother." After failing to conceive, she and her husband enter a long, drawn-out process to adopt a child from Japan.

Without giving away the twist in Orenstein's story, the surprising personal growth that the author experiences while waiting for her first child to arrive concerns much more than motherhood (or the lack of a child) in her life. The struggle and ultimate growth for the narrator occur when she confronts her belief that since she'd always been so competent and successful in everything else she'd tried, becoming a mother should be a snap. When it proves the opposite, and her slog through fertility treatments tests her resolve even further, the author's crisis becomes the need to surrender to a life over which she suddenly must admit she doesn't have control. Here is a telling exchange with her husband, the Oscar-winning documentary filmmaker Steven Ogazaki, while she visits him on a filming location:

> "I've made a decision," Steven said. "I'll only keep trying to get pregnant if you stop caring." Stop caring. He might as well have told me to stop breathing.... "You pretend to talk about normal things, but I can tell you're thinking about

fertility the whole time. You're this angry, bitter person fixated on having a baby." ...I wish I could say that Steven's warning, his pleading, brought me to my senses, made me realize how sorely I'd neglected him. But, perversely, it was my very faith in his commitment to our relationship that had allowed me to abuse it. I had convinced myself that we'd survive the damage I was inflicting, that it was reversible, even necessary.

When a blessed event finally does come to the Orenstein-Ogazaki household, the narrator goes through many of the awe-filled experiences of new motherhood. But as far as the writer is concerned, her central struggle has already occurred. With the necessary internal change made, Orenstein, like her readers, can appreciate the joy that Daisy brings all the more.

> **TAKE IT TO HEART**
>
> "Memoir is how we try to make sense of who we are, who we once were, and what values and heritage shaped us. If a writer seriously embarks on that quest, readers will be nourished by the journey, bringing along many associations with quests of their own."
>
> —William Zinsser, *Inventing the Truth, The Art and Craft of Memoir*

# Dealing with Loss and Tragedy

Writing about loss offers memoirists a safe place to feel and begin to heal from painful experiences. When authors manage to record their trauma with honesty and self-scrutiny, they produce some of the most powerful memoirs that have been published. Among the best in recent years are Joan Didion's *The Year of Magical Thinking* and Kay Redfield Jamison's *Nothing Was the Same*. Both of these books charted the immediate aftermath of losing a husband to a sudden fatal illness. They can be said to map the geography of grief.

Others deal with grief as well as unresolved aspects of the relationship between the memoirist and the deceased. Linda Gray Sexton's latest book combines the theme of grief with an illness narrative of bipolar disorder and the story of a troubled mother-daughter relationship. The resulting memoir, *Half in Love, Surviving the Legacy of Suicide,* offers an explicit—and at times claustrophobic—yet surefooted and ultimately redemptive memoir covering two lives and three generations in the Sexton family.

Through Linda Sexton's eyes we see that death was a demanding creative muse to her mother, the famous poet Anne Sexton. It was also daughter Linda's main rival for her mother's attention, since Anne managed to include young Linda in her creative writing process, going so far as to arrange poetry writing lessons for her daughter. The pull of death was something else entirely, first for the mother and then, in a near repeat of the same tragedy, for the daughter who emulated everything about her.

Sexton begins her story on the evening of her first suicide attempt, when she takes narcotic pills and slits her wrists in the bathtub of her family home while her husband is away on business and her teenage sons sleep in their rooms down the hall. As she sinks into unconsciousness, Sexton remembers the promise she made to her boys that she would never do to them what her mother had done to her and then proceeds to nearly do it. The author describes her loss of resolve with heartbreaking honesty:

> I was ready, at last, to cheat on love. Ready to renege on assurances that now felt as if they had been too easily given to everyone—children, husband, sister, father, friends. Immersed in communing with my mother, I became a small child that night, a vulnerable daughter. She seemed right then to hover in the room, guiding me. I knew that when I finished, she would be waiting to fold me into her arms, and I would go home with her one more time.

The next scene, appropriately, brings us back to the morning in 1974 when, as a 21-year-old college senior, Sexton learns that her mother, by then a Pulitzer Prize–winning cultural darling, has finally—after innumerable attempts—succeeded in killing herself by carbon monoxide poisoning in the family garage.

Over the next several chapters, Sexton recounts her later childhood and teen years at the hands of this often loving but wildly inconsistent mother. By the time the author returns to the night of her own suicide attempt, she is 45, and we are not a bit surprised to learn that she has reached the same age as her mother when she took her life...so strongly has Sexton brought us into her visceral experience of being the adoring, insecure daughter who identifies completely with a beautiful, vivacious, but helplessly narcissistic parent. The fact that it is Anne Sexton's bipolar disorder—never properly diagnosed or treated—producing this deranged parenting is never far from the reader's consciousness. The daughter well understands her mother's feelings of hopelessness; within months Sexton receives the same diagnosis.

The good news Sexton offers in the final chapter of her memoir is the arrival of her own hard-won stability. And then, in a touching and beautifully rendered scene, she shares the conversation she has with her two now-grown sons, in which she asks their forgiveness and speaks openly about the illness for which they, too, are at high risk. The fact that this conversation happens at all offers real hope that the legacy of suicide will, at least in this family, finally be halted.

For aspiring memoir writers, Sexton's memoir offers valuable lessons; it shows us that it can take many years for an artist to find her own voice. In Sexton's case, we appreciate the added difficulty faced by a writer who is the daughter of a famous poet. Her story also reveals many subtleties and difficulties in the complicated process of resolving and achieving distance from our major life relationships, with the bond between mothers and children depicted as the most complicated and formative of all. No wonder parent-child–themed memoirs continue to be among the most popular for memoir writers and readers alike.

## The Least You Need to Know

- The passages that mark a typical life are keyed to common turning points.
- Coming of age represents the most conflict-laden of passages.
- In a successful memoir about a life passage, the writer lets readers see her deepest wound, the part of her that must change if she's going to get what she most desires.
- Memoirs dealing with the death of a parent often represent the culmination of a healing process begun with the writing itself.

# Relationship Memoirs

**Chapter**

# 14

## In This Chapter

- Finding the beats for true love, real and fictional
- How to pick a romance plotline for your memoir
- Giving an old romantic theme a new twist
- Using your personal experience as advice

Memoirists love to write about love. As such, romantic relationships, from the hottest and briefest to the longest and most dependable, fill many pages of memoir. There is much to learn from fiction when you write the intricacies of the human heart in and out of love. In this chapter, we look at the standard romance plots, their variations, and how memoirists apply these plotlines to their real-life love stories. From romance, we look at how some writers have recorded some memorable friendships.

# Real-Life Romance Plots

Although you are writing about a real-life love, you'll find that when it comes to romance, fact and fiction overlap. The romance plot is a subcategory of the three-act dramatic plot—with its own beats and standard variations. Let's look at these structures and how your story might fit the mold.

## The Basic Beats of Romance

The customary steps in a romance plot generally proceed as follows:

ACT I

> Step 1. Boy meets girl (or girl meets girl, boy meets boy).
>
> Step 2. Sparks fly (if one initially resists, he/she ultimately falls).
>
> Step 3. Conflict arises.

ACT II

> Step 4. Boy loses girl until he/she faces fatal flaw (this often takes a long time).
>
> Step 5. Conflict gets resolved.

ACT III

> Step 6. Boy gets girl or someone better.

Does this basic dramatic structure match the sequence of events in your real-life love story? If you think not, try adding one of the following complications to see if it feels closer to home.

## Romantic Complications

There are a myriad of things that can happen to screw up a romance between steps two and five in the three-act plot structure. In the next list, I offer some of the most common themes. Each of these would qualify as the central conflict between two lovers that arises for the first time at the end of Act I. The rest of the story, Acts II and III, is then spent breaking up and making up:

- **Triangle**—A new love develops, but one partner is already taken. Because the new couple is destined for each other, the third wheel must be dispensed with. Ideally she will see the light and find someone else, too. Or the new love interest will be shown to be shallow or in some way unworthy and the original couple will survive and be better off for the near loss of real love. This is an extremely popular plot you'll see in everything from *Wuthering Heights* and *Same Time, Next Year* to the *Twilight* saga.

- **Beauty and the beast**—One of the characters is marred or scarred—usually physically, but sometimes emotionally. Think *Phantom of the Opera*.

- **Cinderella**—A classic plot in which the protagonist (male or female) goes from rags-to-riches and wins a prince or princess after experiencing deprivation and want. Think *Pretty Woman*.

- **Class differences**—One partner is in a different class or world than the other one. This doesn't have to be monetary; the difference could be due to education, lifestyle, or work. Think *Sabrina* and *Working Girl*.

- **Family feud**—Two characters are interested in one another, but their separate worlds seem closed because of family hatreds and misunderstandings. Think *Romeo and Juliet* and *Giant*.

- **A bad boy (or girl) is in serious need of help**—This love plot involves one character who is desperately in need of redemption and a second who is clean-cut and straight-laced and is surprisingly attracted to and interested in the "bad" boy or girl. This is a great plot if one character is a vampire; think *The Greyfriar* where a human female is stuck in a strange world and rescued by a young vampire male.

- **Homebody versus adventurer**—The characters have opposing traits. Which one will change in order to preserve their love? Think *The City Mouse and the Country Mouse*.

- **Crime victim/savior**—One character is kidnapped, mugged, stolen from, and so on. The other character might be the perpetrator, a helper, a detective, or a bystander. Think *The Bodyguard*.

- **Lost or stranded together**—Two characters who were formerly not interested in one another—perhaps couldn't stand one another—are thrown together alone, bringing forced intimacy complete with danger. They learn to get along and, surprisingly, grow in respect and caring. Think *African Queen.*

- **Mistaken identity/secret**—One character isn't who the other thinks she is, or one character has a secret that must not be revealed because all love could be lost. This was Shakespeare's favorite romance plot. Think *Twelfth Night* or *The Prince and the Pauper.*

- **Unknown baby**—A woman has a baby, but the father never knew about it. At a later time, the father and mother meet again, with him still not knowing the baby is his. Think *Thorn Birds.*

Just because these romantic complications are familiar to readers and moviegoers does not make them any less compelling. To the contrary, a reader/viewer enjoys knowing the familiar underlying structure in a story. Then she can relax into the details and thoroughly enjoy the experience.

**QUICK PROMPT**

When you were young, did you believe there was one true love out there for you, a child somewhere in the world to whom you were destined to be married? Many of us grew up believing in this fairy-tale view of love. If this was your fantasy, too, write it as a children's fairy tale. You just might find a use for this memory in your romantic memoir.

## Same Plot, Different Characters and Stories

In fact and fiction, there is rarely, if ever, a love story without complications. As we peruse a few recent memoirs about love, it will not be hard to place each in one of the plot variations you just read. But again, that's often what makes them delicious.

*Kissing Outside the Lines, A True Story of Love and Race and Happily Ever After,* is a new memoir by actress Diane Farr. In it, Farr tells an interracial love story involving her Korean-American husband. Farr uses a classic family feud romance plot but tells her story with two key differences that give this familiar plot structure a distinctive twist.

First, Farr applies a deft sense of humor to her foibles as well as those of her husband and in-laws. Here she sets up her story in the introduction to *Kissing Outside the Lines:*

> My mother claims I am not white. You might be thinking my mother is not all there from the previous quote, but she's right about my skin. My coloring is olive, my hair is dark. I'm taller than most American women, and my body frame is small. You could argue that I look Brazilian or Russian, with the body of a Swede or sub-Saharan African, depending on your frame of reference. But when my Korean in-laws look at me I am most importantly not Asian. Therefore I am white.

Then she captures the moment of love at (almost) first sight:

> Seung never asked for my phone number because he had saved it for over a year, waiting until he thought I was actually interested in him before calling me. Hearing this made my spine turn to cheese dip. I slid down on the well-worn cab seat into my own puddle of happiness. Seung Yong Chung owned me even though I couldn't correctly pronounce any of his three names.

Farr ventures from formula again in this memoir by including brief portraits of other American interracial couples whose romances and complications resonate with those of her own love story. She uses slang in the titles of these chapters to comically announce the racial mix of each new couple, including "Mexican American Loves Palestinian Englishman in Illinois," and "Evangelical White Chick Loves Hindu Indian Man in Maryland." Farr then interweaves different stages of her own romance plot with the other couples, offering a rich menu of variations on her theme: true love conquers all obstacles.

# Marriage and Memoir

There are not many (or any) memoirs about marriages without complications, which is as it should be. Do you know any marriages without problems? As such, I will not offer up any happy marriage memoirs as examples to inspire your own. Instead, I'll draw from the rich pool of memoirs of love found, lost, then found again before it's lost again. Here we're looking not at dating stories, but the kind of drama that occurs solely within the stormy confines of the institution of marriage.

> **TAKE IT TO HEART**
>
> What is your biggest regret in a significant relationship or a past or present marriage? Make it something you did or said that you wish you could take back or something you failed to do or say. Write about the situation, your words and behavior. Then write a letter of apology to the person you hurt. Make it from the heart, no excuses or defenses. How do you feel about it now?

## "Unhappy in Its Own Way"

Tolstoy's famous line states, "Every happy family is the same, every unhappy family is unhappy in its own way." It can be said that the class of memoirs detailing married life is the encyclopedia of all the ways in which these unhappily married couples live together and either confront the problems at the root of their unhappiness or break up.

*Perfection* is the ironic title of Julie Metz's true account of one initially happy but ultimately deeply marred marital union. Her subtitle telegraphs the survivor theme that she places within her romance plot: *A Memoir of Betrayal and Renewal.*

In *Perfection*, Metz gives her readers the bad news first: the sudden death of her thirty-something husband, which then leads to the revelation of his secret life:

> It happened like this: Henry's footsteps on the old wooden floorboards. The toilet flushing. More footsteps, perhaps on the stairs. Silence. Then the thud.

Metz then begins to interweave the present with various points in the past and future—the promising start of her and Henry's love story, the revelation of his numerous extramarital affairs, conversations she had with three of these "other women," her own first love affair with a younger man as a new widow, and ultimately her confrontation with the parts of herself that led her to not see what had been hiding in plain sight. Here she describes some of that self-reckoning:

> While I had wanted to see everything in terms of absolutes, right and wrong, good and evil, it was clear that I would have to settle for something gray and muddled. I could talk to Christine or Ellen or Eliana every day for a year, and still I would never really be able to understand what had happened to Henry, to the marriage I had clung to, to me in the marriage. I would have to go forward into the gray, muddled place and bushwhack some clear path of my own. And while I had scattered moments of gratitude for my "second chance," I was mostly furious, raging and brokenhearted.

Thinking back to the memoir structure and plot discussion in Chapter 8, where would you place this reflective moment in Julie Metz's life journey? If you thought the middle of Act II, when the protagonist must really see her flaw and how much she's messing up her own life by not confronting it, you got it right. In fact, this scene occurs about halfway through. The protagonist has a lot more slogging to go before she gets it and makes the hard change required so she doesn't repeat the same mistakes in her next relationship.

## The Other Woman

The perspective of the mistress is relatively new to memoir, having remained in the shadows of the betrayed wife until fairly recently. As morality loosens and more memoirs are written, we read an increasing number of real-life romances told from the point of view of the character readers used to view exclusively as the "home wrecker," now just one more player in the game of love.

Laura Fraser's bestselling memoir *The Italian Affair* and its sequel *All Over the Map* chronicle her ten-year relationship with a married Frenchman whom she meets in Italy—a man whose name she never reveals, calling him "the Professor." She begins her story of their secret relationship with the end of her own marriage:

> Twelve years ago, after 18 months of marriage, my husband left me unexpectedly, and when I could finally rouse myself to do anything, I booked a flight to Italy. Every time I'd been there, I'd felt happier, more alive, and I hoped that by speaking another language I would become another person for a while, one whose heart was whole.

After a blissful four-day affair on the island of Ischia, Fraser and the Professor part, leaving Fraser alone and feeling blue again, that is until...

> One chilly day that winter, at home, while I was in the midst of moving out of my husband's house and refiguring my finances, a postcard arrived from Paris. "I couldn't forget," the Professor wrote. And neither could I. That spring, we met in Milan. Six months later, we met in London, and the next fall he flew to San Francisco. Over the next three years, we met in Turin, Morocco and Mexico, immersing ourselves in the food, the art—whatever was beautiful and sensual. Always keeping things simple and speaking Italian.

Fraser's talents as a travel and food writer are on display in her two memoirs that share this forbidden love affair as their story spines. In fact, it is the author's undaunted curiosity and love of new places, people, and cuisine that carry her and the reader through the ups and downs of her unconventional love plot. In contrast to *Eat, Pray, Love*, this is a romantic memoir about going off to heal after a divorce, having an affair, and coming home—without the happily ever after.

Her second memoir ends poignantly with Fraser, still single, visiting the Professor—now divorced and married again to another woman— one last time at his hospital bedside a few weeks before his death. At this point, Fraser's story becomes a celebration of the deep friendship that exists between two grown-ups, one that more than survived the romance that initially brought them together. Booklist called *All Over the Map* "a winning coming-of-middle-age memoir." Fraser's work demonstrates again that, when handled well, having more than one theme in a true-life story only deepens and enriches the reader's experience.

**QUICK PROMPT**

Picture your closest friend as an older child or teenager. Describe her in detail—her hair, her features, and the clothes and colors she always wore. Then write a conversation between the two of you, whatever comes to mind, as if you are a fly on the wall that has traveled back in time. Capture the essence of that friendship in 300 words or less.

# Best Friends

Long-term friendship between two men or two women is another favorite theme of fiction and memoir writers. Stories of friendship share some elements of the romance plot, especially when friends become possessive or competitive or when one betrays the other, leaving the two to make up or break up. But friendships tend to be more stable than romances, resembling the warm and fuzzy feelings of long-time married couples more than the roller-coaster highs and lows of newly in-love couples.

In *Let's Take the Long Road Home, a Memoir of Friendship*, Gail Caldwell tells the story of her relationship with fellow memoirist Caroline Knapp, the author of *Drinking, A Love Story*, who died at 42 of lung cancer. Caldwell portrays the extraordinarily close bond between the two women as a character in its own right, describing it with all the intensity of a lover:

> From the beginning, there was something intangible and even spooky between us that could make strangers mistake us as sisters or lovers, and that sometimes had friends refer to us by each other's name…. Finding Caroline was like placing a personal ad for an imaginary friend, then having

> her show up at your door funnier and better than you had conceived. Apart, we had each been frightened drunks and aspiring writers and dog lovers; together, we became a small corporation.

As the story of their friendship unfolds, Caldwell makes clear that it is their common flaws that allow these two friends to achieve such a high level of mutual understanding. This is emotionally satisfying for readers, just as it is instructive for storytellers. Every novelist must understand his protagonist's fatal flaw, since it is the thing from which the central conflict of the novel will flow. Likewise, a memoirist, as the protagonist of her own story, must be able to identify her central flaw, and then reflect it in the main conflict of her memoir. For Caldwell, the central flaw is an inability to face painful emotions.

In *Let's Take the Long Way Home*, Caldwell deals with Caroline's death in similarly fresh and surprising terms:

> Before one enters the spectrum of sorrow, which changes even the color of trees, there is a blind and daringly wrong assumption that probably allows us to blunder through our days. There is a way one thinks that the show will never end—or that loss, when it comes, will be toward the end of the road, not in its middle.

Caldwell depicts the excruciating experience of seeing her friend through the final days of stage-four lung cancer in as blunt terms as have ever been used to describe what it looks and feels like to watch another person die. Before picking up this book, as readers and writers we might not think there is much new to say about friendship or grief. By the time we put down her memoir, Gail Caldwell has trampled this assumption.

**POTHOLE AHEAD!**

When writing about another person's medical experiences, you must get the patient's and the doctor's permission to use their names. In many cases, medical personnel prefer to go unnamed rather than be quoted out of context. An option then is simply to use a pseudonym—for example, Dr. M.

# The Last Passage

In her most recent book, *Passages in Caregiving*, Gail Sheehy combines memoir and a compendium of self-help advice to write about her husband Clay Felker's long illness and her trials and personal growth as she unexpectedly becomes his caregiver. With irony, Sheehy describes herself before and after she got the bad news about Felker's turn for the worse:

> What was I thinking in that beauty salon just before Clay's surgeon called to announce, two years after the fact, that we had a new visitor in our lives—cancer? A profound issue: whether I could fit into last year's theater suit. That night, we were joining friends for Zubin Mehta's farewell concert at the New York Philharmonic. As I hung up numbly, I remember thinking, "We will never be carefree again."

Describing her experiences over the next 17 years while caring for her chronically ill husband, Sheehy shares many realizations that will ring true to many of her fellow Baby Boomers. Chief among these is that, as a generation, they have never imagined that they would find themselves in this position with a loved one. Therefore, many, like Sheehy, are woefully unprepared for the marathon that ensues.

At the conclusion of her memoir, Sheehy tackles another taboo when she speaks directly to her husband about his fear of dying and reveals it on the page. We are fortunate that she chose to share this incredible conversation between herself, Felker, and his doctor. The physician speaks first:

> "Are you afraid of dying?"
>
> Clay nodded yes.
>
> "What is your biggest fear?"
>
> "Being alone."
>
> Again, we reassured him that would not happen. Dr. M would alert me and I would be there. Dr. M asked what else worried him.

"Dying in a hospital." We could assure him that wouldn't happen (although most Americans don't have a choice).

"Some people worry about what it's going to feel like, the process, the symptoms," Dr. M said.

After more words of candor between doctor and patient, Felker, with his wife as witness, gains some ease with the idea of letting go. Here's how Sheehy finishes the scene:

> I asked if he'd like me to read poetry or Shakespeare. Clay said it was just hearing my voice that made him feel good. And music. That squared with Dr. M's private instructions to me: The last sense to go is hearing, so don't say anything in front of the dying that you don't want them to hear....

Sheehy's latest "Passage" shows how a master memoirist can craft a piece of writing that is both powerfully intimate and of service to others. Don't be afraid to share the important lessons that you, like Sheehy, gather from weathering a life crisis. Put this acquired wisdom on the pages of your memoir. Your readers will thank you.

## The Least You Need to Know

- The basic romance plot is the same for fiction and nonfiction: boy gets girl, boy loses girl, boy gets girl back, or someone better. The variations on this structure are many.

- There are very few memoirs about carefree happy romances and marriages. Many more are written about love gone bad and marriages gone askew.

- The point of view of the "other woman" has only recently entered the genre of romance memoirs.

- There are endless variations on the classic love story to make yours worth telling. Find the particulars to hit a universal chord.

- Adding a second theme—such as friendship or grief—on top of a romantic plotline adds depth and meaning for readers.

# The Illness Narrative

**Chapter**
# 15

## In This Chapter

- Deciphering the meaning you give to illness
- Seeing how a patient's story impacts treatment and cures
- How your illness narrative determines plot
- Trying out the three plotlines for your illness memoir

Stories chronicling a person's journey through medical and mental suffering, told from the point of view of the sufferer or caretaker, now occupy a large percentage of memoirs. Memoirists approaching the subject of illness might think they face a simple task. All they have to do is describe before and after. A narrator would begin by establishing her good health and then show the moment when she noticed the suspect symptoms. There would be a diagnosis, followed by effective treatment and the return of good health. Without question, this plotline can produce a compelling illness narrative. However, different people interpret the same symptoms and illnesses differently. This changes their memories of the experience. In this chapter, we look at how different perspectives and illness narratives present different choices for the memoirist trying to make sense out of a personal medical or mental health challenge.

# What Is an Illness Narrative?

Over the past two decades, the concept of an illness narrative first emerged, not in a literary context, but in psychotherapy and medicine. Narrative therapy uses the ideas of a person's choice of "narrative identity" and how people tell their life stories to help them reframe difficulties and adopt a more positive attitude. In medical schools, the illness narrative has been applied to the training of doctors, teaching them to communicate better with patients by understanding the various meanings patients give their illnesses and helping patients change their narratives toward more successful outcomes.

It has been found that a patient's illness narrative can have a real impact on treatment and survival. Studies show, for example, that when a wife includes her husband in the story of her breast cancer, in effect turning the protagonist in her narrative from *I* to *we*, treatment becomes more effective and her chance of survival improves.

Before writing a memoir about the experience of surviving a grave illness, it is useful for a memoirist to identify what story he has told himself about his illness and how this choice of a storyline might have shaped the outcome.

## An Interactive Story

Frank describes an illness narrative not as an externalized construct but as an interactive experience that the ill person enters. From within this story, the patient then finds others—patients like him, medical providers, caregivers—with whom he interacts, using the illness as a primary focal point for those interactions.

How family and friends react to an illness affects the stories a patient tells himself and others. For mental illnesses, addictions, or the more mysterious physical illnesses—for example, chronic pain syndrome—there is often a stigma attached. This stigma can then shape our personal narratives by adding guilt or shame to the mix, which in turn can turn us into unreliable narrators.

The relational nature of the illness narrative concept is strikingly similar to the bond that exists between a memoirist and a memoir's readers, especially when the focus of the memoir is on an illness or addiction. The memoir is not just any story—the reader is very aware that it represents the author's true life story of struggle and survival. This fundamental fact changes everything about the writing and reading experience. This specialness then extends to any other forms of interaction the memoirist has with readers—as part of a community of writers, in book talks, online, and so on.

# Three Plotlines for an Illness

Frank defined three types of illness narratives, seeing them as the frameworks or plotlines that the ill person uses first to understand and then to explain her illness. If you are writing an illness memoir, you will likely discover that one (or more) of the following three narratives mirrors the storyline you once lived and are now writing.

## The Restitution Narrative

This is the most familiar and socially condoned type of illness narrative. A restitution narrative tells the story of a patient being restored to good health due to the marvels of modern medicine. These are the gee-whiz recovery stories that we often read about in the popular press. In this story model, the illness is seen as transitory. As Frank put it, "It [the patient's thoughts, feelings, and actions] is a response to an interruption, but the narrative itself is above interruption." It is all about the body returning to its former image of itself, before illness. The illness has been managed, the body likened to a car that has broken down and been repaired.

The memoirs written using this story model are about achieving complete remission—for example, from a virulent form of cancer or a brain tumor—and being none the worse for the experience.

## The Chaos Narrative

In contrast, the narrator in a chaos illness narrative takes a radically different and more chaotic path. The illness moves randomly, so the patient goes in a zigzag story line, one that progresses from bad to worse and back to bad before getting worse again. The storyteller is without hope; he imagines his body and life never improving.

If you were constructing a memoir about your years in a downward spiral dealing with a less familiar ailment such as chronic fatigue syndrome or fibromyalgia, you would likely be writing a chaos narrative. Chaos narratives describe the experience of having a disease with no cure and perhaps only unreliable treatments. It is the story of AIDS in the '80s and early '90s. It also describes the old medical model used for treating severe mental illness or long-term addiction, which aimed for maintenance, not improvement, as the goal of treatment. For many in mental health care, this old model has been replaced by a recovery model. A patient shifting between these models can be seen as changing his story from a chaos narrative to a quest narrative.

## The Quest Narrative

Frank described the quest illness narrative as when "the ill person meets suffering head on; they accept illness and seek to use it. Illness is the occasion of a journey that becomes a quest."

The narrator in a quest narrative shows us what it's like to be in pain. She shares her hopes, and fears, and sense (or lack of sense) about the meaning of suffering and the possibility of death. Rather than telling others what they should do in order to return to their former state, quest narratives bear witness to the experience and share wisdom. It's not that the person doesn't wish to be well. She might in fact achieve wellness; but, more importantly, she accepts what is. Wellness is not defined as the state the ill person occupied before the illness struck. It represents the claiming by the narrator of a newer, wiser state.

Frank demonstrates the quest narrative in action when he writes to his younger self, the person he was before the onset of his testicular cancer: "For all you lose, you have an opportunity to gain: closer relationships, more poignant appreciations, clarified values. You are entitled to mourn what you can no longer be, but do not let this mourning obscure your sense of what you can become. You are embarking on a dangerous opportunity. Do not curse your fate; count your possibilities."

The point of applying one or more of these models to a memoir documenting your personal journey through a medical or mental health crisis is to help you get a better handle on how best to structure your story. If, for example, you had one of the many types of cancer that now have a high rate of remission when they are treated early, a restitution illness narrative could well be an appropriate plot structure for your story.

# Putting It All Together

Let's go a little deeper into how plot and other story elements work together to achieve *narrative coherence* in the three illness narrative structures introduced.

> **DEFINITION**
>
> We say a story has **narrative coherence** when its parts work together smoothly to take a narrator on a journey: the narrator's voice fits the protagonist as he changes; other characters, including an antagonist, are present to ensure complications; and a recognizable plot hangs on key turning points. Lastly, all these elements support the memoir's desired theme.

## Starting with a Restitution Narrative

Scenario 1: In a restitution illness narrative for breast cancer, the following would happen:

- The author would participate in a plot sequence that unfolds according to a set of fixed responses to what is found in the analysis of her breast tissue.

- The author would visit an oncologist, a radiotherapist, and a surgeon and would have ongoing relationships with them depending on how the illness plot unfolds.

- The author's family members would be given a set of roles to play and events to expect.

- The feelings of everyone involved would include sadness, anxiety, worry, and fear, producing a predictable character arc for the narrator as well as other characters around her.

- The author would have feelings of extreme fear, but because her disease is familiar and is known to have a cure, there would be a clear, uplifting conclusion to the plot.

## Switching Illness Narratives

Scenario 2: But what if the author-patient eschews conventional treatment and opts for an alternative, natural cure for her breast cancer? This author-patient could quickly find herself in a chaos illness narrative. In this story the following would happen:

- The author would go through a less predictable series of medical events, and, given the greater unknowns, she would be likely to experience different emotions.

- It would not be clear who the principal characters in the story should be (besides the patient). What kind of specialists might she consult? Where would she have to go?

- She would likely receive less support from those around her in this scenario. Unsupportive family members who disapprove of her choices might become antagonists in her story.

- How the ill person resolves ensuing conflicts would shape the plot in significant ways. A family estrangement complication might take over the narrative for a period.

- The author would have to find new ways to chart her progress or lack of it. How would she interpret any temporary improvement or sudden decline in the course of her unconventional treatment?

- In this chaos illness narrative, there might be no clear point of remission. How would the memoirist bring her narrator to a climax and resolution of the story?

If she is writing a memoir about seeking an unconventional path for treating an illness or about getting treatment for a rare illness, the memoirist is by necessity laying a mystery story on top of a chaos illness narrative. In such a narrative, she might need to find an alternative climax to replace achieving a cure. One can imagine this alternative would have something to do with a radical acceptance of what is. But this would depend entirely on how the patient-author experienced and interpreted the events in question.

> **QUICK PROMPT**
>
> Remember your scariest experience as a patient. What was your worst fear? Do you think you had a particular illness narrative (conscious or unconscious) for what was happening to you? Was being restored to health a sure thing in your narrative? If not, describe the chaos you felt without having that certainty. Try to re-create a key conversation between you and a doctor. See if this scene has a place in your memoir.

# When No Cure Is in Sight

Author Melanie Thernstrom wrote a remarkable book that looks at how someone goes about choosing an illness narrative as a patient and author. In *The Pain Chronicles: Cures, Myths, Mysteries, Prayers, Diaries, Brain Scans, Healing, and the Science of Suffering*, she explores the subject of unrelenting, incurable pain from the perspective of someone who joined the ranks of pain sufferers due to a degenerative spinal condition, which first manifested when she was in her 20s.

To investigate possible treatments for her condition and to understand the science of pain, Thernstrom went to seven pain clinics where she listened in on hundreds of interviews between doctors and patients. One clinic at Stanford she cites as exemplary for its interview techniques. Doctors there work to discover the patient's perceptions of pain—in effect identifying the patient's personal illness narrative—before treating him. What does the patient think caused the pain? What meaning does the patient draw from this cause?

One purpose for this line of questioning, Thernstrom explains, is to make sure the patient isn't conjuring a sinister cause for his pain. Doctors know that when patients do this, their treatment is not as effective as it would be if they understand the pain for what it is—for example, a result of nerve damage. The goal, these doctors tell Thernstrom, is for a patient to understand that "although chronic pain feels like an alarm bell, it is often a false alarm signifying only that the alarm system is broken."

Here, Thernstrom interweaves the personal and scientific threads of her memoir, showing us how exposing the illusions in a long-term romantic relationship figured into her process of awakening to the shortcomings in the (restitution) illness narrative she had been using to understand her pain:

> The relationship with Kurt—the long false relationship— was over, I realized. Of course, of course, of course. I had deluded myself about the relationship, just as I had deluded myself about the pain. The two had seemed so confusing— confusing and confused—but now they were clear. My pain was not a manifestation of a personal, spiritual, or romantic problem and could not be alleviated by thinking of it that way; it was a biological condition, plain for a stranger to see.
>
> "Questions?" the doctor said affably, and sat down at his desk. "Come now. What about what I said don't you understand?"
>
> "Will it get better over time?"
>
> "It's degenerative."
>
> "Can't it be fixed?"
>
> "No, it's structural. Do you see?" He paused. "You need a new spine." He smiled.
>
> I almost asked whether as it degenerated, I would have more pain, but I was too afraid of the answer.
>
> I broke up with Kurt that night.

This scene, which comes about a third of the way into Thernstrom's memoir, marks the first crisis-change point in her narrative. Afterward, she creates a new illness narrative, accepting chaos for a time, before shifting once more into a quest narrative. She's not looking for a cure. Ultimately, she finds a way to manage her condition using medication and neuroimaging to change her perception of the pain she still suffers on a daily basis. Today, Thernstrom thrives as an author and a teacher who is also married and the mother of twins.

# When Hope Is All That's Left

David Sheff's bestselling memoir *Beautiful Boy: A Father's Journey Through His Son's Addiction* tells the harrowing story of the battle Sheff waged over his son's meth habit. As Sheff recounts it, his son Nic's addiction to speed began when he was midway through high school, and it gained a fierce stranglehold on him almost immediately. The book details the stages of addiction for the son and the progressive loss of denial by the father.

Sheff initially is helpless to understand his son's disease. Not knowing how he can help Nic survive, let alone thrive, makes this father's journey nearly unbearable to witness as a reader. It's a testament to Sheff's storytelling ability—especially his willingness to confront his own failings and most difficult emotions—that he keeps you with him on this journey.

As years go by, with Nic's sobriety lost repeatedly to a succession of relapses, Sheff and his family are lost in a chaos illness narrative. The story's major crisis point comes when Sheff realizes he's enabling his son's behavior and has to stop sending him money or otherwise bailing Nic out so that the boy might hit his own rock bottom. This, we learn along with Sheff, is the necessary prerequisite to standing firmly on his own feet. It's easy enough to understand intellectually, but brutally difficult to pull off for both father and son. Sheff makes us see and feel how terrifying it is for a parent to be in this position, when letting go means the real possibility of losing a child forever.

As father and narrator, Sheff ultimately releases Nic along with any illusion of his control over the monster of his son's addiction. As he tells this part of the story, Sheff also acknowledges his unreliability as a narrator—because he has been fooled by misguided hope several times before. Here, he's at a rehab center with Nic:

> Parents are suckers. I am a sucker to contemplate opening to the idea of healing. And yet…. Suddenly I recall when I prayed for Nic. I never planned to pray. I just looked back and realized I'd been praying. What did I pray for? I never said Stop taking drugs. I never said Stay away from meth. I said Please God heal Nic. Please God heal every ravaged person on this planet, these dear, wounded people. I look around at them. They are brave. They are here. However they got here, they are here. They are here and so there is a chance.

David and Nic Sheff's story ends as inconclusively as it began, with son hanging on to a fragile recovery and father grasping at whatever hope he can muster. As readers, we sense as we leave these two—stripped down to essentials and without any illusions to cloud their vision—that this family does in fact have a real chance.

## The Least You Need to Know

- Illness in memoirs can be treated in many ways depending on the meaning an author gives to her illness.
- A restitution illness narrative makes modern medicine the hero of the story, and a return to how the patient was before is the prize.
- The chaos illness narrative tells an opposite story, where hope for a cure doesn't exist and the future is unknown.
- In a quest illness narrative, the author-patient reframes her experience and makes wisdom the overarching prize.
- Authors often shift illness narratives midstream, giving up on a chaos narrative and committing to a quest.

# Travel and Adventure

## In This Chapter

- The creative uses of a travel journal
- How to write for travel guidebooks and magazines
- When travel meets science and discovery
- Writing a memoir of love, food, and travel
- When extreme adventure leads to self-reckoning

Travel writers are a breed of memoirists unto themselves. They combine their love of writing with an insatiable curiosity about new places, new cultures, and the challenges of an unfamiliar setting. Some travel writers move permanently to a new location—say Tuscany or Provence—and become students of the local cuisine and lifestyle, using their writing to express their love of a second home. In addition to travel writing as a popular genre for writers and readers, this chapter also covers the work of some memoirists who've shared an incredible experience in an exotic or distant place. These memoirists have faced down a formidable enemy, whether an invading army or Mother Nature. Their stories tend to revolve around the theme of survival.

# The Many Faces of Travel Writing

Traveling can be an end in itself, a break from routine or a long-term cure for what ails you. When writing and travel are strictly personal, keeping a travel journal allows you to experience a physical journey on a deeper level. You have the luxury of spiraling down into feelings and self-discovery without regard for other readers. A change in scene can bring a new perspective about life back home. Processing these thoughts and feelings in your journal gives you a valuable record of the moment when an internal realization meshes with a new vista.

When travel writing is done for an audience, you enter a large genre encompassing a number of styles that can range from the nuts and bolts of a guidebook, to a journalistic account of a place or people, to a literary-style narrative. In tone, travel writing is all over the place: it might be folksy, fact-filled, reverential, or funny.

Travel writing is often linked to the tourism industry. Subgenres of writing fall into subcategories of tours—for example, eco-tourism, culinary, historical, and archeological themes. Each of these specialties offers opportunities for writers to write reviews of hotels and restaurants, information-rich instructional articles, and inside scoops on a particular locale or opportunity for adventure.

Effective tourism-bound travel writing should allow readers a vivid preview of the location being described in a way that is useful and entertaining. Travel writing of various degrees of quality can be found on websites, in magazines, and in books.

## The Traveler's Journal

Traveling is one of the best antidotes to writer's block. Whether you are heading to a faraway place or to a nearby destination, a change of scenery can be just what you need to ignite new ideas and get you writing in your journal.

Keeping a travel journal is as easy as maintaining your regular journaling practice; all you need is a notebook, a pen, and a little inspiration. Make a temporary adjustment so your writing practice becomes an enjoyable part of your vacation experience and not an annoyance or obligation. Switch to evenings or mid-day breaks if that fits the climate and lifestyle where you are traveling. Or limit your writing to train or plane rides, using that time to reflect and muse.

One of the simplest ways to get the words flowing in your travel journal is to write what you see. Take your journal to an outside café or an urban park and observe the people, dress, language patterns, and smells around you. Focus on the cultural details most different from your own, and describe them in detail.

Don't feel as though you need to exhaustively cover every event on your itinerary, unless that's your preferred style. Use exercises to root out those aspects of the place that touch you the most memorably.

**QUICK PROMPT**

Pick one stranger you either meet and speak to or simply watch on your travels. Describe him in detail. Try to surmise a biography tied to specific observations of his manner, appearance, and any words spoken. Fill as many pages of your journal as you can with this exercise in character development. Pull it out when you get home and see if it has a place in your personal essay or travel article.

## Mining the Unexpected

Sometimes your vacation doesn't go exactly as planned. Travel writer's goldmine! Perhaps the tour bus broke down in the middle of nowhere. So, get busy and...describe nowhere! Talk to your fellow passengers. These conversations can be a rich source of material for travel pieces when you want to contrast your response with others from different cultures or even your own. There is an incredible, albeit transient, intimacy created with fellow travelers participating in tour groups together. The instant relationships you form or avoid tell you much about yourself and your preferred traveling style. Are you a loner who wants to savor places and new experiences without constant chatter? Or do you revel in the group happening? More great material for your travel journal.

**TAKE IT TO HEART**

Save yourself the trouble of sorting through ticket stubs, postcards, boarding passes, and other mementos from your trip when you get back home. Bring a small pair of scissors and a glue stick, and simply paste your souvenirs in your travel journal as an ongoing collage.

A funny thing happens to many travelers who enjoy writing about their trips and adventures: after a certain amount of time on the road, they find what's happening inside themselves much more interesting than what's taking place on the outside. This is the point at which travel writing becomes a travel narrative or simply a memoir.

# Travel Narratives

Authors who write in the armchair travel genre are meeting the needs of readers who like to learn about exotic places but don't want to leave home to do it. In the armchair travel genre, two things are essential: an interesting topic and the ability to write a memoir that reads like a novel.

Writing that mixes travel and memoir, which is valued as literature in its own right, may be referred to as travel literature. Perhaps the most renowned author of this category is Paul Theroux, who in 1975 set off on an epic journey by train from Great Britain through Asia. His account of this journey was published as *The Great Railway Bazaar*, his first major success as a travel writer. It has since become a classic in the genre. It recounts Theroux's four-month train journey, travelling through Europe, the Middle East, the Indian subcontinent, and Southeast Asia, before returning to the United Kingdom on the Trans-Siberian Railway. The route to India follows the so-called Hippie Trail, the favored route for young backpackers of the '60s and '70s who were in search of the meaning of life but more than willing to indulge in earthly pleasures along the way.

In Theroux's writing, his often cutting observations about others are matched by the process of self-discovery that he wrote about in the same critical terms:

> The farther one traveled, the nakeder one got, until, towards the end, ceasing to be animated by any scene, one was most oneself, a man in a bed surrounded by empty bottles. The man who says, "I've got a wife and kids" is far from home; at home he speaks of Japan. But he does not know—how could he?—that the scenes changing in the train window from Victoria Station to Tokyo Central are nothing compared

to the change in himself; and travel writing, which cannot but be droll at the outset, moves from journalism to fiction, arriving promptly as the Kodama Echo at autobiography. From there any further travel makes a beeline to confession, the embarrassed monologue in a deserted bazaar. The anonymous hotel room in a strange city.

Peter Mayles is another immensely popular armchair travel writer whose work qualifies as literary in quality. Mayles had been an advertising executive who left the United Kingdom and the business world behind in order to live someplace simple and beautiful where he could write. His 1989 book *A Year in Provence* chronicled the year he spent in Ménerbes, a village in France. The book became an international bestseller and led the way for a wave of travel/expatriate diaries that have followed.

---

**TAKE IT TO HEART**

If you are a fiction writer as well as a memoirist, you can use your exploration of a new location as a research mission for your next short story or novel. Tour a castle or a monastery, or stop in at the local police station. While there, imagine what your characters would be doing and saying. Once a writer, always a writer.

---

# Love Abroad

Mixing travel, food, and romance is a favorite concoction for memoir writers. One recent book to succeed in this large subgenre is *Lunch in Paris: A Love Story with Recipes* by Elizabeth Bard. The author's reason for being in France when the stars align to change her life forever is a stuffy academic conference on computers and art. She comes for the art history; her future French husband, Gwendal, is there representing the computer side of the equation. That's where their romance takes off, although, as Bard recounts, she isn't entirely sure (at first) whether she loves him or Paris or learning to cook French food more. Here she describes one of their first dates, which, of course, takes place in a fabulous Paris restaurant.

The waiters looked like they had a train to catch. Dressed in white shirts and black trousers they wove in and out of traffic, often holding a dozen escargots, a boeuf bourguignon, and a baba au rhum in the crook of a single thumb....The tables were small enough that if you put your elbows on the edge you'd have a hard time not holding hands with the person across the way.

Bard's enthusiasm for Paris and French culture, combined with an eye for detail and sharp sense of humor, make her account of a much-written-about place feel fresh and new:

In Paris the past is always with you: you look at it, walk over it, sit on it. I had to stop myself from grabbing Gwendal's arm as we walked up the narrow passage to the entrance: Pardon me sir, I couldn't help but notice; the cobblestones outside your door are older than my country.

Many of us have had this same thought while traveling in Europe, but Bard's way of bringing us into the experience succeeds like all good travel writing must—as though we are there standing on those cobblestones, seeing them anew through her eyes.

# Adventure Travel

The polar opposite of an armchair traveler is the adventure traveler. These outdoors lovers leave civilization behind to explore remote caverns and caves, search for wildlife, and climb steep rock faces. Aron Ralston is one such outdoorsman who, at 27, was on a day hike in a narrow Utah canyon when a falling boulder wedged his right hand against the canyon wall. If you've read *Between a Rock and a Hard Place* or seen the movie version *127 Hours*, you know the harrowing experiences that came next. In the book, Ralston uses those five days of being physically stuck in the rock face to go back over his past and into the future, reviewing how he got there and then how his life changes after he gets out. Finally, with no rescuers or options left and in searing pain, Ralston uses his pen knife as a surgeon's blade. Here the surgery is finally complete:

I AM FREE. This is the most intense feeling of my life. I fear I might explode from the exhilarating shock and ecstasy that paralyze my body for a long moment as I lean against the wall. No longer confined to the physical space that I occupied for nearly a week, I feel drugged and off balance but buoyed by my freedom....

He pauses; mesmerized by the sight of the hand and wrist he must leave behind...

My glance lingers and becomes a stare. My head whirls, but I am fascinated, looking into the cross section of my forearm. "Okay, that's enough. You've got things to do. The clock is running, Aron. Get out of here."

Ralston's account starts as a casual adventure and becomes a story of courage and survival. The awful choice he must make in order to live becomes a narrative through line, organizing everything else in his life as either before or after. He is forever changed—making this true-life adventure the basis for an amazing memoir.

## The Least You Need to Know

- Journaling while on the road can be especially fruitful as insights about self mix freely with observations about new places and people and give you a new perspective on your own life and changes.

- Literary writers such as Paul Theroux and Peter Mayles breathed new life into the subgenre of the armchair travel narrative, using fictional storytelling techniques and introducing their own inner lives into the story.

- Adventure travel becomes memorable when accidents happen and the adventurer's survival is threatened.

# Business Memoirs

# Chapter 17

## In This Chapter

- The right reasons to pen your business life
- Finding the story behind a business
- Why rags-to-riches is still a winner
- Taking homespun to the top
- Outrageous claims that become bestsellers

This popular category of memoir gets behind the scenes and into the head of inventors, entrepreneurs, successful CEOs, and anyone else who thinks outside the box in the world of free enterprise. A book of this type can size up an entire life spent building one company—for example, McDonald's founder Ray Kroc's *Grinding It Out: The Making of McDonald's*. It can alternatively tackle a brief period in an executive's tenure that was marked by controversy, such as displaced Hewlett Packard CEO Carly Fiorina's *Tough Choices: A Memoir*. Many entrepreneurs starting new businesses publish memoirs as self-marketing tools, and retiring CEOs like to leave a legacy to mark the secrets behind their success.

## Why Write a Business Memoir?

In a word: *self-promotion*. Now that a career is rarely spent in the confines of one company, a successful businessperson builds his own brand, and having a book is one of the best ways to identify the strengths of that brand.

These are the usual motives that get business types putting pens to yellow pads, including

- **Public relations**—A business memoir can reach out directly to potential customers and potential business partners by putting your story into the marketplace and calling attention to it.

- **Media relations**—With the right news hook, a published book can get you on one of the business cable channels or in the pages of *The Wall Street Journal*, *Business Week*, or *Fortune* magazine.

- **Public speaking**—A business memoir calls attention to your expertise, be it a product or a style of management. Your natural audience is then identified within a business sector, with the book serving as a natural entrée to speaking gigs.

- **Giveaway, promo, or premium**—A loss leader is the gadget or book copy you give away to get customers to buy something more expensive, such as your consulting services or a widget you've manufactured.

- **Gifts**—Enthrall family and friends or business contacts with a gifted copy of your book. It's an excellent networking device, especially with your personal inscription on the title page.

- **Keepsake at tradeshows**—Put your book up there as a freebie next to chocolate candies and free promotional pens.

- **Promotion and advertising**—Mail copies with your business proposals. Use reviews of your book to generate buzz.

- **Getting ready for an initial stock offering (the IPO)**— A copy makes a nice add-on with your business prospectus.

- **To hawk on television, on radio, and in print appearances**—With a book, you have a reason for being on the air or in print to comment on the story behind your story.

- **So you can be called an "expert"**—Nothing spells expert like authorship.

Of course, these purposes overlap and feed each other. Self-publishing a business memoir is highly conducive to targeting business audiences and the lecture circuit.

**POTHOLE AHEAD!**

Just because you can sell a raincoat to a duck doesn't mean you also write well. If you have a good business story to tell but writing isn't your thing, hire a ghostwriter who specializes in business titles and memoirs.

# Types of Business Memoirs

Even if the purpose of your memoir is professional self-promotion, it still has to be about something. Here are some story angles used in many business memoirs.

## The History of a Business

Although these memoirs are often bland exercises in self-flattery, some take on a harder edge, looking at the perils of success and concurrent personal trials and tragedies.

In *All in the Family Business: A Personal Memoir and Corporate History*, George Raymond tells such a tale of mixed blessings. As a teenager, Raymond went to work for his father's firm, The Raymond Corporation. He rose to become its president, developed a revolutionary product (the narrow-aisle forklift truck), and made the company a premier manufacturer of materials-handling equipment. Just as he was starting to enjoy his success, tragedy struck: a murder shattered his family. Having remarried and reached retirement age years later, Raymond picked a CEO for his company who became an adversary. Finally, he was compelled to sell his family-owned company.

## A Different Business Model

In *Pour Your Heart Into It: How Starbucks Built a Company One Cup at a Time* by Howard Schultz, the chairman and CEO of Starbucks traces the growth and development of his brand from a single store in Seattle, which in 1973 sold only dark-roasted coffee beans, to the international business it has become today. Schultz effuses passion for good coffee and his company. He recounts his initial goals: to introduce Americans to really fine coffee, provide people with a "third place" to gather, and treat his employees with dignity. His kinder, gentler philosophy of business becomes as much his brand as the dark roasts whipped up by his baristas.

The founder's business approach was made explicit in a subsequent memoir written by Shultz's number two, Howard Behar. Behar wrote *It's Not About the Coffee: Leadership Principles from a Life at Starbucks* offering further insights on the same egalitarian themes.

## A Winning Philosophy

This type of business memoir is popular for retiring executives seeking to leave a self-defined legacy. Jack Welch, former CEO of General Electric, has created a mini-empire out of his business philosophy with *Straight from the Gut*, *Winning*, *Winning International*, and other books. Welch, who was known as an exceedingly tough-minded and quick-to-fire top executive, has many fans and an equal number of enemies, but his opinions are universally noted for one reason: he achieved extraordinary levels of success for himself and GE.

## Rags-to-Riches with Good Works

When the businessperson-memoirist wants to leave a life story that inspires, she writes along the lines of *Four Seasons: The Story of a Business Philosophy* by Isadore Sharp. Sharp tells the story of his astonishing rise out of the Toronto ghettos to become the founder, chairman, and CEO of the Four Seasons Hotels and Resorts, the largest group of five-star hotels in the world. Born to Polish-Jewish immigrants, Sharp began his career building apartment buildings. He chose midsize and luxury hotels as the focus for his untested hotelier ambitions, and he emphasized exemplary service.

When a successful businessperson also wants to promote a personal "pet" project or cause, she might follow Sharp's lead again. Sharp shares how, as his Four Seasons business grew, he shifted his attention to charitable pursuits and founded the Terry Fox marathon to benefit cancer research.

You might not be a Fortune 500 CEO, but these books and their story angles can be useful in suggesting a focus and story structure for your business memoir.

> **TAKE IT TO HEART**
>
> Successful business memoirs can change public perceptions about a CEO and help build or rebuild brands. Howard Shultz's well-timed and well-received story of how he built Starbucks by caring about his employees helped revise public opinion just when customers started baulking at his $4 cups of coffee and the claim that Starbucks was opening a new store somewhere in the world every day.

# Homespun with an Edge

Barbara Corcoran has a hit reality TV series and a bestselling business memoir of the same name—*Shark Tales*. Her memoir combines a rags-to-riches theme with a business philosophy that reeks of competitive spirit, a surprising combination for the memoir of a working-class girl with no education and an amazing success story. Her meteoric rise can be summarized as follows: after failing at 22 jobs, Corcoran borrowed $1,000 from a boyfriend, quit her job as a diner waitress, and started a tiny real estate office in one of the toughest markets in the world—New York City.

Using her homemaker mother's unconventional wisdom, Corcoran traded on that modest start to create a $6 billion business empire. What was Mom's secret? To make everyone feel that they had a special talent that simply had to be put to work, with Mom's agenda served at the same time.

The chapters in Corcoran's memoir demystify how this simple philosophy can work to turn virtually any situation to business gold by alternating each stage of her success with a theme-matched childhood vignette and lesson from her mother's bustling household. The content focus of her memoir is ostensibly entrepreneurial sales techniques, but with bits of wisdom applicable to virtually anyone, it becomes much more than that. Chapters have irresistible titles like "You Have the Right to Be There," "When There Are Three Buyers and Ten Puppies, Every Pup Is the Pick of the Litter," and "You've Got to Bully a Bully." Clearly, there is a philosophy of life at work here, too.

Here, Corcoran describes a tough time of stalled growth for her real estate business (well after its initial success had been reached) and an old lesson from Mom she used to make it through:

> I thought back to my memory of my mother quietly hopping back to the kitchen as my dad sat in his La-Z-boy. Mom's unspoken words still echoed in my memory: "In a family, everyone helps mash the potatoes."

> For the next six months I fed my after-tax income back into the Corcoran Group, earning the needed cash that bought my struggling company some time. ...My willingness to go out and take a second job to keep us afloat set an example that was noticed by everyone at the company.... They formed listing teams, taught workshops, helped each other negotiate, supported cuts in advertising and even took pay cuts. Nothing is more powerful than a team working together.

Corcoran also makes clear she was not a nice boss just for niceness sake. Here, from the chapter titled "Shoot the Dogs Early," she shows us how she roots out the best employees from the nonstarters:

> Firing people is the worst part of running any business, but I got good at it. When I spot a chronic complainer, I can't wait to fire him, as one complainer quickly recruits another to join his pity party, and that will rot a business faster than anything else. People who are usually good at hiring are terrible at firing because firing someone is also an admission that you hired the wrong person in the first place. And people don't readily admit to being wrong.

Corcoran closes her entertaining and enlightening business primer with an update on Mom and Dad (retired in Florida, Mom happily washing beach towels for her 26 grandchildren) and the graduates from her Shark Tales entrepreneurs boot camp.

# Write a Business Memoir to Get Rich

Another inspiring and wildly successful business memoir, *The 4-Hour Workweek*, is at first glance unbelievable from beginning to end. In it, Timothy Ferriss, a Princeton graduate in the seemingly unlikely fields of neuroscience and East Asian studies, tells how he went from being a $40,000-per-year cubicle resident to one of *Forbes* magazine's "Names You Need to Know in 2011."

Ferris is now an angel investor for such companies as StumbleUpon, Facebook, Digg, and Twitter. However, it's important to note that Ferriss' wealth came initially from sales of his self-help memoir, which became a number one *New York Times*, *Wall Street Journal*, and *BusinessWeek* bestseller.

In a nutshell, Ferriss teaches his eager readership by his own example of how to specialize, find virtual assistants, and outsource their way to fame and fortune at an early age. The author is a master of self-promotion. Critics say he uses his "sham businesses" to hawk self-help seminars that simply rehash old ideas. Even if that's true, Ferriss would certainly not be the first media-savvy expert-author to get rich by offering a promising brand of self-help.

Here is some of that formula for success in the author's own words:

> The most fundamental of American questions is hard for me to answer these days, and luckily so. If it weren't, you wouldn't be holding this book in your hands. "So what do you do?"

After pointing out that he is not a multimillionaire (he just lives like one), Ferriss explains that his formula for success is about working smarter, not harder. He equates wealth not to amassing dollars, but to having more time and mobility:

> How can I possibly explain that what I do with my time and what I do for money are completely different things? That I work less than four hours per week and make more than I used to make in a year?

In less than 200 pages, Ferriss then provides the essential details of his "get rich by not getting rich" scheme. Judging by the hundreds of animated reader reviews generated on his Amazon page, the author appears to leave his readers either stoked or steaming. Nonetheless, with impressive chutzpah and a great title, Ferriss has given us a bold model of what a memoir can do to stir things up in the business world and beyond.

## The Least You Need to Know

- Writing a memoir, either at the start or end of a career, has become de rigueur in today's business world.
- For the entrepreneur just starting out, a memoir that offers inspiration, a new management model, or a winning sales strategy can jump-start a career.
- For successful CEOs either retiring or chased out of a job, a business memoir can settle scores and save a reputation.
- Business memoirs need not all be written in MBA parlance.

# Getting Read

You might or might not wish to publish your memoir and distribute it around the neighborhood or out to a wider world, but you will want to share it with others. That can be simply family and friends, or it could include thousands of people you don't now know. You might wish to help others or simply entertain. As soon as your memoir lands in other people's hands, you are in an interactive relationship with readers. For many memoirists, a writer's group provides an ideal first audience. In this final part, you learn about your choices if you wish to pursue publishing, electronically, online, or as a printed book. You'll soon discover that your options are numerous. It's a great time to be writing memoirs.

# Keeping It Close to Home

## In This Chapter

- Finding usable memoir material in your journals
- Turning diary entries into well-crafted poems
- Learning the differences between personal essay and memoir
- Knowing the essentials for any family history
- Digging deeply into favorite family topics

Now that the average life expectancy has shot up to 77 years, we have much more time to ponder our lives and consider the legacy we'll leave behind. If you are writing a memoir that you intend primarily for the eyes of family, this chapter is written especially for you. Although many requirements of good memoirs and writing still apply, there are different expectations, ways to share, and possible forms that your life story can take when it's going to stay in a smaller circle of readers. For one thing, you can reasonably expect it to be hand-delivered from one generation to the next as a family heirloom. You can allow yourself to envision future descendents 100 years hence reading what you've written and gaining a unique window on their roots—a precious gift given and received.

## Journal Writing and Memoir

Journal writing, that modest daily practice requiring no fancy tools or skills, is the basis of many privately held memoirs. Even if diaries are seen by no one but the writer, they can be a wonderful venue for creative expression. As noted previously, they also grant the diarist the scientifically proven health and mental health benefits that come from a practice of life-writing.

Writing that goes into a daily journal is usually raw and uncensored. A journal is a place for strong emotions to be safely expressed. Difficult or confusing thoughts and feelings can be untangled in the acts of writing, reading what you've written, and reflecting. By definition, a daily journal records the details of events, conversations, and feelings while they are still fresh in your memory.

> **TAKE IT TO HEART**
>
> The first two things that should go at the top of every new page in your journal are the place and date on which you are writing, including the day and year. You can't notice patterns or properly record your personal history without paying attention to these fundamental facts of where and when.

# Giving Shape to Journal Writings

At some point, most journal keepers feel the urge to put their diary entries into a longer and more structured format, with an eye toward sharing them. Perhaps the writer is ready to show some of this personal writing to select family and friends. It might be the right time to join a writers group. If you are at such a point with your journal writing, there are several formats you can try. Any of these can be conducive to taking your journal writing to the next level.

Journal writing comes in many forms or no form at all. Perhaps your diary is written in complete sentences with perfect grammar and punctuation. If so, you're probably in the minority. For most who keep a journal, free-writing is exactly that. Free of the formalities of normal expository or narrative prose meant to be read by others. In addition to all the other benefits of having a place to privately record your innermost feelings and thoughts, a journal can contain pieces of writing that are ripe for conversion to poetry.

## Crafting Poetry

If you've never imagined being a poet, now just might be the time to do so. A poem can be short or long, 5 words or 500, written in free verse or rhyme. In recent decades, poetry has returned to its ancient roots as a medium of oral performance. Its fans consider hip-hop music to be a form of urban poetry. Poetry performances can now be seen in a wide range of public places both real and virtual—among them street corners, cafés, and YouTube.

The wave of poetry popularized by the revered 1960s poets Sylvia Plath and Anne Sexton was called *confessional* precisely because much of what the academic community had previously recognized as great poetic writing was not as stark and personally revealing as the work coming from Plath, Sexton, and others of their generation. Certainly both of these poets broke taboos against women (especially) addressing the darker side of their natures, including their perceived failures as mothers and wives, abortion, addiction, debilitating depression, and ultimately the consummated wish of both to die by suicide.

Notice in the few lines from "The Division of Parts"—the Anne Sexton poem excerpted here—how details help drive home the universal resonance of this painful moment she describes during the aftermath of her mother's death. The sentences and sentiments they contain could have easily been plucked from a memoir, if Sexton had written one:

> A week ago, while the hard March gales
> beat on your house,
> we sorted over your things: obstacles
> of letters, family silver,
> eyeglasses and shoes.
>
> Like some unseasoned Christmas,
> its scales
> rigged and reset
> I bundled out with gifts I did not choose.

The journal writer with years of diaries sitting in a drawer might find that by lifting phrases and whole sections from her journal writings, she has the makings of one or more deeply personal auto-biographical poems. For inspiration, she might want to seek out the work of poets like Sexton who've pioneered this form.

## Writing Personal Essays

Personal essay is another format for life-writers that works well as a vehicle for expanded journal entries. As a form, it encourages the diarist to refine and shape memories into a narrative that deepens the meaning of what he has already put to paper. The personal essay has a beginning, middle, and end structure but uses a smaller word count than that of a full-length memoir. An average length for a personal essay is between 800 and 1,200 words. This is typical of magazine essays such as those appearing under the banner of "Lives" in the *New York Times Magazine* and "My Turn" in *Time* magazine.

In literary journals, both online and print, longer lengths of between 2,000 and 5,000 words are often permitted. When personal essays run this long, they can be referred to as *creative nonfiction*. The higher word count of creative nonfiction permits the use of more fictional techniques, such as scene and dialogue.

Personal essays are also the form used by columnists in major news-papers, although some of these have a more political, less personal, slant. Like memoir and longer creative nonfiction pieces, personal essays depend to a great extent on their narrator's voice. In *The Art of the Personal Essay*, Phillip Lopate refers to this as "the need to assert a quite specific temperament." In the shorter lengths, this narrator's voice must be asserted immediately.

Adair Lara's personal essays appeared for many years as a twice-weekly column in the *San Francisco Chronicle* before she turned to the book-length memoir form. In her guide to personal writing in both forms, *Naked, Drunk, and Writing: Shed Your Inhibitions and Write a Compelling Personal Essay or Memoir*, Lara distinguishes two main stylistic differences between the short and long forms of life-writing.

In the personal essay, Lara points out, in addition to the assertion of a distinctive narrative voice, the writer must quickly spell out the problem to be confronted by this narrator. Then, just 1,000 or so words later at the essay's conclusion, this same narrator should experience a big epiphany. This is the moment when he gets it, meaning the solution to the problem set up at the beginning. Lara says that for a personal essay to satisfy its readers, this epiphany needs to work as an unmistakable final turning point.

**POTHOLE AHEAD!**

If the protagonist's problem is too complex and thus not resolvable in 1,500 words or less, the writer has two choices: he can simplify the conflict (situation) or write a book-length memoir instead of a personal essay.

One of the many excellent examples of personal essays collected by Lara in her book is by San Francisco essayist Bonnie Lach. In it, Lach quickly establishes a distinctive voice as she describes her struggle with post-partum depression, a condition she quickly shows to be a formidable inner antagonist:

> Even in places where I should have felt some kind of kinship— new moms classes, support groups—I was an outsider. Happy new mothers made my flesh crawl. Trust me when I tell you that nothing can drive a depressed mom to the bottom of a shame spiral faster than a circle of blessed-out breast feeders happily comparing burping techniques, smug and satisfied in the certainty that they are exactly where they're supposed to be, doing exactly what they're supposed to be doing. Saying that your infant feels like one of those animal leg traps, and that you're contemplating chewing off your own foot to get away from it, isn't exactly the stuff of baby chitchat.

Of particular note is just how much Lach accomplishes with this one powerful paragraph. We are ready to follow her narrator anywhere to find out how she solves this tough problem.

## Using Social Media and Blogs

With the advent of the personal blog, writers of memoirs have found another natural home for their writing. Some of these are where a blogger posts personal news intended primarily for family and friends. In decades past, the same exchanges took place via letters. Some families went so far as to send out an annual "newsletter," usually at the holidays, containing headlines of each member's big event from the previous year. My guess is that a lot less of this snail mail activity goes on now. In addition to blogging for the benefit of readers already in their inner circles of family and friends, an increasing number of online writers offer their personal news in the form of blog postings for anyone in the digital universe to read and enjoy—even comment on.

Now that sharing personal news, recipes, birth and wedding announcements, graduation photos, and pieces of creative writing has become easy enough for anyone to do, many bloggers offer what amounts to wall-to-wall coverage of their lives. For those who don't want to take the time to keep up a personal website or blog, social media sites such as Facebook do 99 percent of the posting and communicating for you. Just adjust your personal settings and your online world is an open book.

One clear result of all this sharing is the quickly collapsing sense of propriety that used to keep us from sharing things publicly that we considered too embarrassing or shameful to admit—for example, being jobless or homeless. By going public, some bloggers without jobs or homes have received help for their plights from complete strangers; job offers and book deals have even come for a lucky few.

What, you might wonder, does all this have to do with journaling and memoir writing? Everything! Among the millions of new websites and blogs popping up every month are online communities dedicated to the posting and discussion of life-writing in the form of memoirs, journals, personal essays, and poetry. These virtual groups are on AARP and Yahoo! among other web destinations. They're made up of both published and aspiring memoirists who post their work, conduct webinars to discuss craft and content, and give each other a break from the loneliness of the writing life.

# Finding the Best Forum for Your Work

None of these forms or forums for containing or sharing your writing is inherently better or more valuable than the others. Some people are content to stick with their private journals. Others will put a toe in the water by penning an essay and mailing it in the form of a letter to a friend. Many more are venturing online and clicking "publish now."

While each of these formats for life-writing can stand on its own, they are also mutually supportive. The journal writer might decide to craft a personal essay and share it via the mail or a personal blog. She may send her best writing to a literary journal or the local newspaper. Regardless of its destination, you'll find that by upping the ante and putting your work out there for others to read, it improves. As you revise it one more time, you discover the main point that might have been hiding from you before. This discovery and the reactions of new readers will lead many a shy writer to gather the nerve to tackle a longer version of the same personal story.

# Writing a Family Heirloom

For many life-writers, the whole point of writing a memoir is family, meaning its subject matter and primary readers are people to whom you are related. When you write something that contains genealogical information that will be of interest to subsequent generations of your family, you have a greater level of responsibility to get the details right. You will probably want to include more factual details. This means dates of birth—perhaps the precise times of birth, too (in case your future relatives are interested in astrology)—and names of any ex-wives and important significant others who did not become legal spouses. Certainly it means including children born of out wedlock; adoptions; geographic moves your family made along with employers, the reasons for the moves, addresses for homes, and burial sites.

There might be military service records and acts of courage and tragedy on and off the battlefield, or perhaps a crime committed with some jail time resulting, or the unexplained absence of a relative you feel compelled to investigate. It's the stuff of Greek tragedies, soap operas, and families everywhere. And if you're brave enough, it makes perfect sense that it also lands in your memoir.

## Family Medical Data

One very important function served by writing a family history is to create a repository of medical data for the benefit of future members of the family. An accurate evaluation of a young person's genetic risk for a disease that "runs in the family" often depends on how many family members might have had it or a related condition. For physical diseases, there's usually a cause of death obtainable from an official death certificate. That is, unless the individual had a socially less acceptable disease, such as AIDS. Then the impetus to cover up that person's sexual preference can cloud proper reporting of his cause of death. The same goes for determining whether a death deemed accidental might have actually been a suicide. Coroners frequently go along with family wishes to keep such things quiet.

These are the sorts of family secrets that end up causing grief, resentment, and confusion for family members for generations to come. It might land on your shoulders to decide whether the truth needs to come out about a particular long-held secret. It might not please certain members of the family to make such information public, even among their own blood. How important is the truth to you as the writer? There's no easy answer to this question.

## Mental Health Complications

Not knowing whether a family had a past illness comes more into play around mental illnesses, where the lack of diagnosis and treatment was and remains more the norm than the exception. Without proper diagnosis, you and other relatives are left to make educated guesses about what might have made Uncle Bob spend most of his days alone in the attic or caused Granny to check the stove some

20 times before leaving the house. The technical term used in the mental health professions for this sort of after-the-fact evaluation of a deceased person's mental health is *psychological autopsy*.

**TAKE IT TO HEART**

An Internet resource for inputting and storing family health and mental health information is offered by the U.S. Surgeon General's office. The website allows family members to input information into the record, making it easier to collaborate. The U.S. Surgeon General's online family health history-keeping online tool is free at https://familyhistory.hhs.gov/fhh-web/familyHistory/familyHistory.action.

By laying the foundation of your memoir or family history with basic factual information, you are free to explore the other events and important passages that most compel your attention.

# Favorite Topics for the Family Memoir

As we've covered from many angles in previous chapters, every memoir starts with you. In a family-oriented memoir, the focus then moves outward in concentric circles to include your closest family and other personal ties.

## Writing About Family

For most of us, memories of childhood begin at or around five years of age. Your first images of your parents, those sense memories that have remained with you all this time, are rich veins for digging further into childhood. As you go through the next series of questions and prompts, make use of your golden notebook. Give each family member a few blank pages and record anything that comes to mind. Questions and suggestions are organized by various family relationships and topics. But don't stop with what you find here. Allow yourself to go off on whatever tangent occurs to you. This is free-write territory!

## Parents and Grandparents

What is your first memory of your mother? As time goes by, our first images become fused with our favorite family photographs. You can make that work for you when you're digging up early memories. Take out your family photos and let your eyes lead the way for the rest of your senses. Go back to the time and place when a favorite photo was taken. See yourself as that five-year-old sitting on your mother or grandmother's lap. Was there an ice cream cone in your hand? Remember the sweet taste and the feeling of cold ice cream on your tongue. Use all your senses to go back there.

Then remember:

What color, smell, and fabric do you associate with Mom? How about Dad?

Remember a time when you hurt yourself (a bee sting, scraped knee, broken arm, and so on) and your mother comforted you. Go through that incident by giving it a beginning, middle, and ending. How did she make you feel better?

What special treat do you associate with your grandmother?

Some of the best pieces of memoir are about grandparents. These relationships tend to be less complicated than those we have with our parents. After our parents, they were often the first people we adored and who adored us in return. How did it feel to be in Grandma's kitchen or Grandpa's garage?

## Courtship and Marriage

Who was the first person you ever kissed? (You can record other sexual firsts, as you wish.)

Did you attend your senior prom? Whether you did or not, that night is a memorable one for many of us. (I considered myself too cool to go to mine and then moped around all evening wishing I'd gone.)

An amazing number of people say they knew the instant they met their future beloved that he or she was "the one." Describe the moment when you laid eyes on your first adult love. Was it love at first sight or something else?

Write about your wedding day from the moment you woke up until your head hit the pillow next to your new spouse. Many people admit to having had last-minute doubts on that big day and remember having the temptation to be a runaway bride or groom. Were you one of those? If you married more than once, you might compare the experience of getting hitched each time.

Did you lose a beloved to illness? Writing about such a loss is one of the most healing things you can do. Whether you ever share what you write with another soul, do it for yourself.

## Including History—Personal and Global

A wonderful device you can use to establish a setting for your life is to obtain page one of *The New York Times* for the day of your birth. If another newspaper closer to where you were born offers archives, get its first page instead or in addition.

Another revealing perspective from which to view different times in your life is to write about where you were when you received the news of an important national or international event. Who were you with, and how did you react? Ten years after September 11, 2001, people still speak at length about their experience of that awful day.

Have you ever experienced a natural disaster? I'll never forget my first earthquake as a new resident of Los Angeles in the 1990s. It was the Northridge quake. For a native New Yorker, to have my house start shaking violently in the middle of the night was one of the most disconcerting (read: terrifying) things I'll ever experience. One unforgettable image was the time, 4:20 A.M., frozen on my alarm clock. It was unforgettable because it took three days for the electricity to come back on, thus the clock wasn't about to change anytime soon. What in your life represents such an image of sheer terror?

### Your Proudest Accomplishment

Out of modesty or a desire to keep work at work, many people don't share the details of their worldly achievements with even close family members. This makes the inclusion of these details of someone's business or professional life doubly important when these individuals (or their relatives) decide to write a memoir. If it's your father's or mother's accomplishment you want to include in family memoir, after you've learned everything you can from inside the family, seek out business associates who can give you a fuller picture of the deeds in question.

What are you most proud of in your work or community life? Take a few pages to toot your own horn. When we underplay our achievements, we don't leave a model behind for younger people to emulate.

## Genealogical Discoveries

The research techniques offered in Chapter 3 for discovering factual information about the lives of your ancestors are invaluable for creating family histories for heirloom purposes. Pay special attention to immigration records so that you can also use social history to establish the probable setting for a great-grandfather's first steps onto American soil.

Who were the first immigrants to America in your family tree? Once you fill in these slots, you might wish to actually draw a tree or use one of the computer programs that can help you compile all the branches of the family with names and photos attached.

## Soldier Stories

War stories occur in nearly every decade and mark nearly every family. Many veterans who fought in World War II, Korea, or Vietnam have maintained a wall of silence about their experiences. This makes any stories they tell even more precious to their children and grandchildren. By all means, record what you've heard and, if the veteran is still living, gently ask for his personal memories of war.

Some ways to open up these delicate conversations include

How did you feel about going to war?

What was your proudest moment as a soldier?

I know it's painful, but can you share your saddest memory?

If the person says no, of course you should respect his wish to let the past go unmarked.

## Sharing Matters of Faith

Matters of religion and faith are important in family memoirs; even the choice not to practice a religion frames your life in a way that reveals an important piece of information about who you are. Write about the religious beliefs held in your family of origin and how they shaped you growing up.

Write down your earliest or most memorable experience in a place of worship. Was it a first communion, bar mitzvah, confirmation, or baptism? These are often the markers in our lives that help establish a timeline for key turning points.

If you had one, share a memorable religious experience. If it was a profound one, go into detail and show us the profundity as it played out for you. For me, it was more comical—at age seven, during my first confession, in my nervousness I blanked out on the list of sins I'd planned to tell the priest and then quickly made some up so as to avoid further embarrassment. I never told a soul about that incident until I wrote it in a memoir.

### Nothing Less Than a Miracle

For your reader to appreciate how your spiritual beliefs have shifted from childhood to adulthood—if they have—you need to establish what you first believed as a child. Do you remember the words of your first prayer? Speak the prayer aloud and write it down. See what thoughts and emotions come up for you. Is it a feeling of fear or a sense of comfort?

Describe the moment when you personally became convinced (or ceased believing) in the existence of an almighty God. Did you have a revelation? By all means, tell us about it.

### Sharing Our Losses

We all lose people we love; it's a universal experience we never seem to grow tired of reading about in other people's memoirs.

Describe your first experience of death. Who did you lose? How old were you? If you were a child, who explained where that person went after she died? What image did you have of Heaven or the afterlife? How has it changed?

Have you ever experienced a miracle? Please share it.

# Creating a Family Heirloom

Once you've completed your family memoir—meaning it has been written, revised, and hopefully copy edited and proofread by someone you trust—you might want to print a limited number of copies. You probably will want to include photographs. If you're creating an heirloom that you hope will last for generations and be read by your descendents, you might want to go to some expense to have it printed on the highest-quality paper. You might then invest in a secure binding, and finish with a printed dust jacket or a leather cover. When you're finished, you'll have an elegant gift for family and friends and a container worthy of your efforts.

## The Least You Need to Know

- If you put raw and uncensored life-writing in a personal journal or diary, you will have a rich source of material for poetry, personal essays, and memoir.

- Blogs and social media websites have replaced letter writing and family newsletters as a way of sharing personal news and family record keeping.

- Online communities of journal keepers and memoir writers have sprung up for sharing writing, classes, and support.

- Family histories do a great service for those who come later when they contain medical and mental health information going back generations.

# Getting Published

Are you ready to publish your memoir? There are two aspects to this question. The first concerns your readiness for possible rejection and any impact publication might have on your closest relationships—if they are treated in the memoir. The other has to do strictly with the manuscript—is it as polished as it can be before you send it out into the world? We'll take on both aspects of the readiness question in this chapter.

# Personal Readiness

For new writers, visions of their books on display at the local bookstore and in the hands of anonymous readers represent long-held dreams. But when we're just starting out, venturing from our private writing garrets and critique groups with a first book, there are many things we don't realize. First, we don't expect to find the army of gatekeepers whose job it is to screen out from 95 percent to 99 percent of all books written—before anyone else has a chance to read them.

These are the agents, editors, and even some fellow writers who occasionally show their darker, competitive sides by telling new writers that what they've written doesn't make the cut. And even if a new writer realizes that the judging of any piece of writing is a highly subjective process, the pain of rejection can be devastating. That's why it's important to know what to expect, and be prepared. The name of the game of publishing is rejection. Develop a thick skin, or don't even imagine getting into it. The potential rewards are rich, but they don't always come when and where you think.

## What and Who Gets Published?

The odds of getting a first book published are very small. But wait, you say, what about all those success stories we hear about debut books hitting the bestseller list? First, you should know that just because a book is called an author's "debut" doesn't mean it's the first that individual has written. Very often, the debut author has three or more rejected manuscripts sitting in a drawer.

Then, the number of books reaching bestseller status in any given year is miniscule compared to the total number of books published (nearly 200,000 in the United States). In fact, the average number of copies sold of a *trade-published* book is said to be 2,000. If you take into account the blockbusters whose sales are in the stratosphere, there are quite a few books that don't top 100 copies sold.

**DEFINITION**

**Trade publishing** refers to the business of producing books by companies that acquire, edit, print, and market anywhere from 5 to 5,000 books a year. In trade publishing, the author is usually paid an advance by the publisher and then receives a royalty payment, generally from 7 percent (for paperback printed books) up to 25 percent (for e-books) of the sale price from every book sold, with middlemen (such as distributors and booksellers) taking a slice before the author gets his percentage.

## The Ascendancy of Memoirs

It's fair to say that few if any of the brightest lights in publishing predicted the popularity of memoirs. True-life stories now sell better than novels. Nothing seems to make memoirs less popular with the reading public. Not even the widely reported scandals involving incidents or whole stories touted as true-to-life accounts of real people's lives that turn out to have been fabricated.

James Frey's *A Million Little Pieces* continues to sell well after Oprah scolded the author on her show for calling his fictional addiction tale a true story. It turns out that he originally wrote *A Million Little Pieces* as fiction, but then someone convinced him it would sell better as a memoir. Could the subsequent buyers of the book have missed that Oprah episode and the massive media fallout that followed? Or did they simply not care, having decided that a good story is worth reading, regardless of whether it's true? For his part, Frey has returned to writing fiction.

For those of us who continue to write true memoirs, more immediate and personally relevant questions remain. With the thousands of true-life stories already in print, what makes one worth publishing now? How should a writer decide if her memoir is publishable?

Here are some considerations when deciding if the trade publishing route is right for you and your manuscript:

- Does your memoir offer a unique take on an important (not necessarily new) topic? Examples might be a woman in a traditionally male profession or a man in a female-dominated profession.

- Is there a timely topic that's part of your personal story? An example is growing up as an Arab-American youth post-9/11.

- Does your memoir break some taboo? Some memoir topics that broke previous taboos include an ex-wife writing about her life in a polygamous household and a mother who gave up her children to pursue a life of adventure.

- Is there a ready-made audience for your memoir—for example, aficionados of a particular sport, hobby, or avocation or the practitioners of a specific profession who constitute a large enough special interest group to buy and read it? This special-interest group could be anything from microbrewery operators to skydivers or model train collectors.

- Is your life or adventure story truly extraordinary?

- Is your writing about a universal experience truly extraordinary?

You might not have an objective enough perspective to be able to judge whether your writing meets any of these criteria. A sure way to find out is to begin sending the manuscript to agents. You will probably get a clear and rapid response, one way or another.

# Legal and Ethical Issues

As covered in Chapter 2, a memoirist can face a sticky situation when and if he discloses to family members that they appear in an about-to-be-published memoir. Siblings and parents can object on principle to the idea of allowing strangers to read about private family matters. Even though you as the writer might consider a portrayal positive and flattering, there's no guarantee that the person involved will agree with your assessment. So what do you do?

Most likely you will have a good idea ahead of time whether the material you've written will cause the other person major upset. If you don't travel in the same social circles or live in the same geographic area, you could gamble and simply not tell that person. Obviously, there's an inherent risk in this strategy. The individual can eventually hear about it and be doubly upset with you for not providing a warning ahead of time.

Whether this awkwardness goes beyond the family sphere and becomes a legal issue is hard to predict. Very few memoirs provoke lawsuits, but there are reasons to be cautious if you are reasonably sure that the publication of your material is going to upset others.

## Can You Be Sued?

The worst-case scenario would be someone suing you for *libel*. One way to view this dilemma is that you're always better off telling the truth than lying. However, things might not be as black-and-white as that. Can you prove that something took place as you remember it, particularly if the events occurred many years ago? Are you depending on repressed memories that have come out as a result of hypnosis and/or a psychotherapy process? If so, it can be difficult to know for certain if these memories are absolutely true or whether they might have been tainted by a therapist's suggestion. The tide that once favored plaintiffs in sexual abuse cases has turned in the opposite direction, with courts and juries less willing to accept repressed memories as dependable evidence.

**DEFINITION**

**Libel** is a form of defamation, meaning you've disseminated potentially damaging lies about someone. The verbal form of defamation is called *slander*.

In summary, there are ethical concerns and, in rarer cases, legal issues that should be clearly thought through before you publish a memoir containing strong accusations against another person.

## Options if Your Story Disturbs

If you have grave concerns about someone's reactions to your memoir or, more importantly, if you harbor doubts about the accuracy of your memories, you have a few options:

- You can acknowledge your doubts in the text of your memoir. State your case, but leave open the possibility that events did not transpire exactly as you remember them.

- Change the names of certain characters in your memoir. This doesn't preclude a close family member (or even someone else) suing you for libel, but it can give her less impetus to begin the process.

- If there is a specific institution—for example, a school or hospital—which could view something you write as derogatory, it would be best to not use the real name of the institution or company. The same goes for any product or brand names. When in doubt, change the name and tell the readers that you have done so.

- Another option when the concerns involve an individual would be to wait until the person whose reaction you fear is deceased. Most legal experts agree that you cannot libel the dead. And although some descendents have attempted to sue authors on behalf of their ancestors (particularly when they represent the estate of a famous person), they have generally not succeeded in those libel cases—unless they could prove an intentional falsehood was told. When in doubt, consult a libel attorney.

- If you don't want to wait to publish your memoir and you have no doubts about the veracity of your memories, then you should consider showing the specific pages to the other person and see how she reacts. She might offer you a valuable perspective that you might wish to include, and this can appease her. Alternatively, the person might be ready to admit that the event happened exactly as you wrote and even apologize to you for her wrongdoing. At least by sharing the material, you will get a preview of the reaction you can expect if you go forward. Many times, people simply appreciate being forewarned of something disturbing.

If you have any trepidations, it would be prudent to consult an attorney with libel and slander experience. There is a type of insurance you can take out in advance of publishing a potentially libelous printed work, although it tends to be expensive. If you are very concerned, investigate your situation as regards the particulars in your manuscript with experts in these areas before you publish it.

**TAKE IT TO HEART**

The safest route and the one required by most trade publishers of memoirs is to obtain a signed release form from any person who appears in your memoir being quoted or paraphrased in private situations. A copy of this release form is included in Appendix C.

Even if you are not concerned about the reactions of other people who appear in your memoir, it is a good idea to obtain and keep as much documentation as possible of any events that might prove to be controversial or be in any way challenged. With the accumulation of contested memoirs in recent years, there can come a time when book publishers will require the same fact-checking standards for published memoirs as are currently applied to articles published by major print magazines.

# The Nuts and Bolts of Copyright

Should you copyright your memoir? Yes. Contact the Library of Congress for instructions on how to register an original work. Then always use a copyright symbol © at the bottom of the first page when you send it out or publish online.

## Intellectual Property

A few other legal issues can get an inexperienced author in trouble if care is not taken before his work is published, either online or in print. The first is copyright, and it comes up when an author chooses to use an excerpt of someone else's published writings in his own work—for example, if you were to use a part of a novel, a play, or another memoir in your memoir to establish it as something that inspired or influenced you in some way.

To make a long story short, most recently published writing is owned by someone, usually the person who wrote it, his publisher, or estate. Any literary work, like other forms of art, is legally identified as "intellectual property."

## Public Domain

When the author's ownership in the intellectual property has been forfeited or expired, the work is considered to be in the public domain. Generally speaking, materials published before 1922 in the United States are in the public domain and need no permission to reprint them.

As a result, most books and plays written one or more centuries ago might be reproduced or performed without paying for that right. Jane Austen's novels, for example, are in the public domain. So if you'd like to use a large chunk of *Pride and Prejudice* in your memoir, you might do so without worries—assuming of course that there is some creative justification for its use.

Other older works still require permission and payment for their use or performance. An example is the play *Peter Pan*, or the *Boy Who Wouldn't Grow Up* written by J. M. Barrie. Royalties must be paid to perform *Peter Pan* so long as Great Ormond Street Hospital, to whom Barrie gave the rights to his play, continues to exist.

## Fair Use

Another aspect of copyright is known as *fair use*. An example of fair use occurs in this book with the brief excerpts I've reprinted from published memoirs and books about the craft of writing. Generally speaking, fair use of a preexisting work is defined as extracting fewer than 500 words, unless it is a much shorter work and the amount excerpted is significant in relation to the length of the original source.

Here's a last note on the topic of copyright. If you are using someone else's writing in your memoir—for example, a poem or letter written by a member of the family other than you—you need her written permission for its use. And when it comes to correspondence, even if the letter's recipient holds the only copy, she does not own its contents; only the letter writer has the right to publish it. As long as that person is still living, you need her permission.

# Manuscript Readiness

After you've gotten feedback from some trusted readers and revised your manuscript accordingly, congratulate yourself for having gotten this far in the process. Then take a deep breath. Much as you'd love to pack up several copies of your memoir and send them off to the 10 top agents on your carefully researched list, *don't do it yet.*

Any objectivity you might have once had is now gone. As such, the worst thing you can do is rush your completed memoir out the door. The best route is to put the manuscript in a drawer and stay away from it for at least a week, preferably a month. This will give you a modicum of objectivity that is vitally important after you've been intensely reading, getting critiques, and rewriting this work for months and possibly years.

You will be amazed after you return to it at the number of obvious fixes that will leap out at you. You'll cut, cut, cut; you'll excise whole chunks and then add missing transitions. After this is done, you'll get to the point where you'll need another outside opinion. Rather than return to your writer's group, whose members have probably read your manuscript more than once already, this would be a good time to engage a professional freelance editor.

## An Objective Opinion

A freelance editor is usually a published writer or an editor who once worked at a trade publishing house. Freelance editors advertise their services at writers' conferences or through author membership organization websites (see Appendix A). You should interview and make a selection of a freelance editor based on the individual's track record with memoirs written in the same genre as yours. An equally important factor is whether you feel comfortable with the editor's temperament and work style.

There are two categories of editorial services you can consider buying. In the first, you pay the editor only to evaluate your manuscript and produce a written description of its strengths and weaknesses. If you agree with the editor's suggestions, you'll go back and make changes based on this guidance.

Either before or after doing these revisions, you can choose to engage the same or a different editor to perform a line edit. At this stage, the editor will go page-by-page, cleaning up awkward sentences and making further suggestions for cuts or additions. You might opt to then have the same editor give the manuscript a final proofread. Another option would be for you to hire a proofreader, usually at a lower cost, to take one last look after all the editing and revising is complete. This is the icing on the cake. At the end of the process, you should have a manuscript that meets the requirements of publication—of course, still beholden to the same subjective criteria of individual literary agents and acquisition editors.

## Do You Need a Ghostwriter?

If you are committed to having your story told but have gone as far as you can as its sole writer, you might consider bringing in a *ghostwriter* to finish the job. Traditionally, ghostwritten memoirs have been written "by and about" politicians and entertainment or sports celebrities—people like Andre Agassi, Keith Richards, and Sarah Palin.

However, with the growth of self-publishing options and the seemingly inexhaustible public hunger for real-life stories in print, non-celebrities with unique stories to tell are also now engaging ghostwriters to pen their memoirs. At all times, the subject of a memoir remains its *author*.

> **DEFINITION**
>
> The person whose story is told in the memoir is referred to as the **author**. A **ghostwriter** is the writer-for-hire who executes the memoir according to the specifications of the author who pays him to do the work.

Prior to hiring a ghostwriter, an author might have already completed a first draft of the memoir on his own or have made extensive notes toward that end. The ghostwriter's role is to flesh out the story and write a first full draft. A ghostwriter's name does not appear on the cover of the completed book.

The distribution options for ghostwritten memoirs are the same as those written by the subject of the memoir. Some of these authors intend to market their memoirs for conventional trade publishing distribution. Others will self-publish, while still others will want only to preserve their stories for family and friends.

# Testing the Water Online

One of the best ways to test potential readers and trade publishers' reactions to your memoir is by publishing parts of it on the Internet. You can offer your writing on a personal website or blog, or you can share pieces on one or more community sites where writers and readers gather to exchange writing and offer comments. Examples of such websites include redroom.com and scribd.com. Writers can obtain quite a few readers this way; one unpublished fellow writer in a memoir workshop I attended told the group he had amassed a tally of 10,000 loyal readers, with the page views to prove it, for his memoir published on scribd.com. Beyond publishing one's own material, these websites offer a community of writers with online forums and chat rooms for communicating on creative and business topics.

# The Trade Publishing Route

Hundreds of books and magazine articles are available to help new writers crack through the gatekeepers and get a book deal with one of the big publishing houses. But where do you start? For this section, we'll go right to the source: top literary agents Marilyn Allen and Coleen O'Shea, authors of *The Complete Idiot's Guide to Book Proposals and Query Letters*.

## Why an Agent?

First, you might wonder, why do I need an agent? Can't I just send my memoir directly to an editor at one of the trade publishing houses?

Usually, the answer is no. Due to the sheer numbers of authors seeking publication, only a very small number of publishers accept un-agented submissions. So an agent is an inevitable gatekeeper, but also a strong potential ally for a new author. An agent will hold your hand through the pitching, negotiation, and publication process.

## Answers from a Top Literary Agency

To help you find the right agent for your memoir and make your presentation irresistible, I asked Allen and O'Shea some pointed questions about how memoir writers should position their books for presentation, first to agents and ultimately to editors:

**Question: How do you define memoir?**

Allen and O'Shea: A *memoir* is a narrative that focuses on a personal time, experiences, or people in your life. The story may be all about you, but it has to be universal enough to interest other people besides your wife, your husband, or your Uncle Bob. (Think *A Year in Provence* by Peter Mayles.) Don't confuse a memoir with an auto-biography. An autobiography of a famous person is dependent on the profile of the subject; the memoir is often driven by the broad appeal of the story and the writing.

**Question: How do editors from the publishing houses feel about memoirs?**

Allen and O'Shea: Memoirs can be tricky. Many editors and agents consider them a hybrid of fiction and nonfiction, but a key point for a memoir is the quality of the writing. [Unlike other nonfiction books] some publishing professionals might want to see the entire manuscript of a memoir before saying "yes." Before you send off your memoir query, make sure you have at least half of it written; a proposal might not be enough.

**Question: After the memoirist is sure the book is ready, what are the steps for submitting it to you?**

Allen and O'Shea: Your first step is to write a query letter. A query letter is a brief presentation of your book concept that invites the interest of an agent or editor in seeing more material, with the ultimate goal of introducing your book to publishers. In a memoir query, you need to get right into the elements of the story that demonstrate why your experience would be compelling to an audience. The writing must make the reader care. By its very nature, a query letter is short. But therein lies the challenge: within a few paragraphs, you have to sell your idea, sell your experience to write it, and sell your book's potential popularity.

Here, from Allen and O'Shea, is an annotated example of a bad memoir query letter, followed by a good one:

Dear Mr. Little,

I've just finished writing about my life, a story of sex, drugs, and greed that everyone will find inspiring. **[Another one? What makes this one more than just another cliché?]** Several people I know have read it and think it's really good. **[Of course they did—they know you.]**

Please let me know if you'd like to read it. I'm almost done with the writing! **[Too little information about your life, what you are doing now, and what the book is about.]** You can reach me at carlrichards@downonthefarm.com.

Thanks! **[The exclamation mark is unnecessary.]**

Carl Richards

Dear Mr. Little,

There are hundreds of stories about overcoming addiction, but mine is a little different: I spent 20 years as head of a Fortune 500 company without anyone noticing my problem. **[An interesting twist!]**

I am no longer at the company. I've found peace in a quiet life in the country, running a small B&B and an organic farm where our guests work in the field during the day, learning about raising their food. We have received national awards and media coverage, pulling visitors from around the nation. My memoir, called *Down on the Farm: From Crackhead CEO to Contented Country Life*, not only details how I hid my addiction while in a high-pressure job, but also what my guests are like—and how I handle them—at the B&B and farm. I am in discussion with a film company that will produce a documentary about our work. **[A second good twist. It could create some good subplots. And an exciting marketing and publicity opportunity if the documentary is done.]** I've included a photograph of last week's guests and harvest. **[The visual will add authenticity and help the query stand out in the agent's or publisher's mind.]**

I've written three quarters of the book and a detailed outline of the remaining chapters. **[That should be enough to make a decision.]**

You can reach me at carlrichards@downonthefarm.com or at 999-555-1234. **[Two choices are better than one!]**

I hope you'll want to see my work, and thank you for your consideration.

Best,

Carl Richards

**Question: If an author catches your interest with her query and you ask for a book proposal on her memoir, what should it contain?**

Allen and O'Shea: A book proposal is the fleshed-out presentation of a book in development. Writing the proposal is often harder than the book itself because you have to conceive of the entire project and communicate the content and your expertise in writing the work in a short and compelling manner. Here's an overview of the crucial sections that any strong proposal should include:

- **Overview**—This is a snapshot of what the book is about; if it's original and marketable; and if you, the author, are marketable.

- **About the Author**—Here's your opportunity to prove that you're the best person to write the book by showing your credentials.

- **About the Market**—This section provides plenty of credible stats to prove to a publisher there's a ready-made audience for your book, reviews the competition, and discusses relevant market trends.

- **Platform marketing**—A strong platform shows a publisher that you can help sell your book through media contacts, public appearances, media opportunities, a popular website and/or blog, seminars and lectures, a client base, and so on.

- **Expanded Table of Contents**—This gives an overview of the logic, flow, and content of the book, with brief descriptive paragraphs presenting the content of each part and chapter title of the work.

- **The nonfiction (memoir) writing sample**—Finally, here is where you show agents and editors that you can really write.

As you research your book idea and project, you will need to keep all these proposal categories in mind. You might want to establish folders for each section where you can keep and collate relevant documents, notes, and ideas. Investigate what other writers in your category are up to, and keep an eye on relevant current events.

**Question: What should writers do while they're waiting for a response from an agent or editor on their submission?**

Allen and O'Shea: It may take months or even years to get an agent (and then a book deal), and you may have to deal with many rejections before you get to "yes." Bear in mind that many of the greatest books and most popular authors have gone through the same ordeal! Be prepared and be patient. While you wait, continue to develop and polish your work. Share your work with objective readers and keep writing.

Once you have an agent, help her sell your book by strengthening your platform. Work on your website, blog, and e-mail list, and continue to build your business.

Thanks to Marilyn Allen and Coleen O'Shea for that great advice. When you're ready to craft your query letter and proposal, it will be well worth your investment to purchase *The Complete Idiot's Guide to Book Proposals and Query Letters* to get more of their specific instructions and helpful examples.

## The Least You Need to Know

- A professional editor and/or proofreader can provide the necessary final editorial input and polish to make the text shine.
- Your memoir should either be of extraordinary quality or have a unique angle on its subject to rise above the 95–98 percent of manuscripts rejected by agents and editors.
- Libel is knowingly putting into print something that is untrue and potentially damaging to another person.
- Agents function as gatekeepers and business allies for authors and can help you navigate the publishing process.

# Self-Publishing

**Chapter**

# 20

## In This Chapter

- Deciphering your options for self-publishing
- Finding out what goes into printing a book
- Learning how print on demand can work for you
- Comparing the print versus e-publishing routes
- Getting real about marketing your book

Self-publishing eliminates the gatekeepers separating you from your potential readers. To self-publish a printed or electronic book, an author does not need an agent or a book proposal. Nor does he require the assistance of a publishing company. The author controls all aspects of the book: its content, cover design, printing, price, distribution channels, and marketing. As such, self-publishing adds many tasks to the author's to-do list. If you're ready to take on some or all of these tasks, self-publishing might be for you. On the other hand, the sheer size of such a project can overwhelm someone with a demanding day job and personal responsibilities. In this chapter, self-publishing is demystified, so you can decide for yourself if it's the right way to get your memoir into readers' hands.

# What Is Self-Publishing?

*Self-publishing* is a catch-all term for various combinations of services available in the marketplace to authors and small businesses who want to independently produce and market their books. Although the self-publishing business has been in existence for two decades, huge technological strides over the past five years have brought exponential growth in this area of publishing.

With the ever-growing market segment of consumers and professionals who are now willing to use electronic devices to read books, the self-publishing trend will only keep accelerating. The impact of e-publishing has only just started to ripple through every part of the book business. The number of consumers buying e-books jumped with a gain of 164.4 percent in 2010.

In fact, more than a few authors have used a successful self-published e-book to leverage their way into a major book deal with a conventional trade publisher. Others have decided that self-publishing is a great long-term solution for getting their books into the marketplace.

# The Language of Self-Publishing

Although it can feel daunting at first, there are really only a handful of new terms an author must decipher to enter the world of self-publishing. Here is the primary cast of characters.

## ISBN

The International Standard Book Number (ISBN) is a 13-digit number (it used to be 10 digits) that uniquely identifies books and booklike products published internationally. The purpose of the ISBN is to establish and identify one title or edition of a title from one specific publisher; it is unique to that edition, allowing for more efficient marketing of products by booksellers, libraries, universities, wholesalers, and distributors. Any author-publisher can purchase ISBN numbers from R. R. Bowker (the U.S. agency licensed to sell them) or from one of their authorized agents, which include subsidy publishers and print-on-demand (POD) publishers.

## Subsidy or Vanity Press

A subsidy, or vanity, press is a publishing company that applies its ISBN to a book and charges the author for the cost of production. The author receives a certain number of copies of the book and is paid royalties on those copies that are sold by the subsidy press. The use of the term *vanity* implies that the published book has no value other than to stroke the author's ego.

As in any business niche, there are good companies and some bad ones. However, at least in their early years, many of these vanity presses earned negative reputations for overpromising and under-delivering to their customers.

**POTHOLE AHEAD!**

Never give away the copyright to your book. Even trade publishers paying advances don't take over the ownership of an author's work. They simply contract to distribute a book for a limited period of time. Compare prices on each service a self-publishing company promises. You should not be paying upward of $10,000 for a box of your own printed books and a vague promise to sell a few more.

Past problems with subsidy/vanity presses usually resulted from the presses taking large sums of money from authors, promising to market and promote their books. Some have taken over the author's copyright and failed to sell more than a handful of books. Authors, alone and in groups, have fought back by posting their negative experiences online in an effort to prevent other would-be self-published authors from making the same mistake. One reliable website that lists the good and the bad among vanity (and conventional trade) publishers is called PredatorsandEditors.com.

## Print-on-Demand Publisher

A *POD publisher* is one who publishes books strictly on an as-needed basis using a POD printer. These publishers carry no inventory. While a handful of legitimate POD publishers do exist, most POD publishers are vanity press publishers who charge authors a premium to publish their books.

## Book Packager

A *book packager* acts as an independent contractor to bring a prede-termined number of your books into being. All the books belong to you. Book packagers work for a preset fee, and all the profits belong to the author.

Not long ago, I served as ghostwriter for book packager Booktrix. com to produce a book for a nonprofit foundation devoted to stop-ping child sexual abuse. This group wanted to turn the life story of its executive director into a memoir in order to help pass new child protective laws and promote awareness for their cause. The nonprofit paid all the costs, including writing, editing, printing, and marketing fees. The book packager hired and managed these roles, including mine, and got the book distributed through standard channels such as online and bricks-and-mortar booksellers.

# Producing a Printed Book

How a book is transformed from the completed manuscript sitting on your desk to a bound and printed set of pages in a reader's hands has changed in some ways, and not in others. A printed book must come in a designated size and binding. It must have a cover, either hard or soft. Every book cover is different and must be designed and printed—separately from the printing of the book's inside pages.

## Compositing a Book

*Composition* is the name of the process for laying out printed text onto pages of varying sizes. This book, for example, is 6"×9", thus the compositing for its pages will require a different process than that for a book that's 9"×12". A compositor makes sure that the text on each page is balanced in proportion to the page headers and footers. With e-books, the process is more complicated, as new capabilities—for example, clicking on a word to look up its definition, saving text, and highlighting text to save for later—are integrated into the composi-tion process.

# The Printing Process

Although printing and publishing are sometimes conflated into one operation, they are different processes and businesses. The *printer* is the company that owns the printing press. The printer sells printed books to the *publisher* or the company that bundles services for self-published authors. Very few publishers have their own printing presses. So in this sense you as a single book publisher are not all that different from Penguin USA, the publisher of this book. You both take prepared manuscripts to a printing company to have them produced in some quantity. The main difference between you and a big publisher is the size of your print runs.

There are two ways to print a book:

## Offset printing

*Offset*, or conventional, printing has changed little since the original steam-powered offset press was first developed in 1906. It involves a mechanical process of applying layers of ink to paper with a series of rollers. Each roller has its own specified ink. As these rollers pass over the page, they transfer ink and build layers of colors, resulting in complete images and text on the page. For offset printing to be cost-effective, the number of books to be printed must usually be more than 500.

## Digital printing

*Digital* printing eliminates the numerous steps involved in the offset printing process, such as creating films and plates for ink rollers. Most digital presses today apply ink in a single pass from a single ink head, similar to the common inkjet printers found in homes and offices. The advantage of digital printing is its lower cost and greater speed. Less setup and maintenance (no films/plates) results in cheaper pricing and a quicker production turnaround.

The major propelling factor behind the growth in self-publishing has been the reduction in the unit production cost required to print a book as a result of digital printing. When printing can be done cheaply in small quantities, you have print on demand. This means the publisher prints only as many books as you have customers to buy them. It also means less warehouse space is needed to store large quantities of printed books. And, because of the speed of print on demand, bookstores keep fewer copies of books on hand.

More and more, your local bookstore is the entity that takes and places orders with a publisher and holds a book for customer pick-up. When there is no bookstore involved—for example, if you are selling your book through a website or through one of the major online booksellers, such as Amazon.com and Barnes and Noble (BN.com)—mailing costs for the publisher are less. Although you might assume that all the big publishers exclusively use the offset printing process, the fact is that because of all these advantages, many also use digital on-demand printing services, especially when they want a smaller first run or reprint of their books.

The most important thing is that at the end of this process you have a book—*your* book—in a customer's hands.

# Print on Demand

To take advantage of POD to produce a limited number of printed books—anywhere from 50 to 500 (as would be the norm for a self-published author)—services can be purchased directly from vendors. Or the author can do as most self-published authors do today and work with a single company set up to offer services in bundles.

As the dust settles on these early years of self-publishing, some POD companies have emerged as trustworthy vendors. They offer fair prices and a dependable menu of services. The most popular is Lightning Source, owned by Ingram—the largest book distributor in the United States. The model used by Lightning Source, and replicated by several smaller and medium-size POD companies, offers many advantages to the author-publisher. For example:

- Author control of each step in the process, with different bundles of services offered to meet different author needs. For example, a memoirist who wants fewer than 100 copies of her book for family and friends might choose a package emphasizing a higher-quality cover with heavier, more durable paper. But this author would not need any of the marketing or ongoing POD costs related to marketing and distribution.

- The purchase and registration of an ISBN number, the code required for every printed book in the United States, is offered at a cost of around $100.

- A low-cost composition service, usually under $500, is offered along with the production of proofs for author examination prior to printing. Most POD companies also provide basic cover design services at a reduced cost.

- POD companies provide a low cost/high return for each book sold to readers via bookstores, online sales, and so on. For example, one author-publisher of a book about computer repair writes in a testimonial that he produced a 168-page book through Lightning Source for $3.82 per unit and then offered it for sale on his website for $14.95. After paying a 35 percent discount to Lightning Source for printing and sending the book directly from the POD location, this author-publisher netted a total of $6.63 on each copy. Compare that to $1 or less—the royalty he would have received in a standard trade publishing arrangement.

- If the book is ordered on a site such as Amazon (where self-publishers sell in anywhere from decent to great numbers), the consumer places the order online. The order is then sent electronically to the POD printer, which prints and ships the book within 24 hours. The publisher (you) is then paid the difference between the wholesale price and the cost of the POD printing.

- The company keeps a digital file of your book and charges a cheap storage fee of around $15 per year. This permits a quick turnaround of a POD order of anywhere from 1 to 50 copies.

This business model is especially suitable for small businesses and authors who have a few marketing channels available to get books out through professional and personal relationships. Whereas it was once thought that a stigma applied to self-published books, that attitude is rapidly disappearing in the face of mounting sales and the diversification of purposes that authors bring to self-publishing.

Essentially, it boils down to this: if a reader gets the book he wants, who cares how it gets into his hands?

# Getting Into Bookstores

There's absolutely nothing stopping you from approaching your local or regional bookstores and personally offering your book for sale. Often, booksellers, particularly independents, like to play up a local angle for sales. Go right in and make the sale!

If you want your book to be available to hundreds of bookstores and other bricks-and-mortar outlets, you will need the services of a distributor, such as Ingram or Baker and Taylor. A distributor typically takes a 60–75 percent discount off the retail price to get your book placed in the various wholesale and retail databases so that it is available to the bookstore buyers. Getting a distributor does not guarantee you any actual sales. It does make it easier, however, when you get enough publicity to create a demand for your book. A true distributor works on a commission based on the total sales of the book. In other words, the distributor is not making money unless you are. Beware of those who say they want to distribute your book but want you to pay $500–$1,500 to get you "set up."

All distributors have a review committee to decide which books to take and which to decline. Most will accept only about 10–15 percent of the submissions they receive; the rest are sent a letter and an evaluation form explaining why the distributor decided not to offer a contract. Overall, the goal is to offer contracts only to small presses that publish books they believe they can sell through retail and online bookstores.

Here are the primary reasons for a distributor declining a self-published book, as offered by the POD company Self-Publishing Inc., on its website:

- **Market**—The trade book market, including all the big publishers, is very competitive; the distributor might feel that your book can't compete or that the market is flooded with similar titles because it is of too narrow interest or too much like other books already in distribution.

- **More suited for a specialty distributor**—Your title might be better suited for the academic or religious market. You might consider selling directly through or to religious bookstores, direct mail, lectures and seminars, regional bookstores, and online retailers to best reach your audience.

- **Basic book requirements not met**—For example, no ISBN, no bar code, no price on book, price too high, price too low, and so on. The price on your book must be competitive for your category, page count, and format.

- **Lack of marketing and promotion**—The book does not appear to be supported via advertising, marketing, or promotion. Books do not sell just by being on the bookstore shelf or through word of mouth alone. They must have a solid promotion planned in advance of any sales efforts or publication.

- **Poor design**—The production value of your book is not competitive with other books in the category. With the vast quantity of books published every year, packaging is important to sales. Design elements over which to maintain high quality include the typeface, jacket, layout, photo reproduction, table of contents, index, and other features. A spine with the title is essential for placement on store shelves.

- **Limited subject matter**—Many distributors will tell you that poetry and personal memoirs are very difficult to sell, so your best options are your own website, online retailers, and local bookstores.

- **Rights/publisher problems**—The applicant is not the owner of the book or ISBN prefix. Publishers, not authors, must apply for distribution.

- **Future publishing plans**—There is no indication of future publishing plans, and the title submitted is not strong enough on its own to support full distribution efforts. Or future plans are not focused enough to build a program upon; the publisher should choose a niche market on which to focus its efforts.

An alternative to working through a traditional printed book distributor is to use CreateSpace, an Amazon-affiliated company that also takes upfront fees to print, store, and mail your book when it is ordered online.

# Self-Published E-Books

Electronic, or *e-book*, publishing is growing rapidly alongside POD publishing as a book production and distribution channel for independent authors. E-books cannot be topped for efficiency, cost, and speed. For these reasons, e-publishing is becoming an increasingly popular method of getting memoirs into the marketplace. Amazon offers one of the most popular programs for the uploading of, handling the sales of, and the downloading of e-books for its Kindle, as does Apple through its iBookstore for the iPad. Both of these giants are facing competition from other mobile platforms. This is all rapidly changing, so do your homework when you're ready to self-publish, and find the right solution for your needs.

# Self-Marketing and Promotion

No matter which company you use to print and distribute your book, sooner or later you will face the herculean task of promoting it. However, the same is true of authors published through trade publishing companies.

## Think Like a Brand

As an author, you are a brand. Your book sales depend on you forming a relationship with your readers. You must have a web presence and, if you're not already, become an active opinion leader in the online communities that relate to the subject matter you write about. Another term for building a brand is having an author *platform*.

 **DEFINITION**

**Platform** is your credibility and following in a particular subject area. The size of an expert's platform is measured (these days) by the number of hits on his website and how often his Twitter posts are retweeted. Ultimately, platform drives the sales of a book.

In the case of memoirs, this can be as varied as a self-help topic tied to your story or the particular genre, setting, and theme of your book.

Wherever you go and whomever you meet, talk with them about your book. Yes, this constant book hawking can seem distasteful at first. Writers are not often the best self-promoters. But it is a skill that can be learned like any other.

## Getting Started in Self-Promotion

When starting out, here are a few strategies worth pursuing to get your feet wet:

- Create a website for your book. Include excerpts and some background information about you and why you wrote it. Include the web address on business cards, in handouts, and in the book itself. Refer everyone you meet, e-mail, and talk with to your website.

- Go to your local bookstore and see if you can arrange for a book signing.

- Go to your local library and look in the List of Associations. Find the groups that relate to your book and join these organizations with an eye toward speaking about your book at an upcoming meeting.

- Write articles for your local paper or trade association newsletter.

- Seek reviewers to read and comment on your book in other venues. If they are authors, volunteer to read and review their books in exchange.

All of these strategies add up to the creation of your brand as an author with a distinct niche in the marketplace of ideas and books.

# Is Self-Publishing Right for You?

As you can see, there are many ways to self-publish a memoir, some modest enough to be available to virtually anyone. Before you take on an ambitious plan to self-publish and distribute beyond your own social and professional circles, consider these questions:

- How many titles have you published in the past? If you are new to books and self-publishing, you will have a learning curve and much trial-and-error ahead before you find out what works for you. Take a long view.

- Where do you reside? Geography matters only somewhat when selling a book, and soon it might not matter at all. Large cities provide more retail outlets for book sales. On the other hand, less urban areas can provide more opportunities for community gatherings, such as fairs, festivals, and parades, where you can hawk your book.

- Who do you feel is your primary market? Is it family and friends, business associations and other professionals, or the general public? Always build your marketing campaign so that it is in line with whomever you are trying to reach.

- Do you have any experience in sales and marketing? Selling is an art form. With prior sales experience, you have a leg up when you begin selling your own book. On the other hand, if you have enough passion for it, your enthusiasm can get you a long way.

- How much time do you plan to spend on the production and sales of your book? Do you plan to spend as little time on it as possible, evenings and weekends, or none at all? This is a time-consuming project. Adjust your expectations accordingly.

- How do you plan on funding your publishing project? If you've set aside funds for book promotion, that is great. If not, save a little at a time and do it consistently. That's a far better approach than one blast of effort, followed by lulls and absences.

# Celebrating Your Success

It's important to take stock at the end of a project of this size, especially one with as much meaning as your personal memoir holds for you. My own memoir, *A Lethal Inheritance*, took me ten years to write and another two to sell to a publisher. I am only now planning a marketing and promotion campaign. To accomplish it, I'm calling on everyone I know, all across the country, to help get the word out. But I'm also focusing on the broad organized community of parents and family members of the mentally ill. I plan to speak to many small groups, not just about my book, but about the common ground we share as parents and individuals who've made it through something really tough and triumphed on the other side.

Whatever your story and the obstacles you've overcome and then written about, this is a time to celebrate. By putting your own narrative frame on your life, you've empowered yourself in a way that no one can do for you. The memoir that you've written is one manifestation of that enormous growth process. Celebrate every day. Share it with those whom you think might appreciate it. Most of all, be proud of your success.

## The Least You Need to Know

- Self-publishing adds many responsibilities to the author that were traditionally handled by publishers.
- Print on demand is a process by which independent authors can get their books printed digitally in small quantities whenever they have an order to fill.
- Self-published authors might be able to get their books accepted for distribution to retail and online outlets through a major distributor.
- Along with self-publishing comes self-marketing and self-promotion for you and your book.

# Resources

**Appendix**

**A**

Here are some of the best websites and books to help the memoir writer learn the craft, receive inspiration, and enjoy being part of a community of memoirists.

# Websites and Organizations for Memoir Writers

AARP Memoir Writers Online Group (Public)
www.aarp.org/online-community/groups/index.action

International Association of Journal Writers
www.iajw.org/

Martha Alderson's Blockbuster Plots, a book, DVD, online course, and website
www.blockbusterplots.com/

Women's Memoirs
www.womensmemoirs.com

Memory Writers Network
memorywritersnetwork.com/blog/

National Association of Memoir Writers
www.namw.org

Story Circle Network (for women only)
www.storycircle.org/index.php

Writing Through Life
www.writingthroughlife.com/

Yahoo Groups Lifewriter's Forum
groups.yahoo.com/group/lifewritersforum/

# Books for Memoir Writers

Abercrombie, Barbara. *Courage and Craft: Writing Your Life Into Story.* Novato, CA: New Work Library, 2007.

Allen, Marilyn, and Colleen O'Shea. *The Complete Idiot's Guide to Book Proposals and Query Letters.* New York: Penguin USA, 2011.

Barrington, Judith. *Writing the Memoir: From Truth to Art.* Portland, OR: The Eighth Mountain Press, 2002.

Cameron, Julia. *The Artist's Way: A Spiritual Path to Higher Creativity.* New York: Jeremy P. Tarcher/Putnam, 2002.

Dillard, Annie. *The Writing Life.* New York: Harper Collins, 1989.

Goldberg, Natalie. *Writing Down the Bones: Freeing the Writer Within.* Boston: Shambala, 1986.

Gornick, Vivian. *The Situation and the Story: The Art of Personal Narrative.* New York: Farrar, Straus and Giroux, 2002.

King, Stephen. *On Writing: A Memoir of the Craft.* New York: Scribner, 2000.

Lamott, Anne. *Bird by Bird: Some Instructions on Writing and Life.* New York: Pantheon Books, 1995.

Lara, Adair. *Naked, Drunk and Writing, Shed Your Inhibitions and Write a Compelling Personal Essay or Memoir.* Berkeley: Ten Speed Press, 2010.

Lippincott, Sharon. *The Heart and Craft of Lifestory Writing.* Pittsburgh, PA: Lighthouse Point Press, 2007.

Murdoch, Maureen. *Unreliable Truth: On Memoir and Memory.* New York: Seal Press, 2003.

Meyers, Linda Joy. *The Power of Memoir: How to Write Your Healing Story.* San Francisco: Jossey-Bass, 2010.

See, Carolyn. *Making a Literary Life: Advice for Writers and Other Dreamers.* New York: Random House, 2002.

Stanek, Lou Willet. *Writing Your Life: Putting Your Past on Paper.* New York: Avon Books, 1996.

Zinsser, William. *On Writing Well.* New York: Harper and Row, 1976.

———. *Writing About Your Life: A Journey Into the Past.* New York: Marlowe and Co, 2004.

# Memoir Must Reads

Beah, Ishmael. *A Long Way Gone: Memoirs of a Boy Soldier*. New York: Farar, Straus, Giroux, 2007.

Beck, Martha. *Expecting Adam: A True Story of Birth, Rebirth, and Everyday Magic*. (Paperback reprint) New York: Three Rivers Press, 2011.

Caldwell, Gail. *Let's Take the Long Way Home: A Memoir of Friendship*. New York: Random House, 2010.

Corcoran, Barbara. *Shark Tales: How I Turned a $1,000 into a Billion Dollar Business*. New York: Portfolio/Penguin; Revised edition, 2011.

Costello, Victoria. *A Lethal Inheritance, A Mother Uncovers the Science Behind Three Generations of Mental Illness*. Amherst NY: Prometheus Press, 2012.

Didion, Joan. *The Year of Magical Thinking*. New York: Alfred A. Knopf, 2005.

Dillard, Annie. *An American Childhood*. New York: Harper Perennial, 1988.

Farr, Diane. *Kissing Outside the Lines*. Berkeley: Seal Press, 2011.

Fraser, Laura. *An Italian Affair*. New York: Vintage, 2002.

———. *All Over the Map*. New York: Broadway, 2011.

Karr, Mary. *Liar's Club: A Memoir*. New York: Penguin, 2005.

———. *Lit, a Memoir*. New York: Harper Perennial, 2010.

Lara, Adair. *Hold Me Close, Let Me Go: A Mother, a Daughter, an Adolescence Survived*. New York: Broadway, 2002.

Lauck, Jennifer. *Blackbird: A Childhood Lost and Found*. New York: Pocket Books, 2000.

————. *Found: A Memoir*. Berkeley: Seal Press, 2011.

Monroe, Debra. *On the Outskirts of Normal: Forging a Family Against the Grain*. Dallas, TX: Southern Methodist University Press, 2010.

Metz, Julie. *Perfection: A Memoir of Betrayal and Renewal*. New York: Hyperion, 2009.

Nabokov, Vladimir. *Speak Memory: An Autobiography Revisited*. New York: Random House, 1967.

Ralston, Aaron. *Between a Rock and a Hard Place*. New York: Pocket Books, 2004.

Sexton, Linda Gray. *Half in Love: Surviving the Legacy of Suicide*. Berkeley: Counterpoint, 2011.

Sheehy, Gail. *Passages in Caregiving: Turning Chaos into Confidence*. New York: William Morrow, 2010.

Sheff, David. *Beautiful Boy: A Father's Journey Through His Son's Addiction*. New York: Houghton Mifflin, 2008.

Waldman, Ayelet. *The Bad Mother: A Chronicle of Maternal Crimes, Minor Calamities, and Occasional Moments of Grace*. Harpswell, ME: Anchor, 2009.

Walls, Jeannette. *The Glass Castle: A Memoir*. New York: Scribner, 2005.

# Standard Release Form

Give this form to persons who appear in your memoir and ask them to sign it and return to you.

Author's Name

### RELEASE FORM FOR PERSONS INTERVIEWEWED

I (name of person appearing in memoir) hereby consent to be quoted in whole or in part or to have my comments paraphrased by the author in his/her forthcoming memoir titled (title of memoir).

I understand the book may or may not be published in printed form and/or distributed electronically worldwide.

I further understand that (author's name) will hold copyright to the whole work titled (title of memoir) and all parts thereof, and I will not materially benefit from the sale of the book or from the licensing of any rights thereto.

Signed: (person appearing in memoir)

Print Name

Date

# Index

## Numbers

# S